Grass Flats

Grass Flats

Birds of Warren County, Pennsylvania,
Including Notes on Other Species Observed
at Presque Isle, Erie County, Pennsylvania.

From the 1890–1923
Journals of the Naturalist,
Ralph Bernard Simpson.

William N. Hoover

iUniverse, Inc.
New York Lincoln Shanghai

Grass Flats

Birds of Warren County, Pennsylvania, Including Notes on Other Species Observed at Presque Isle, Erie County, Pennsylvania. From the 1890-1923 Journals of the Naturalist, Ralph Bernard Simpson.

All Rights Reserved © 2003 by William N. Hoover

No part of this book may be reproduced or transmitted in any form or by any means, graphic, electronic, or mechanical, including photocopying, recording, taping, or by any information storage retrieval system, without the written permission of the publisher.

iUniverse, Inc.

For information address:
iUniverse
2021 Pine Lake Road, Suite 100
Lincoln, NE 68512
www.iuniverse.com

ISBN: 0-595-28749-2 (Pbk)
ISBN: 0-595-65848-2 (Cloth)

Printed in the United States of America

For Henry Franklin Britt

“There are too many people in the world—we ought to give the birds a chance.”

~ *Pittsburgh Press*, June 10, 1956

Acknowledgements

I am indebted to the Warren County Historical Society (WCHS) and its Board of Directors for permission to publish the species accounts and journals of Ralph B. Simpson; Rhonda J. Hoover, Executive Director of WCHS, for her humor, insight, and encouragement; and the WCHS staff who soon grew accustomed to my daily meandering and mumbling as research was accomplished. Also thanks to Jim Henderson, grandson of Ralph B. Simpson, for sharing family stories and memorabilia; Mary Grishaver for her expert knowledge of ornithology which she readily shared; and Tom Curtin for permission to publish excerpts from his article, *Priceless Legacy*.

Contents

Images and Maps

Prologue

These are the journals of Ralph Bernard Simpson. They are the meticulous documentation of Simpson's scientific observations of 218 species of bird life in Warren County, Pennsylvania, with additional observations of bird life at Presque Isle Peninsula, Erie, Pennsylvania. Ralph B. Simpson was a wildlife expert and a remarkable naturalist, particularly of the avian realm.

The Simpson journals cover the time period of 1890 to 1923. Simpson dates the journals October 1, 1923. There are a few notes prior to 1890, and all post-1923 entries added by Simpson are included and noted as such. His observations are so complete that it appears some years were spent entirely in the field surveying and collecting. R.B. Simpson puts it best:

> A few of my notes were taken prior to 1890, but mostly since. During the 1890s, also 1901-02-03 and 1904, I seldom missed being out a morning during the spring migrations in March, April, and May, and whenever there was anything like a flight I usually spent the day down the river. In this way I got very complete migration notes, especially in regards to dates of first arrivals and last seen.

Simpson knew the terrain he traveled in great detail, and his uncommon powers of observation regarding nature were astounding. Simpson began honing these skills as a young man, as the following true tale reveals.

A story told by Jim Henderson of Warren concerning his grandfather, Ralph B. Simpson, gives insight into the budding naturalist. Ralph, at age 10 or 11, was attending Sunday school when the teacher, being of some social prominence, entered the classroom wearing a new fur coat. The teacher, proud of her fur, explained to the class that her husband, upon his return from an important business trip to New York City, presented her with this fine gift—a mink coat. She proudly displayed it to all of the students.

Ralph, being well trained and mannered, knew that one needed to tell the truth—especially in Sunday school. Being ever observant and eager to clear the murky waters of confusion, he explained to the teacher that her new and highly prized coat was not mink at all—indeed, it was dyed muskrat fur. Convinced that Ralph's intentions were honorable, but that he was certainly in error, she explained the classroom events to her husband later that day. Upon his return to New York City, the husband, convinced that he had not been hoodwinked, had the coat examined by a professional furrier. Ralph was found to be correct in his assessment as the mink coat was genuine muskrat. Ralph's career as a noted and ardent naturalist had begun.

At the time of his birth there were only 37 states in the Union—Ralph B. Simpson was born November 20, 1874, in Reading, Pennsylvania. He moved to Warren, Pennsylvania, with his family at the age of five.

Warren, in 1895, when Simpson was deep into his study of birds and doing much field work throughout the county, was a bustling, growing community. An 1895 promotional advertisement of Warren states the following facts, of which the community was undoubtedly proud:

> Warren is the county seat. Its county buildings (courthouse) cost $150,000. Warren has 13 churches; eight hotels; three and one-half miles of electric street carlines which will be doubled this year. Principal business streets are paved with brick. The town has nearly seven miles of sewerage. Streets are all lighted with electricity and gas. There is free mail delivery to all parts of the city. The YMCA will erect a $30,000 property this year.
>
> The population is growing: 1880, 2810; 1890, 3415; and 1895, 7,500. City properties, including city buildings, are valued at $27,500. Warren has four banks with combined capital and surplus of $805,000 and deposits of $2,225,000.
>
> There are four fine school buildings with 1600 scholars and 40 teachers. School property is valued at $147,120. The water works provide a bountiful supply of good, pure water. Fire protection includes six volunteer fire companies—a reserve reservoir with 130 pounds water pressure and one Silsby Steamer.
>
> There are three railroads. Freight and passenger business is the largest in point of receipts of any town between Buffalo and Pittsburgh, Erie and Williamsport. Warren has natural gas—two competing companies with direct lines to the largest supply of natural gas in the United States. Manufacturers are over forty in number.
>
> The Warren library building and Opera House are owned by the municipality. They cost $80,000. The seating capacity of the Opera House is 960; the free library containing over 8,000 volumes. There are three daily newspapers and four weeklies.

There is no doubt that Warren was a thriving community as Simpson was beginning his career. It is certain that these comforts and conveniences of civilization were duly noted by Simpson, but not of great importance, as it was to the remaining wilderness where the birds and beasts had dominion that Simpson was drawn each day. This book takes its title from such a favored and frequently mentioned haunt of Simpson's. He says, "About 5 miles below town…is a large tract of wild land known along the river as the 'Grass Flats.' This has always been a favorite hunting and collecting ground with me."

In 1961, Tom Curtin, teacher and historian, published an article about Ralph B. Simpson. It is particularly poignant and offers additional insight to Simpson's life. Below are excerpts from Curtin's piece, titled *Priceless Legacy:*

> Forming such a detailed interest in nature this early in life left R.B. Simpson alone most of the time, except when he went on field trips with older enthusiasts. Loneliness had seemingly little effect on Simpson though, for until his dying day he would devote his spare time to advancing this interest and yet he would receive little recognition for his efforts because of his self-desired obscurity.
>
> Simpson acquainted himself with nature in general, but his greatest interest was the study of birds: ornithology. At the age of sixteen he saw his first paper published in an 1890 issue of *Oölogist*, a publication which was dedicated to the study of birds and eggs. This was just the beginning, for during his lifetime he had over eighty professional papers published on ornithology. Not only that, but he gave numerous authoritative notes to the Carnegie Museum, the Philadelphia Academy of Sciences, and the Smithsonian Institute.
>
> Anytime during the year was suitable for one of Simpson's field trips, and anytime that was his own was time devoted to his interest.
>
> When on these trips Simpson would take specimens, notes, and photographs of every type of bird that passed through Warren County.…Simpson had a way of hunting down nests and finding eggs that was seemingly comparable to a sixth sense. He also knew and could give most of the bird calls of the birds in this area.
>
> Upon returning home from a field trip Simpson would put his proficient ability in the art of taxidermy to use; creating an unequalled collection of birds and mammals of the area. As he worked diligently away, constantly improving this priceless collection, he did it quietly and strictly out of self-interest, and so recognition of his great achievements never came to him in his lifetime.

The understanding of birds of every conceivable species in Warren County became Simpson's passion, which he pursued with unmatched vigor. During most of his adult life he was closely associated with W.E. Clyde Todd, a leader in ornithology and at that time curator of the bird section of the Carnegie Museum in Pittsburgh, one of the finest natural history museums in America. While looking at some family memorabilia with Jim Henderson, a carefully hand-written letter revealed itself. Jim kindly shared the letter with me. It was from W.E. Clyde Todd to Mrs. Ralph Simpson, after the death of her husband on March, 30, 1960. With Jim's permission, I include part of that letter. Todd writes:

> I first met Ralph one June day in 1895, when he called me in from Tiona and I came to visit him at his home. He took me out in the rain, in my traveling suit, to look at a Magnolia Warbler's nest he had found. I tore my trousers on the trip and had to stay in bed the next morning until his mother could fix them.
>
> While I was in Washington *(D.C.)* in the 1890s, and after I came to Pittsburgh, he used to write me long and interesting letters about his finds. You will see that I used a great deal of this information in compiling my book. It was very generous of him to present his egg collection to the Carnegie Museum *(Pittsburgh, Pennsylvania)* some years ago. I assure you that it is and will be properly taken care of here. I learned that his collection of mounted birds is to be given to some local institution where it will be useful.
>
> My suggestion would be to have all his records, notebooks, and journals kept together and deposited in some safe place, for the benefit of those who may come after. Considerable change in the bird life has taken place since the early days, and his records are valuable.

Todd was a couple months older than Simpson, being 85 at this writing. Mr. Todd was an enormously respected ornithologist. The book he refers to is the 1940 *Birds of Western Pennsylvania,* the most important study of birds of this region. Many references to Simpson's work occur throughout Todd's book. In Todd's recognition of contributors to his book he says the following about Simpson:

> ...With thanks especially due Ralph B. Simpson, Warren, for the most comprehensive and carefully prepared list of birds from any locality in western Pennsylvania. Mr. Simpson has an extensive private collection of nests, eggs, and mounted birds, which it has been the privilege of this author to examine. Lately his interest has inclined

> more to photography, and he has supplied some excellent pictures of nests and eggs taken by Harry Granquist and himself."

Todd and Simpson had much in common. Both were self-educated in their specialty of birds. Neither man ever went to college to study the subject. Todd started his study of birds in 1887, while Simpson began his study earnestly in 1890, though his journals indicate his systematic study began as early as 1888.

In his journals when writing about the Olive-sided Flycatcher Simpson says:

> On coming back from West Virginia in the spring of 1900, I began to look these flycatchers up. In June I located a pair in the vicinity of our old camp at the head of the Tionesta while on a trouting trip. I wrote to Todd, of the Carnegie Museum, Pittsburgh, who had been trying for several years to get a pair from this state, and he came up. I took him over and he secured the birds for the museum.

This was the unassuming nature of Simpson—he assists an internationally recognized ornithologist in collecting needed specimens as if it was any day in the field. As I read the original Simpson journals this aspect of his character stands out—his lack of ego. He so loved the work, and he carried it out with scrupulous accuracy and painstaking care.

As W.E. Clyde Todd's letter indicates, considerable change in bird life has taken place making the Simpson records valuable. These journals have become ever more important in the nearly half-century since Todd wrote that letter. There is a wealth of information provided of interest to novices, advanced birders, and ornithologists; additionally there is also the sense of a man with a quiet calm about him—a character trait not often found today.

In his accounts Simpson speaks of the status of species through the seasons, habitat preferences, changes in avifauna, while at the same time offering a view of the natural world with a bit of whimsy—as in the following May 9, 1909, observations of the Screech Owl.

> I found the second nest of the Screech Owl that I robbed this spring. I knew of an old Flicker's hole nearby, and on going past I saw feathers about the edges so I investigated and found a Gray Screecher at home. She made no resistance so I reached in and counted five eggs under her, petted her, and left her.

Ralph B. Simpson did his field work and specimen collecting by the highest professional standards. Permits were required for collecting as this was a special privilege and responsibility. Each year he was specially licensed with a certificate granted by the County of Warren, Commonwealth of Pennsylvania. Simpson's September, 1893, certificate states the requirements as "...where written testimony from two well known scientific men was presented..." and where he "...executed a bond in the sum of fifty dollars as required...as witnessed by the Prothonotary." Simpson was then permitted to collect birds, their nests or eggs, for strictly scientific purposes by the Act of May 14, 1889, P.L. 218. These certificates permitted bona fide researchers to capture, mark, and hold live specimens; to salvage dead specimens; and to collect specimens, their nests, and eggs.

Ornithology at this time was still in its infancy; in fact, the first systematic list of birds of Pennsylvania was not published until 1845. The earliest information was gained through collecting bird skins, nests, and eggs. Study skins still provide value in research on birds in the field as well as in taxonomic investigations. When Simpson first began collecting in 1890, Benjamin Warren's book, a report authorized by the Commonwealth and titled *The Birds of Pennsylvania,* was just being published. This was the first thorough reference on the state's birds and it marked a new era in ornithological history. Simpson's scientific work contributed significantly to the next standard ornithological text in the Commonwealth, which was produced fifty years later, W.E. Clyde Todd's *Birds of Western Pennsylvania.*

Barbara and Richard Mearns report in their book, *The Bird Collectors,* that the first Roger Tory Peterson field guide was not published until 1934. Previous books were large, costly and not generally affordable, and impossible to use for species identification in the field. With the addition of the Peterson guides the "shotgun was being replaced by binoculars." The collection of species was no longer necessary to identify birds in the field, even though it was the only means available for centuries. In the early years, besides identification, species collection was used by professionals such as Simpson for study, examination, and classification.

From *The Bird Collectors:*

> Until well into the early decades of the twentieth century, the field ornithologist carried a gun for the same reason that an ornithologist now carries binoculars—it enabled him to identify what he saw.
>
> A few of the early ornithologists carried a telescope as well as a gun, prism binoculars were not invented until the beginning of the 1900s and they were expensive until after the First World War.

In the later years of his career, Simpson, along with his good friend Harry Granquist, used photography increasingly in the field. Simpson introduced Granquist to the world of birds on many field trips. Granquist became very interested in the feathered tribes and with Simpson produced many fine photographs. The addition of photography to Simpson's documented observations and specimen collection is noted often in the journals. Photography was an exciting addition to his field methods, and Simpson thought nothing of climbing to perilous heights to obtain a fine photo, as evidenced by this entry regarding the Tufted Titmouse.

> April 1, 1928, I saw and listened to one at Grass Flats. Later we saw it again and began watching and found there was a pair. Afterwards we watched for them and finally were rewarded by detecting them building. This nest on June 3 contained 7 eggs and we got a fine photo. It was 30 feet up in a Butternut tree—in an old Downy Woodpecker hole in a dead limb. The nest was a mass of shreds of bark, fur, and fine woody material. This is my first nesting record.

A little information as to the organization of *Grass Flats* is necessary. As part of his data collection Simpson provided measurements for many of his species accounts. Four numbers are the usual format and the measurements are in inches. The measurements will appear similar to this: 26–36–10 3/4–5 1/2. If a number is missing you'll find an "x" in its place. The numbers are length, wingspan, wing, and tail. The procedure he used to obtain the measurements is as follows: length is measured from the tip of the bill to the tip of the tail; wingspan is measured from wing tip to wing tip; wing is measured from the bend in a folded wing to the tip of the longest primary feather; and the tail is measured from the point at which the middle tail feathers emerge from the skin to the tip of the longest tail feather.

For some bird species Simpson also provides the date the specimen was taken, the sex, and whether it was a young bird or an adult; the weight of the bird; and on occasion the contents of the stomach. Simpson provides dates of arrival, departure, size of flocks, habitat, nesting, and feeding habits. Also observed are patterns of behavior, increased sightings or fewer sightings for different years, record flocks, and weather conditions. Severe storms are noted, and the resulting hardship and death to the feathered fauna are documented. Simpson continuously comments on the status and distribution of birds in Warren County and often at the Peninsula at Erie, Pennsylvania. Maps are provided to assist the reader on locations where data and species were gathered.

For each species, except the Presque Isle birds, Simpson provides the common name of the bird and the scientific name. I have added the newer common name, where different, in addition to the common name used a century ago. Some name changes are rather dramatic. The common name "Snowflake" of Simpson's time is now known as the "Snow Bunting." Also the updated scientific name has been included where applicable. The format for each species account is as follows:

Simpson common name | Current common name

Simpson scientific name | Current scientific name

For example, it would appear as follows for the Merganser:

American Merganser | Common Merganser

Merganser americanus | Mergus merganser

Species split, names change, and changes in taxonomic sequence over time accelerate. Every effort has been made to maintain accurate reference to modern and past naming conventions. For convenience there is an index provided for all common and scientific names, both historical and current. Also a list of the breeding birds of Warren County, as documented by Simpson, is provided.

Maps and images are either original creations by the editor or drawn from the extensive archives of the Warren County Historical Society. They are reproduced here with the kind permission of the Board of Directors. An index of maps and images is included.

Some geographical information was obtained from the *Gazetteer* appended to Todd's *Birds of Western Pennsylvania,* while other localities were obtained from county and township maps. Allegheny River islands were primarily identified and placed from the 1855 *Allegheny Pilot,* by E.L. Babbit, which contains a complete chart of the Allegheny River, showing the islands and bars and low water channels from Warren to Pittsburgh. Fixing the position of some remote locations has been a challenge, as Simpson includes mountains, hills, forests, hollows, islands, eddies, sand bars, swamps, ponds, runs, streams, rivers, lakes, lumber mills, crossings, bridges, homesteads, and villages. Many locations do not appear on any official topographic map or survey. Enough information is provided that the reader should feel comfortable at all times knowing what stream, creek, or river he is on—whether the compass points you east or west from Grass Flats—which side of the Allegheny River Simpson is roaming—and whether you are in the Conewango, Allegheny, or Tionesta drainage. To some readers these will be essential details; others will seek the adventure of birding in the virgin timber of the Wildcat Run—climbing 70 feet up a giant hemlock to peer into a Sharp-shinned Hawk's nest—or navigating a narrow precipice in Goshawk Basin, with little or no concern for their latitude and longitude. Simpson provides for those wanting early morning sub-zero hikes looking for Long-tailed Ducks during the blizzard of 1895, as well as for those readers eager to know dates of first arrival for each species.

The Table of Contents, minus the listed indices, prologue, and epilogue, is directly from the journals; book sections appear in all CAPS. Individual species accounts maintain Simpson's numbering order. Comments within parenthesis and in italics are by the editor. Comments within parenthesis, but not in italics, are from Simpson's journals. These unique documents are assembled here for the first time; minimal editing was done, and only for the sake of clarification. All photographs and drawings are by Ralph Simpson or Harry Granquist, unless otherwise noted.

As editor and publisher of *Grass Flats,* I accept all responsibility for error or omission, but remember valued reader,

Whoever thinks a faultless work to see,
Thinks what ne'er was, nor is, nor e'er shall be.
In every work regard the writer's end,
Since none can compass more than they intend,
And if the means be just, the conduct true,
Applause, in spite of trivial faults, is due.
W.J. McKnight

It is the editor's intention and desire that the publication of *Grass Flats* brings recognition to the life works of Ralph Bernard Simpson. It is also hoped that the information contained in the journals will benefit those working to preserve the natural world—and those recognizing the need for wild places. Simpson recognized early on, before there were any popular movements, that species became rare, some even extinct, through man's destruction of habitat. He understood, as W.E. Clyde Todd believed, that education is the best way to do something for bird life.

What follows are the words of Ralph Bernard Simpson, naturalist extraordinaire.

W.N. Hoover, editor and publisher

Ralph Bernard Simpson
September, 1897, 22 years of age.

MAPS

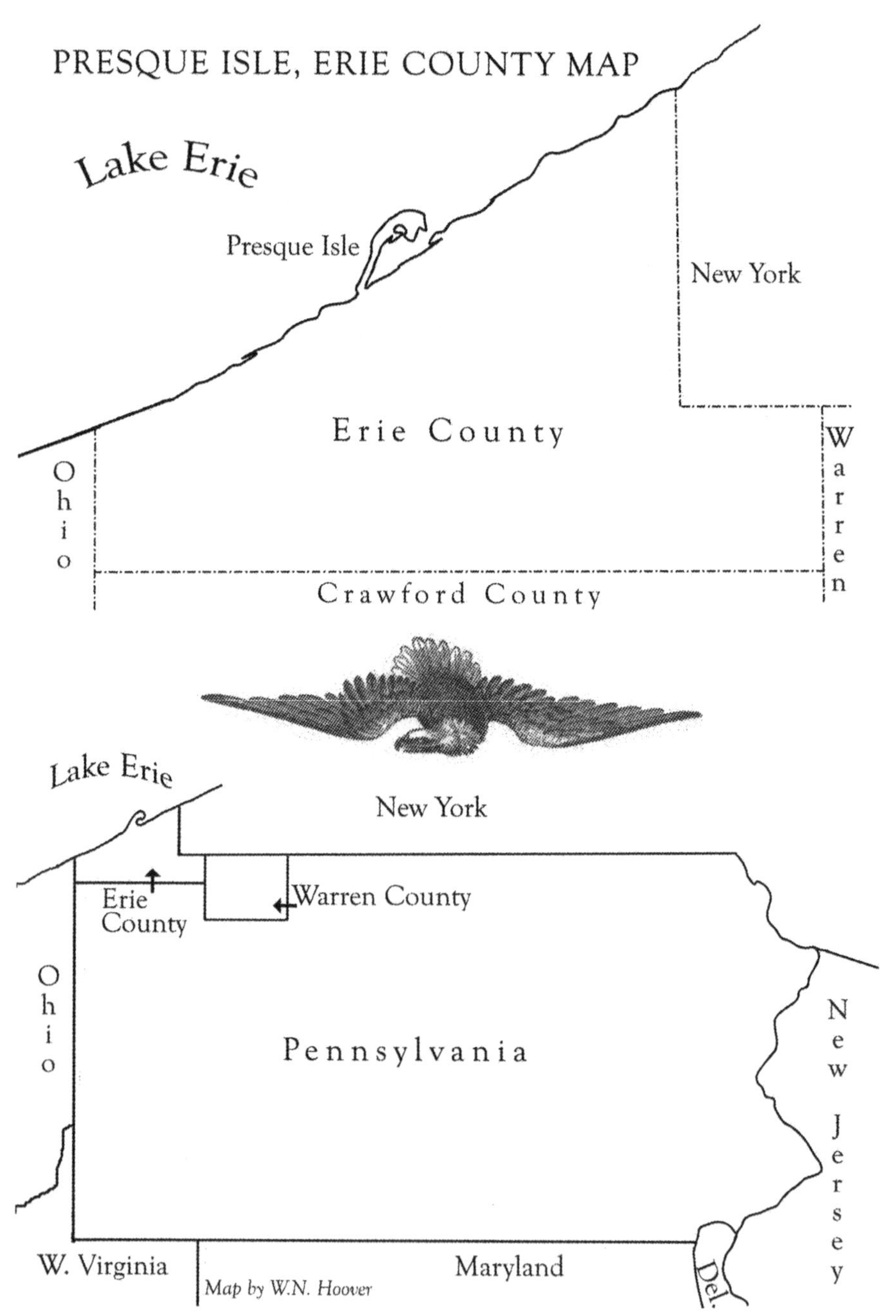
PRESQUE ISLE, ERIE COUNTY MAP
Lake Erie
Presque Isle
New York
Erie County
Ohio
Warren
Crawford County
Lake Erie
New York
Erie County
Warren County
Ohio
Pennsylvania
New Jersey
W. Virginia
Maryland
Del.
Map by W.N. Hoover

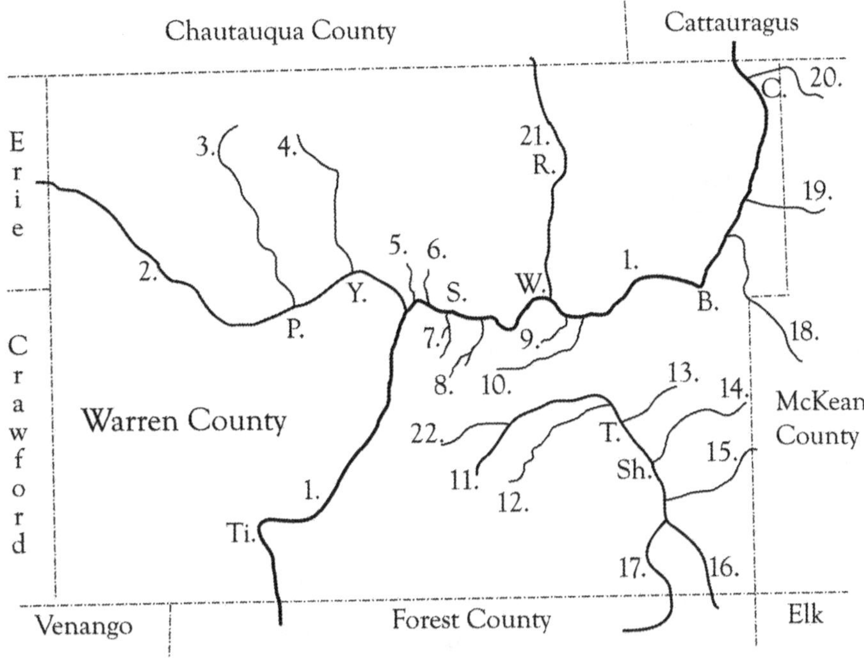

WARREN COUNTY MAP

Map Legend

Numbers are waterways. Letters are towns.

1. Allegheny River
2. Brokenstaw Creek
3. Little Brokenstraw
4. Matthews Run
5. Irvine Run
6. Scott Run
7. Grunder Run
8. Sill Run
9. Ott Run
10. Morrison Run
11. Head of Tionesta Creek
12. Farnsworth Branch
13. Six Mile Run
14. Four Mile Run
15. Two Mile Run
16. S. Branch Tionesta Creek
17. Tionesta Creek
18. Kinzua Creek
19. Sugar Run
20. Willow Creek
21. Conewango Creek
22. Wild Cat Run

B. Big Bend
C. Corydon
P. Pittsfield
R. Russell
S. Starbrick
Sh. Sheffield
T. Tiona
Ti. Tidioute
W. Warren
Y. Youngsville

NORTH

Map by W.N. Hoover

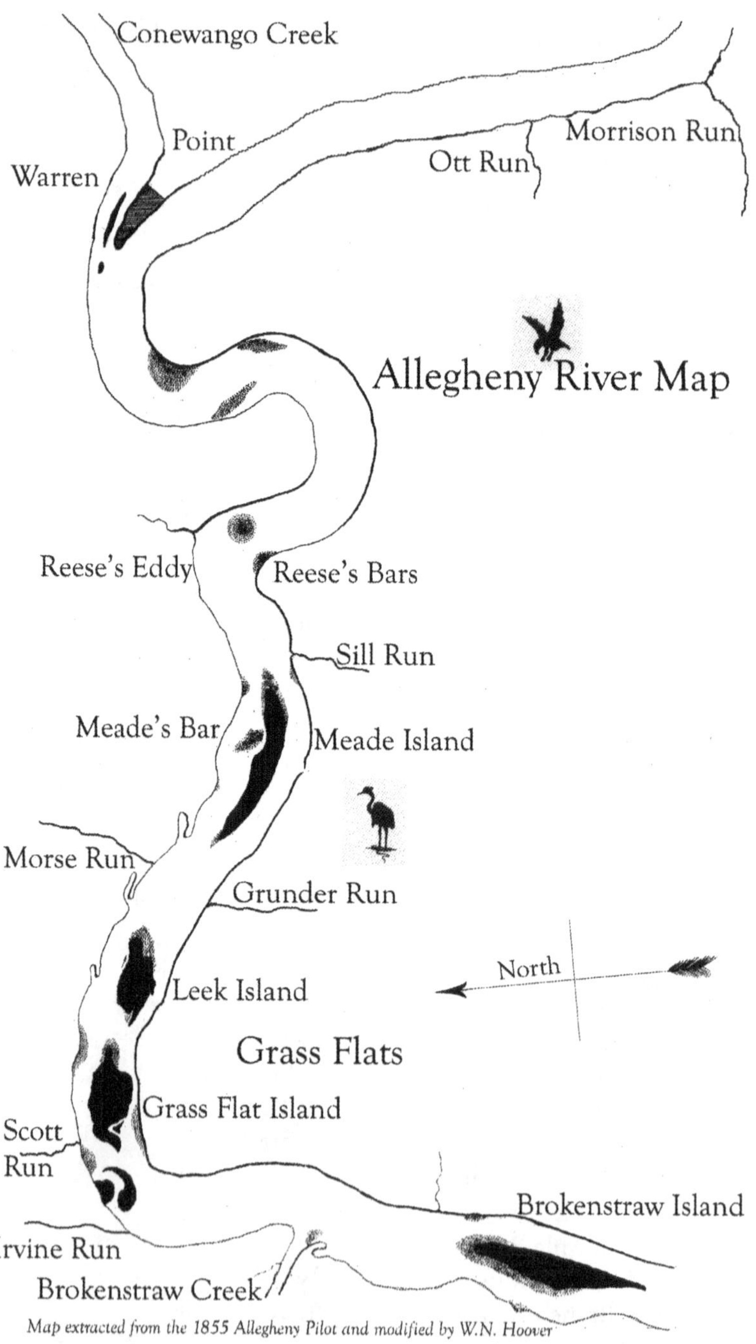

Map extracted from the 1855 Allegheny Pilot and modified by W.N. Hoover

WARREN COUNTY, PENNSYLVANIA

Situation—

Warren County, Pennsylvania, is in the northwestern corner of the state on the western slope, or foothills, of the Allegheny Mountains; the northern boundary is the boundary line between New York State and Pennsylvania, the parallel of 42 degrees north latitude. On the east it is bounded by McKean County, on the south by the northeastern corner of Venango County and Forest County, on the west by Crawford and Erie Counties.

The county measures about 36 miles across from east to west, about 25 miles across north to south, and contains somewhere around 850 square miles. The county line on all sides has been surveyed. No natural boundaries.

Surface—

Laying on the western slope of the Alleghenies the county is naturally quite hilly, rough, and elevated. On the east, along the McKean County line, the country is especially mountainous; the summits reaching an elevation of better than 2100 feet. Towards the west and northwest the elevation becomes less. The slopes of many of the hills are very steep, but there are no real cliffs. The summits of the hills are usually plateaus, the hills not running much to ridges or peaks.

At Warren the low water mark on the government river gauge in the Allegheny River is 1170.5 feet above sea level. Where the river leaves the county the elevation is a little less.

Along the river and larger streams are valleys, quite wide in places, and in other places the hills rise from the water's edge. The soil in places in the low lands and on the more gentle slopes is quite rich, but there are large areas in the mountains that are very rocky. In many places in the mountains huge boulders lie about, some 40 to 50 feet high.

Waterways—

The Allegheny River is the main waterway. It enters the county from New York State on the north, close to the northeastern corner of the county, and flows southwesterly through the county in an erratic and zigzag manner, leaving toward the southwest corner and dividing the county into two unequal parts—the larger part, maybe 5/8th, laying to the west. The river is a succession of rapids and eddies—the eddies vary in length—some are nearly a mile long and of good depth.

At the head or foot of many of these eddies are islands. The largest of these islands is Meade Island several miles below Warren. This is the largest island in the whole length of the river.

(In Todd's 1940 book, Birds of Western Pennsylvania, *Meade Island is described as the largest and most valuable of any island on the river below Warren. It is about 1 mile in length, contains about 300 acres, and is valued at $7,000. Meade's bar extends from the island about one-fourth of a mile below the head. It reaches nearly half way from the island to the north shore, and throws a strong current into the north bank. It is located opposite Starbrick, Warren County.)*

The Conewango River or Creek, the outlet of the famous Lake Chautauqua in New York State, enters from the north and forms a junction with the Allegheny at Warren.

The Brokenstraw and Tionesta Creeks are both large streams.

The county is very well watered by many smaller creeks and runs. Throughout the hills are many fine springs. Due to the mountainous nature of the county, ponds are scarce, except artificial bodies, and the swamps are rather insignificant.

The beds of the streams are mostly rock and gravel; mud or sand bars are not common. In the wilder eastern part of the county many of the mountain streams flow over beds of white sand and gravel.

Vegetation, Past and Present—

When white men first set foot in Warren County it was one unbroken forest of mostly great pines and hemlocks, with many great ridges of beech, and large tracts of oak, chestnut, and other hardwoods, but the bulk of the forest was coniferous. As time passed and the country began to be settled, lumbering became an important industry.

Most of the timber was cut into logs, made into rafts, floated to Pittsburgh and Ohio River points and sold. The men who took these rafts down in the early days were compelled to walk back the entire distance from Pittsburgh, 185 or 190 miles.

After the Civil War lumbering became a very important business with hundreds of rafts going down the river every spring. Sawmills sprang into existence in the towns and back in the mountains, and the deforesting of the county proceeded more rapidly.

The Pennsylvania Tanning Company bought large tracts of hemlock, peeled the bark, and left the great hemlocks lie on the ground to rot. The decayed remains can even yet be seen lying about in some regions. At present there are sawmills in the towns, but back in the woods now, here and there, is an occasional small mill that does business only for a year or so.

Rafting is now a thing of the past. At present the largest stands of virgin timber are on the Forest and McKean County lines and in the vicinity of Sheffield. It is about all owned by the Pennsylvania Tanning Company. Very large and complete mills at Sheffield and Kinzua will in a few years wipe out of existence about all of the first growth or virgin timber.

There are many tracts of mixed timber which have been partly lumbered off years ago—big woods too, but still not virgin. The land that has been deforested has in many regions sprung up into fine second growth, usually mostly hardwood.

In many regions that have been fire-swept and baked by the sun only scrub-oak, poplar, fire-cherry, and brush grows. Fire and hot sun have reduced some ridges and summits to rocky barrens where nothing much but brake, huckleberries, and sweet ferns can grow.

Mountain Laurel is plentiful in many places and along some of the streams is found considerable Rhododendron. The woods are carpeted everywhere with ferns and mosses, while many different species of wild flowers bloom in season. Of those most sought after are the Trailing Arbutus, Orchids (pink and yellow) commonly known as Lady Slippers, both kinds of Laurels, Trilliums of several species, and beautiful, sweet-scented Azaleas, known by everyone in this region as Honeysuckles.

In virgin forest and heavy timber there is not much brush, the ground being carpeted by moss and ferns and very short brush. In the more open woodland is found much brush—Witch-hazel, Dogwood, etc.

In the bottomlands, especially along the river and larger streams, the vegetation in many respects is much different from that back in the mountains. Regular bottom woodland consists of sycamore, elm, butternut, and a scattering of most of the mountain timber, except the Yellow Pine which is only found on the mountains. The ground in these lowland woods and on the islands is carpeted with a luxuriant growth of ferns, skunk-cabbage, and nettles.

In the spring many of these bottom woodlands are great flower beds, being fairly carpeted with Adder-tongues, Phlox, Trilliums, Blue-bells, and many other varieties. Large thorn trees and Slippery Elm are also common to this bottom woodland.

Along the river on the bars and in the quiet water several species of water plants and rushes grow plentifully. In the few swamps and ponds, cattails and flag flourish. *(Flag is a plant with a bladed leaf.)*

Water lilies are rare in this county and are found in but few places. Mr. S.S. Dickey of Waynesburg, for part of a season, made a study of the tree and plant life here. He found many northern or Canadian species, also much that belongs to the Carolinas. We seem to be quite rich in violets, as in a short time he found 14 varieties. *(Professor Samuel S. Dickey, of Waynesburg, Ohio, was a naturalist of note and writer of bird and nature lore, such as:* The Value of Hawks and Owls, Oölogist, *February, 1915;* First recorded nesting of the Bachman's Sparrow in Pennsylvania, Auk, *April, 1917. Most of S.S. Dickey's writings regarding the birds of Pennsylvania were of Central and Southern Pennsylvania, particularly Greene County.)*

Wild and Farming Districts—

That part of the county west of the river is more or less farming land with plenty of tracts of woodland. East of the river the county is little settled and is nearly all wild land.

Climate—

The climate is rather variable. We have some open winters and some quite severe ones. As a rule we get some very cold weather every winter. During severe winters snow in the hills sometimes gets over 3 feet deep and there is a great deal of below zero weather.

On several occasions the government thermometer at Warren has reached 27 1/2 degrees below zero, while at the Pennsylvania Gas Company station at Roystone—in the mountains near Sheffield and where records must be kept—the thermometer has recorded 35 degrees and more below zero.

Some winters we get a run of sleighing for 3 months. Ice sometimes freezes to a thickness of 20 inches on the open river. I have known the ice to stay in the river until as late as March 18. It has snowed as early as the last week in September and snowfalls, occasionally quite heavy, sometimes occur in October. I have known of 12 inches of heavy snow to fall on October 25.

We always have snowfalls in April and frequently in early May. Snow has fallen as late as Decoration Day. Frosts are apt to occur up to June and again anytime after the first of September. In the summer the temperature does not often go above 95 degrees and seldom reaches 98 degrees.

In the valley vegetation leafs out in May, but back in the hills it is usually the first of June before it is well leafed out. By the first of October the leaves are turning color and by the first of November most of them have fallen off.

Principal Towns—

Warren, the largest town and county seat, is situated in the valley at the junction of the Allegheny and Conewango Rivers. It has a population of over 14,000 and on average is 1200 feet above sea level. The courthouse and main business part of town being 1209 feet in elevation. Sheffield, Clarendon, Kinzua, Corydon, Russell, Youngsville, and Tidioute are the other principal towns. *(The towns of Corydon and Kinzua exist no more. They were flooded by the building of the Kinzua Dam and the Allegheny Reservoir in the 1960s.)*

Migrations—

Stragglers are apt to and do occur at all times of the year. The northern visitors, regular or irregular, are liable to be met with anytime from about the first of November up to and into April. The spring migrations begin along toward the first of March, everything of course depending on the weather conditions that have prevailed during winter.

Crows, Canada Geese, Robins, or Bluebirds are apt to be the first noted along about the first of March. Later on in March the ducks are represented by the appearance of Black Duck, Mallard, and Merganser. During April the principal northward movement of the waterfowl occurs with constant new arrivals and migrations of land species. During early May the largest flights occur, as at this time the warblers are everywhere. The largest number of species seen any one day during migrations was 82 species on May 30, 1907.

By the first of June the migrations are pretty much over—with only a few of the very late ones still being about. In August the southward movement begins with an occasional shore bird, and late in August usually an occasional little bunch of migrants is noted. The southward movement is heavy the latter part of September. Small migrants some days fairly swarm. After October 10 a warbler is seldom seen, but the sparrow tribe is more or less common until November.

Collecting Grounds—

Warren County is a fairly good collecting ground. The Allegheny River is a natural highway for water fowl during migrations. Its general course of north to south and nearness to a great body of water such as Lake Erie are a combination that causes a large variety of ducks, together with some members of the grebe, gull, and loon families, to be found during migrations.

Before spring shooting was abolished good bags of waterfowl were often taken. Our fall duck shooting is not very good. The absence of lakes, large ponds, and mud bars causes but few of the shore birds to stop here, while the absence of swamps of any size is no doubt the reason for the scarcity of many swamp birds such as rails.

As vegetation leafs out first along the river valley, the warblers and small migrants are generally pretty well bunched, especially during the earlier part of their migrations, and some days they are very abundant. What we miss on the water birds here is fully made up in the breeding birds. The conditions in our mountains are very much Canadian and many of the more northern breeders stay and find a congenial summer home. Along the river valley in summer there may also be found some of the Carolinian breeders.

Field birds are not nearly as common as in a more settled community, but all around there is some very good stuff found in this region—including breeders that are rare or wanting in most parts of Pennsylvania.

Observers—

There have been but few observers here in the bird line. H.L. Greenlund was the local taxidermist here for a number of years and his brother for several years after he quit. Both however were in the business for profit only, neither had a private collection. They did not pay much attention to or make a study of small birds, and kept no particular notes or records that I have heard of—although many interesting birds, especially the larger ones, must have passed through their hands. *(B.H. Warren's* List of Authorities, *in his 1888-90 book,* Birds of Pennsylvania, *does give some credit to H.L. Greenlund. He appears among persons who "courteously sent lists of birds found in different counties of the commonwealth or otherwise materially aided the writer in securing much valuable information concerning the avifauna of Pennsylvania." Provisional lists, including natives, permanent residents, spring and fall migrants, occasional visitants, and stragglers were sent to B.H. Warren and used when he compiled his book. Simpson was just beginning his work at this time.)*

A few years ago Professor Roy Homer—then connected with the high school here—interested a few of the students in birds. Several good records were made in this way. At present there are a few persons here who are interested in birds, but none go very deep into the subject. Almost all the notes and data in this list are my own, of course, only a small part of the county has been thoroughly covered. Most of my notes were taken since 1890, although a number were taken prior to that time.

Practically every spare hour for a number of years was spent afield. Most of my long hikes were back in the heavy timber and slashings in the wild lands. During the season for waterfowl I would be out at daylight every morning, also spending many full days in March and April down the river at Meade Island and Grass Flats, my favorite ducking grounds.

Morning after morning I was out at break of day during May looking up the warblers and small migrants. Being out so much practically every day I was able to get almost perfect migration notes as to the date of first arrivals, when most abundant, and when last seen. During the nesting season I paid particular attention to the breeding birds.

During the summer I fish a great deal for bass and trout, and I am always on the lookout for birds and animals. In the fall I always watched for the small migrants, hunted game, trapped fur-bearers, and in mid-winter hunted foxes.

By going out constantly the year round for so many years I got many rare specimens and records and my migration notes were about as perfect as they well could be.

Presque Isle, Pennsylvania—

I made a few trips to Presque Isle in Lake Erie, Erie, Pennsylvania. Some of the records and notes that I made there are very good and as well worth saving as my Pennsylvania records. Some of the Presque Isle accounts, the best of them, will be recorded in this list from time to time.

My trips to the Peninsula, dates inclusive, were as follows: 1900 (September 5-19); 1902 (April 24-27), (September 26-28), (November 17-23); 1903 (April 13-16), (November 10-14); 1904 (July 27), (October 5-8); 1905 (May 16-20), (September 19-23); 1908 (February 22); 1909 (July 6); 1910 (June 2-3); 1911 (May 31-June 3), (October 17-19); and 1912 (April 1-2). *(Presque Isle is also known by many residents of northwestern Pennsylvania simply as the "Peninsula." Simpson uses the two names interchangeably.)*

These trips were made with the purpose of securing new shore birds and waterfowl, but of course I was on the lookout for anything new or unusual in the way of birds. There is always a chance of any of the birds occurring at Presque Isle, and also of occurring along the river at Warren—especially during severe storms. Several species of water birds, including several quite scarce that would hardly be looked for in western Pennsylvania except along Lake Erie, have at long intervals been detected in Warren County, and others no doubt may be detected in the future. *(B.H. Warren,* Birds of Pennsylvania, *states: "There are more numerous species of aquatic birds at Presque Isle Bay than elsewhere in the state.")*

List of Species of Warren County—

Every record in this list is positive. The stragglers are all records of birds that I have taken myself or seen in the possession of the party who took them.

Birds have been described to me that I never met with here, and I have seen and as good as positively identified several species which I have not included in this list, as I did not capture them.

No doubtful records are given.

At present my Warren County list contains 212 species. *(Species 213-218 were added after October 1, 1923, Simpson's original composition date.)*

Thirteen of these I have classed as residents, they being found more or less at all seasons.

Ninety-three occur as summer residents, being more or less common in summer and breeding. I have not classed any bird as a summer resident unless it has been found breeding. Odd birds are frequently found about in summer, but close watching and searching would show that they were not breeding. They were simply left over or wounded birds, or birds that for some reason had failed to finish their journey north.

Seven occur as winter visitors only. Thirty-six occur as regular migrants. Twenty-four occur as irregular migrants not being regularly met with.

Twenty occur as rare visitors, having been met with only at long intervals, not often enough to be called irregular migrants, and most too often to be called stragglers.

Eighteen I have classed as stragglers—they having only been seen at very long intervals or only once or twice in many years. One, the Passenger Pigeon, is extinct.

Of the 212 species known to me to have occurred here I have found 106 to breed, having found eggs or young. *(Breeding species 107-114 added after October 1, 1923.)*

I am very certain that several others—Virginia Rail, Yellow-bellied Flycatcher, Crossbill, Nashville Warbler, and Red-breasted Nuthatch—do or have bred here, but up to date I have no positive breeding record.

Several species of ducks are said to have formerly nested in this county, but so far I have never found a nest or seen a brood of young of any kind. *(RBS later notes in the journals that a brood of Black Ducks was located in Warren County during the season of 1925-26.)*

The raven and Passenger Pigeon both nested here formerly, but I have not included them in this list of breeders, as it has been many years since the raven nested here and the pigeon of course never will again.

The wild turkey may have been found here in the past, but old hunters seem to know nothing about it. I think we have always been a little out of their range. *(The wild turkey is not an uncommon bird today in Warren County.)*

PRESQUE ISLE, PENNSYLVANIA, BIRDS

The following is a list of birds that I have taken personally or obtained at Erie, Pennsylvania. Up to date none of these birds have come to my notice here at Warren, although any of them are liable to be found here as stragglers.

Brunnichs Murre

I have a specimen of this bird in my collection that was taken by the late S.E. Bacon of Erie. This specimen was taken on the Peninsula, November 11, 1900. Several small flights of this murre have occurred along the lake of recent years. *(Samuel E. Bacon wrote about the birds of Erie, for example:* Great Northern Shrike and Robin at Erie, Oölogist, *April, 1888;* Old Squaw, Clangula hiemalis, the Abundance on Lake Erie and Destruction by Fishermen's Nets, Ornithologist *and* Oölogist, *March, 1892.)*

Glaucous Gull

On February 22, 1908, I spent the entire morning lying on the ice along the shore of Erie Bay at the mouth of Mill Creek. There was a flock of 20 or 25 Herring Gulls about the large opening on the bay off the mouth of the creek. With the Herring Gulls was a very large white gull. Some of the Herring Gulls would come in and up the creek and feed up the railroad tracks, but the big white fellow would hardly come closer than 10 or 12 rods. I did not care to try a long shot, as I was in the hopes that sooner or later he would come in with some of the others, and I could make a sure thing of it. This, however, he failed to do, and I finally left without a shot.

I had a number of very good views of this gull. As it was so much larger than the Herrings I think it must have been a Glaucous rather than an Iceland. It was certainly one of the two.

Shoveller Duck

I have taken a female at Erie on this Peninsula, November 13, 1903. This is the only one I have seen there, but it is occasionally taken there and should occur at Warren.

Canvas-back Duck

I have a fine pair from Erie Bay—a male taken December 3, 1903, and a female, December 6, 1904. This duck is frequently taken at Erie. I am surprised to have no records for Warren.

King Eider

I have a specimen in fall plumage that was shot along the outside beach of the Peninsula, December 22, 1904. This species, like the Brunnichs Murre, has occurred at long intervals along the lake.

American Scoter

I have a fall specimen taken over the decoys off Crystal Point in Misery Bay, November 8, 1903. *(Crystal Point, the site of the Perry Monument, at the western entrance to Misery Bay, Presque Isle.)*

Surf Scoter

I have a fall specimen taken in Horseshoe Pond back of the Life Saving Station, November 7, 1903. During this trip I saw outside beach ducks that were scoters, some of which were either the Surf or American.

Yellow Rail

I have three specimens of Yellow Rail from Erie taken on the following dates: September 26, 1900; April 23, 1904; and October 4, 1908. Personally I have not met it. It is very secretive. Most of the specimens taken at Erie were secured by Sam Bacon with the aid of a good bird dog.

Knot

I took a specimen in fall plumage on the outside beach on September 10, 1900. This is the only one I met with on any of my trips up there, and the bird is rare, or has been for a number of years.

Baird's Sandpiper

I took specimens several times during my September trips. I have two in my collection secured on September 10, 1900, and October 7, 1904. They are quite scarce. These sandpipers are found in company with flocks of other small shore birds along the outside beach.

Sanderling

I have found this sandpiper to be very common during the fall migrations at Presque Isle, but have not seen it there in the spring. It was found along the water's edge of the outside beach.

Although common along Lake Erie I have never met with it along the Allegheny River at Warren. I think, from observing its habits at the Peninsula, that it is a bird that prefers large bodies of water. It would not be found inland along the smaller rivers and streams, except possibly during severe storms.

Willet

Apparently I have the only record of the occurrence of this species at Erie, at least of recent years. April 24, 1902, while hunting along the outside beach I saw two large birds standing at the water's edge ahead of me a short distance. At first I took them to be gulls or terns of some sort, but as I drew closer I saw they were not. I kept my eyes on them and soon saw by the way they tipped and by their general appearance that they were large waders of some sort.

As there was absolutely no chance to sneak up on them, I walked along as if to pass at long range. About the time I got in range both birds arose and I fired at once. One fell, but the other kept on, as I was about to shoot the second barrel at this one, it also fell. They proved to be a very fine pair in full spring plumage.

Upland Plover

This plover or sandpiper is found along the mainland regularly in Erie County where it nests or at least used to nest. It is said to be very rare on the Peninsula—preferring the fields on the mainland. I shot one on the Peninsula however on April 26, 1902. It was during a gale and this bird was with a flock of Bonaparte Gulls that were coming in from the open lake and down Niagara Pond to the Bay. I did not know what it was, so as the flock flew past I picked off the odd one. *(Niagara Pond is near the eastern end of Presque Isle.)*

I have two specimens from the mainland, August 19, 1903, and April 9, 1904. I am rather surprised that this bird has never occurred here, but up to the present time I have no Warren County record.

Piping Plover

This pretty little plover I found regularly spring and fall on the Peninsula. It was rare though at all times, and there never seemed to be more than a couple pairs. They were only found on the outside beach. I found a nest of this bird May 31, 1911, on the high beach on the outside. It held 3 fresh eggs. This is the only nest actually found there that I know of. The Semipalmated Plover occurs quite frequently here at Warren and there is a chance for the Piping to occur also, as at Erie I often saw them together. (*RBS notes in margin that:* May 29, 1932, Harry Granquist and I found 3 nests of the Piping Plover on the Peninsula, four eggs in each nest. Also, May 24, 1933, four eggs and May 28, 1933, four eggs.)

Short-billed Marsh Wren

May 19, 1905, I shot a specimen on a grassy meadow at one of the ponds on the Peninsula. In 1932 I found a nesting site in the Niagara Pond Marsh. There were 12 or 15 nests in the long grass, none with eggs.

Gray-cheeked Thrush

In late September, 1900, this thrush was to be found occasionally on the Peninsula in company with other migrating thrush. I have one taken September 18. Although I never saw it here at Warren it undoubtedly occurs. I think a close search would discover it.

BIRDS OF WARREN COUNTY, PENNSYLVANIA

THE GREBES

Of the three species of grebes occurring in Pennsylvania, all have been taken in Warren County. None of the grebes breed here. All occur as migrants and are commonly know as "Hell-divers." Large flights of one species, the Horned Grebe, often occur in April with flights of ducks and other waterfowl.

One remarkable thing in connection with the grebe family here is the number of occurrences of the Holboell's Grebe, a species that is a rather rare occurrence in this state anywhere.

Grebes used to be shot in considerable numbers, especially during flights, by duck hunters. They only furnished amusement however, as they are unfit for food.

Holboell's Grebe | Red-necked Grebe
Colymbus holboelli | Podiceps grisegena

(1.) Irregular migrant spring and winter—throughout Pennsylvania in general the Holboell's Grebe seems to be of rare occurrence, in fact, little more than a straggler in most places. This seems rather strange as I have 22 records of its occurrence in Warren County since 1890.

When seen here during the spring flight I have found it to be quite wary, keeping well away from shore. As they are expert divers and hard to stalk, they are not easily taken.

When found here in winter it is always during severe weather. At such times they are generally not hard to approach, appearing to be in rather bad shape. In one case a bird was picked up alive, but exhausted. This was in the snow—back in the country.

The first time this grebe came to my notice was on April 13, 1892. I had gone down the river on a duck hunt, and I met a friend coming up who told me that there was a large diver of some sort near the foot of Meade Island. I crossed in a boat and hunting along carefully soon saw the grebe. As it was diving and feeding about 50 feet from shore, I ran up a little and hid at each dive until in good range—then a charge of 6 shot stretched it out. This was a fine adult male in full plumage.

April 20, 1892, furnished a second record when an adult was in the river at town. It was shot at several times by gunners, but was not secured.

During the spring of 1893, which was a very good season for waterfowl in general, no less than 4 of these grebes came to my notice here. The first occurred on March 21. There had been a southerly wind with rain during the night, which had brought on a small flight of waterfowl. About 7:30 a.m. I saw a diver in the river above the bridge, by its size and silvery throat patch I knew it to be a Holboell's. About that time a friend of mine came with a gun. We then went after Mr. Diver. He was laying in ambush on shore, while I went out in a boat and tried to work the grebe in to him. Once I got within 50 feet of him myself, but it stayed away from the gun. Very soon another party appeared on the scene with a rifle and opened fire. I didn't like this one little bit so I came to shore and gave him the whole river to shoot up. After an ineffectual bombardment the grebe got below the bridge and escaped. This one was a fine large adult.

On April 1, two were in the river above the bridge. One was shot by a friend of mine, Harry Parks. The other escaped. Both were adult birds.

The fourth, and last for 1893, appeared in the river above the bridge on the morning of April 28. Several gunners got after it, and it was finally killed by John Truby, a young man quite interested in birds at that time. He was taking lessons in taxidermy and practiced on this bird, but with what results I never heard. This was also an adult bird.

None were recorded then for some time. During February, 1899, we had a week of blizzard weather with high northwesterly winds, snow-squalls, and zero temperatures that dropped as low as 25 degrees below one morning. On the morning of February 12 one was seen sitting on the ice on Kings Eddy off the foot of Meade Island. It was some distance from open water and no doubt could have been picked up alive, but it was shot. It was in fall or winter plumage.

Next morning another was picked up by a farmer a long ways from water. It was found in the snow along a road—alive, but exhausted. It was brought in alive and I bought it for 50 cents. I put it in a wash-tub partly filled with water and threw in fine pieces of meat which were greedily devoured.

A florist who had a pond in his greenhouse wanted it, so I let him have it. He put it in the pond with two big Mandarin Ducks and next morning the grebe was dead, having been set upon and killed by the ducks.

The winter of 1903-04, one of the most severe of my time, furnished more records. Two specimens in winter plumage were taken by high school students and were made into skins by Professor Homer.

A third I shot myself on the morning of February 2, 1904. It was bitter cold with a temperature of 10 degrees below zero, strong northwesterly winds, and fierce snow-squalls. It was in a little piece of open water in front of the Water Works plant. I easily approached this Holboell's and shot it. This one was also in winter plumage. I received reports of others being seen, but of course they might have been mergansers or other waterfowl, as the severe weather had driven in various northern and lake birds.

April 19, 1904, quite a flight of water fowl came in following a stormy night of wind and rain. I spent the day hunting ducks down the river, and during the afternoon I saw a fine adult Holboell's in the eddy below Meade Island. Although there was a number of Horned Grebes near shore, this old fellow stayed way out. I went after him with a boat, but he was very wild and escaped by diving and keeping on down the river.

May 3, 1904, I saw one in the river above the suspension bridge after supper. This one was not fully adult. The throat patch and markings were there, but were dull. I would think this a very late date for this grebe to appear here.

March 24, 1905, a day or two after the ice had passed out, I saw one in winter plumage on the overflowed meadows below town. Next day it was still there and was shot by Carl Marsh.

April 8, 1905, I saw and shot at, but failed to secure one in Highhouse's Eddy. This one was in winter plumage.

April 18, 1905, after a stormy night of wind and snow (six inches of snow fell) a fine adult male appeared with a small bunch of Horned Grebes in the river above the suspension bridge. It was shot at a few times without effect, so after supper I took my gun and boat and went right after it. I chased it up to the swift water where it tried to dive around me and get below. I backed up and rowed over a little with the result that the grebe came up within range where a quick shot secured it. It was a very fine adult.

March 1, 1907, I saw a Holboell's in winter plumage in some open water in the Conewango above the North Warren Refinery. I walked out on the ice quite close, but did not have a gun. February 9, 1912, I saw one in the open water below the lower railroad bridge. It was of course in winter plumage. April 19, 1912, there was an adult in the river at town, but as it was in the closed season it was not disturbed.

April 14, 1917, there was a nice adult in the river above the suspension bridge all morning. April 10, 1919, while taking a hike down along the river I saw one in winter plumage. March 28, 1923, a Holboell's in winter plumage was in the river above the new bridge all morning. *(The image that follows shows the old suspension bridge and the new bridge referenced by Simpson.)*

A friend at Erie sent me a Holboell's in winter plumage which he had shot along the Peninsula, November 20, 1912. April 29, 1927, a nice adult was in the river above the new bridge all day. March 24, 1933, I saw one in the river in winter plumage. March 15, 1934, I saw one at town here and on March 18 there were two, all in winter plumage.

Measurements:

April 13, 1892, adult male, 19 1/2–31–7 1/2–x

Old and new bridges from Hickory Street and Pa. Avenue.
Allegheny River, Warren, Pennsylvania, photo taken 1918.
Morning shot from 2nd floor of Consumer Discount on Pa. Avenue.
Removing old suspension bridge (left) which was built 1871-72.

New Hickory Street bridge, officially opened 1918, looking north.

Horned Grebe

Colymbus auritus / Podiceps auritus

(2.) A regular spring migrant, occasional in fall—sometimes seen in the winter. Arrives: March 28, 1891; April 3, 1893; March 27, 1894; March 3, 1895; April 7, 1899; March 26, 1900; April 4, 1902; and March 26, 1904.

This species is more or less common during April, especially during the latter half of the month. It is often met with early in May. Stragglers are seen at times up to June. It is met with singly, in pairs, and small flocks of up to a dozen individuals.

Flights of Horned Grebes sometimes appear in April after severe storms that drive in flights of waterfowl. Large flights occurred on April 16, 1891; April 24, 1892; April 25, 1893; and April 12, 1899.

The great flight of April 25, 1893, was the largest that has occurred in my time. This was really a very great flight. From reports of persons riding on the cars between here and Pittsburgh, a distance of 180 miles, and between here and Olean, 60 miles north of us, the flight appears to have been generally the full length of the river. The grebes were abundant everywhere on the river. The night before had been cloudy with a little rain, but it was not a really bad night.

I spent the entire day down the river at Grass Flats and Meade Island. All day long the grebes were abundant. They were everywhere along the shore and in the brush. Flocks of as high as 50 to 60 were continually floating down in midstream, and large flocks were constantly flying past.

At one time I counted 6 big flocks of more than 30 each flying. All were in sight at once. Along Meade Island I saw a great gathering. Many flocks had gathered on a stretch of quiet water, and after counting a few I estimated that there must have been around 500 gathered there. It was certainly some sight.

At the head of Grass Flats a passing train scared up 8 flocks of from 15 to 40 each and all came up past me—one big flock passing not 30 feet directly overhead as I floated along. At a piece of quiet water along shore at Grass Flats there was always a great gathering. When I took a shot at a duck all the grebes would leave, but would soon begin to gather in again. Other flocks coming in, flying up, would drop in so that in a short time they would be as plentiful as ever. At times there were nearly 300 there at once, and to lay close by and watch them was some treat.

I took a couple of very fine adults, but refrained from shooting at a flock. Late in the afternoon on my way back I succumbed to temptation—I tried a pot shot at a great bunch of grebes as they piled out of the overflowed brush along shore. As a result of that shot 10 grebes lay dead on the water. This shot will give you a good idea of how thick the grebes were, but it did something else for me—it cured me forever of smashing into a solid flock of birds, as I was ashamed of it on looking at the slaughter.

Great numbers of grebes were killed at many points along the river and the flight must have suffered considerable loss. Next day only an occasional grebe was seen.

With this flight there were also large flocks of Bonaparte's Gulls—some flocks numbering up to 75 and 100 birds. There were also quite a few flocks of ducks, mostly Long-tails and Bufflehead, with a few Lesser Scaup, Whistlers, and Black Duck. Also seen were several Ruddy, Mallard, Blue-wing Teal, and 2 White-winged Scoters.

Although the other big flights contained many grebes they were not so great in numbers, nor did they extend over so much territory as did the great flight of April 25, 1893.

During the spring of 1904, two grebes stayed at town on the river all through May and up until June 18. Both may have been wounded birds that couldn't get away sooner.

In the fall they are only occasionally seen. My earliest fall record is November 1, 1894, and my latest December 17, 1894. When seen during the fall it is singly or in pairs, only very rarely in small parties of up to half a dozen birds.

Rarely met with in winter—January 18, 1901, I shot one at town during a spell of mild weather. During the severe winter of 1903-04, two were recorded. I found the first frozen to the ice by its breast feathers, February 2, 1904, the day that I shot the Holboell's previously mentioned. The second was shot in a piece of open water at town, February 26. February 5, 1914, one was found by a farmer alive, but exhausted in the snow.

The Horned Grebe is commonly known as "Hell-diver" and "Red-head."

April 21, 1929, there was quite a flight of waterfowl; among them were a number of flocks of Horned Grebes—8 to 20 in a flock. February 3, 1935, I saw one at town. Once so common they have become rare and seldom seen, however in April, 1947, I saw it on 3 occasions, a flock of 7, a bunch of 4, and on the last occasion I saw a single.

Measurements:

Fall, 13–23 1/2–5 1/2–x

Pied-billed Grebe
Podilymbus Podiceps

(3.) A regular migrant in both spring and fall.

Arrives: March 30, 1899; March 24, 1905; and March 19, 1914. Latest spring dates are April 22, 1901; May 6, 1902; and April 27, 1904.

During the spring movement this grebe is rather scarce, only occasionally being met with singly or in pairs. During the fall movement I have seen it as early as August 28, 1900, and as late as November 14, 1890, and November 18, 1901.

In the fall it is more often seen than in the spring, and it is met with singly, in pairs, and sometimes in little parties of 5 or 6. On September 30, 1901, I saw a flock of 12 and on October 12, 1909, I saw a flock of 13. I have not recorded it in winter, but I have seen it in summer—June 12, 1894, and July 10, 1907.

This grebe does not seem to care for running water, but prefers quiet places along shore and particularly coves and ponds. It is shy and easily escapes notice, and is not often taken.

They have a habit of sitting around under over-hanging bushes and amongst brush, weeds, and reeds. On becoming alarmed it will sink quietly out of sight, reappearing with only the top of his head out of water.

Measurements:

14 1/2–24–5 1/2–x

13–23–5 1/8–x

THE LOONS

Common Loon
Gavia immer

(4.) A regular migrant in spring, very rare in fall, no winter records.

Arrives: April 1, 1891; April 2, 1893; March 29, 1894; March 31, 1899; April 5, 1901; April 5, 1902; April 8, 1904; April 4, 1905; April 5, 1907. I have noted it as late as May 5, 1891; May 14, 1892; May 16, 1893; May 10, 1899; May 20, 1900; May 15, 1901; May 8, 1902; May 8, 1903; May 7, 1904; May 16, 1906; and two adults on May 23, 1917.

In the fall it has been noted several times in November, but is little more than a straggler at this season of the year. It is more often seen some seasons than others.

Most of those seen are in full dress. Occasionally one is seen in spring that is still in the gray winter plumage. Met with here singly and in pairs, only occasionally are 3 or 4 seen together.

On April 19, 1901, there occurred a flight of loons, the only real flight I have seen. The day before a strong, warm, south wind prevailed which brought rain. At night the wind shifted to the northwest and blew a gale, the rain turned to sleet, and by morning a heavy wet snow was being driven along by the high wind. In every eddy there were 2, 3, or 4 loons. With them appeared a few Bonaparte Gulls and a number of ducks. The storm seemed to have caught the loons just right.

During this flight, in the close vicinity of Warren, 13 fine adult loons were shot that I know of—three of these falling to my gun. Most of the loons escaped the gunners by diving and swimming on down the river.

From the severe nature of the storm I expected a flight of waterfowl, so I was on the job at daylight at my old ducking grounds down the river. Before it was really light enough to see much I could hear the weird shrieks of loons. I found the wind, waves, and snow too much for my flat or punt boat, so I took a good skiff instead. I soon saw a big old loon sitting out about 100 yards away. I sent a heavy load of shot at him, and a stray one hit him in the neck at the base of the skull, rolling him over. It was a very long shot, of course, and somewhat of an accident that I got him. During the day I saw over 30 pass and shot 2 more. One tried to fly over, as I lay in ambush in my boat in the brush at the foot of Meade Island. I easily brought him down into the river with a great splash.

The third had been bombarded up above and came along down river—diving, just sticking his head out—but he came too near as he passed and I got him. All three were fine adults, and the largest, a handsome male, weighed 9 1/2 pounds. Of the entire flight I neither saw nor heard of gray ones.

I shot specimens of Black Duck, Ruddy, Bufflehead, Lesser Scaup, and Whistler. Nearly a foot of snow fell during the day and loons were about for several more days. Some more were shot. Before shooting was prohibited along the river at town, loons frequently came into the eddy between the bridges. The gunners would then get on both shores and on the bridges and keep up a great cannonade until the loon either got killed or escaped by diving on down.

When it comes to diving, the loon easily carries off all honors among the birds that visit us here. They are hard to kill and will stand a worse shooting up than any bird I ever saw. Once fired upon they depend on diving to escape, only showing a very little of the head on coming up for air between dives.

From the upper railroad bridge I have several times watched loons diving when the water was clear, and I could plainly see that both wings and feet were used in the progress under water. Their progress was very rapid, too. They are strong fliers and get under considerable headway. I have seen one coming into the river skim along for twenty rods before he could come to anchor. Their cry or call is harsh and weird and can be heard a long way off.

The finest loon taken here that I know of was a fine adult male that I shot at town, March 29, 1894. This was a beautiful specimen and weighed 10 1/2 pounds. I gave it to my friend, A.E. Kibbe, of Mayville, New York, who mounted it, and later sold it to H.D. Kirkover of Buffalo, New York. From 6 to 8 pounds is the average weight, not many get over 8 pounds. *(A.E. Kibbe published this account in the* Nidiologist, *April, 1894. It was titled:* A Young Naturalist.*)*

This past summer, 1923, a loon stayed around the Allegheny River at Big Bend from early May until almost July, and then it disappeared. *(Big Bend is the current site of Kinzua Dam.)*

Measurements:
Adult female, April 24, 1890, 31–54 1/2–13 1/2–3, Wt. 6 lbs.
Gray, April 30, 1892, 30–51–13–2 3/4, Wt. 5 lbs., 6 oz.
Adult female, April 19, 1901, 33 1/2–60–14 3/4–3 5/8, Wt. 8 lbs., 6 oz.
Adult male, May 5, 1903, 33 1/2–61–14 3/4–3 3/4, Wt. 9 lbs.

Red-throated Loon
Gavia lume / Gavia stellata

(5.) A straggler, this loon is a rather rare bird anywhere in western Pennsylvania. At Erie one is sometimes taken in late fall or winter. It is evidently a bird that stays about large bodies of water and does not go inland unless driven by storms.

The winter of 1903-04 was one of the most severe in years. Among other northern visitors we had a Red-throated Loon. On February 12, 1904, one in winter plumage was shot at town by a man named Logan. I heard about it and suspected that it was not a common loon. I hunted him up and sure enough the victim was a Red-throated, which I purchased for my collection.

April 9, 1913, while duck hunting down the river I saw a pair of Red-throated in full spring plumage. One I succeeded in shooting, but the other escaped in the high water and I could not find it again. This I consider one of my very best records for this region. I have heard several times of Red-throated Loons being seen here in winter, but they are useless as records, as the birds seen might have been Mergansers or Holboell's Grebes.

GULLS AND TERNS

Only 3 species of gulls and 3 species of terns occur regularly in western Pennsylvania. *(RBS notes in margin of journal that a fourth species of gull, the Great Black-backed Gull, he mistakenly omitted here. True to the journal it is included later.)* This class of birds as a rule frequents large bodies of water so that an inland point like Warren is only visited by a few migrants or an occasional straggler.

At Presque Isle on Lake Erie, probably not over 50 miles from us in air miles, several species are very common. Owing to our nearness to this large body of water, gulls and terns are apt to appear frequently.

Gulls appear here regularly during the spring migration, but are seldom seen in the fall. Terns on the other hand are more likely to be noted late in autumn rather than in the spring. In winter, especially severe winters, gulls are occasionally noted. I have seen several gulls here that I could not identify.

During the severe blizzard of February, 1895, I saw what must have been an adult Black-backed Gull on February 9. The river was ice-bound except for the usual open water on the riffles. It was below zero that morning and a strong northwest wind was driving a fine, cutting snow. While going along the road at Highhouse's Eddy, I saw a large bird along the opposite shore beating its way down against the storm. The bird had black wings and back, the rest white, and if it wasn't a Black-backed then I have no idea what it could have been. I saw several adult Herring Gulls the same day.

During the blizzard of February, 1899, I saw a gull that I am positive was not a Ring-bill. It may have been a Kittiwake.

American Herring Gull | Herring Gull
Larus argentatus

(6.) A regular spring migrant, rare in the fall, occasional in winter.

The following are dates of first arrival in the spring, following winters during which practically none were seen: April 1, 1891; March 22, 1892; April 1, 1893; March 24, 1901; March 20, 1905; and March 16, 1907. I have seen it here as late as April 16, 1891; May 14, 1892; April 30, 1893; May 20, 1894; April 22, 1901; and April 27, 1904.

Usually seen singly or in pairs, sometimes small parties of 5 or 6 pass by. Once late in March *(March 29, 1895)* just after the ice had gone out, and while there was a flood that almost entirely inundated Meade Island, I saw fully a dozen Herrings on the overflows.

It is only rarely seen in the fall and very irregular in its appearance in winter. During very severe winters it is noted occasionally. During the winter of 1903-04, several were about all through January and February.

Although a number pass each season it is seldom taken, as they generally pass right along, keeping well out and over the middle of the stream. I have taken several specimens, both adult and immature, during March, April, and in winter.

At Erie the Herring Gull is very common both spring and fall. A number are about there in winter also.

April 18, 1927, I counted 45 Herring and 45 Bonaparte's Gulls on the bar at the head of Highhouse's Eddy, by far the largest flock of herrings I ever saw here.

Measurements:

Adult male, 25 1/4–59–17 1/2–7 1/4

Adult male, 24–58 1/2–17–7

Ring-billed Gull
Larus delawarensis

(7.) Irregular migrant.

The following dates will show about what time of the year it is most apt to be noted: March 25, 1893; March 24 and April 20, 1894; March 2, 1895; March 1 and 13, April 5 and 18, 1899; April 5 and 15, 1901; April 8 and 13, 1902.

When seen here it is singly and in pairs. Once, March 2, 1895, I saw 4 together. I have no fall records.

Like the Herring Gull this species passes right along—keeping well out over the middle of the stream. I have never taken a specimen here *(Warren County)*, and I have never known of one being taken.

At Erie this gull is quite common, especially in November. I have taken specimens there in April and November, and I have had plenty of opportunity to become familiar with it there.

Bonaparte's Gull
Larus philadelphia

(8.) A regular spring migrant. No fall or winter records.

Arrives in April: April 4, 1891; April 18, 1892; April 5, 1893; April 4, 1894; April 10, 1895; April 11, 1899; April 9, 1903; April 3, 1904; April 12, 1905; and April 6, 1907.

Noted as late as May 10, 1891; May 7, 1892; April 30, 1893; May 7, 1894; April 30, 1901; May 10, 1902; May 6, 1903; May 13, 1904; May 19, 1907; and May 14, 1909.

At times in the past, when storms have driven in flights of waterfowl, this gull has been plentiful. On April 25, 1893, the day on which the great flight of Horned Grebes occurred, the Bonapartes were abundant. I saw hundreds of them that day, many large flocks passed, several of which contained at least 100 birds each.

On April 24, 1894, these gulls were also very abundant, and on that day I also saw several very large flocks. They often alight on the water, on bars along shore, and off the foot of islands. They spend some time feeding as they pass and are not at all shy. They keep their winter plumage quite late sometimes. Some of my latest May records were birds in winter plumage.

Measurements:

April 19, 1901, adult male, 13 1/2–32–10 1/4–4

April 17, 1903, W, 13 1/2–33–10 1/2–4 1/4 *("W" is for winter plumage.)*

Caspian Terns
Sterna caspia

(9.) Straggler.

At Erie this tern occurs as an irregular migrant in late September and early October. I have seen this bird at Erie in the spring also, but according to others who have had better opportunity than I to observe the bird life of that region, this tern is rare there in the spring.

It seems that the shores of Lake Erie are about the only place in Pennsylvania where this tern is apt to be seen. I have taken several nice specimens on the Peninsula at Erie, both adult and immature—and have had considerable opportunity to observe and to become familiar with them.

I have never seen the Caspian Tern here at Warren but once. On the afternoon of May 7, 1908, while doing some work on the East Side along the Allegheny River near the Hammond Iron Works, a friend told me there was a flock of large gulls about the head of Mile Island. He said at noon there were 7 and the last time he looked there were still 3 there.

I walked out to the river and took a look. I saw 3 large birds. They were not far away and a single glance showed me I was looking at Caspian Terns instead of gulls. They stayed until about five o'clock. As the Herring Gulls and Caspian Terns associate together at Erie, the 4 birds that left before I saw them may have been gulls.

Recent record: on April 21, 1945, I recorded the Caspian Tern here for the second time. This bird was a fine adult specimen. I watched it for 15 or 20 minutes, as it circled about over the shallow water around the head of Daly's Island. It repeatedly caught minnows just below the surface of the water.

Measurements:

September 17, 1900, adult male, 20–50–16–5

September 17, 1900, young, 20–49–15–5

Common Tern
Sterna hirundo

(10.) Irregular migrant, spring and fall.

At Erie this tern is very common during the migrations. A few pairs, maybe a dozen, nest on the outside beach of the Peninsula, or at least they did last season, 1922. As they are so common at the Peninsula, I think they must keep pretty close to the lake or they would occur in Warren County more often.

The following dates are from my notebooks: June 20, 1903, saw 1; May 20, 1907, saw 1; May 16, 1909, saw 1; May 18, 1917, saw 2; May 20, 1917, saw 10 about the Town Eddy all morning; and July 3, 1922, an adult was about town all day. In the fall I have noted it occasionally on dates ranging from August 3, 1891, to late September.

1932—quite a large colony now breeds on the Peninsula at Erie, Pennsylvania. On May 29, Harry Granquist and I visited the colony and saw many terns inside the sanctuary wire. We found 4 or 5 nests outside where we took photos.

May 9, 1940, ten were seen in Grunderville Eddy.

Measurements:

Young, 12–28–9 1/5–4 1/2

Black Tern
Chlidonias niger

(11.) Rare visitor during migrations.

I have seen it here but a few times. At Erie it occurs regularly, and during severe storms in September it is abundant.

On April 24, 1892, there occurred a large flight of waterfowl, and among other birds it brought 2 adult Black Terns. These were about for some time. They were the first I ever saw here. May 30, 1895, there was an adult flying about the river at town for several hours. August 5, 1904, I saw two flying about the river and the mouth of the Conewango Creek. One was in almost full adult plumage.

August 20, 1905, I saw 1 in fall plumage; September 11, 1907, saw 2 in fall plumage; August 22, 1915, saw 1 in fall plumage; and August 25, 1922, saw an adult in apparently fall plumage. It was about the river and the mouth of the creek all day. May 16, 1942, about the head of Daly's Island, I saw several Common Terns and a fine adult Black Tern.

CORMORANTS

Double-crested Cormorant
Phalacrocorax dilophus / Phalacrocorax auritus

(12.) Straggler.

Mr. Frank Kranking, who did reside on Dartmouth Street this city *(Warren)*, had a specimen of this bird mounted in his home. This cormorant was shot on the river from the Glade Run Bridge *(see following image)* in the fall of 1890—the exact date was not kept.

May 1, 1903, was the second day of a quite hard northwestern storm. The wind was very high and it had become much colder (28 degrees) with light flurries of snow. Early in the morning I was at King's Eddy, just below Meade Island, on a gunning expedition to see if the storm had driven in anything unusual.

In the eddy I saw a fine Double-crested Cormorant in full dress. It was very restless, and before I could get a shot it arose and flew down the river. A careful search for 4 miles down river failed to find further trace of it. This is up to date the only one of these birds I have ever seen alive in this state.

During the open winter of 1931-32, I found on my several trips to Erie that 4 or 5 of these birds lived about the head of the bay with the swans, gulls, ducks, and other waterfowl.

January 3, 1934, I saw one in company with swans, ducks, and gulls at an open piece of water in Thompson's Bay on the Peninsula, Erie, Pennsylvania. April 20, 1936, I saw an adult in Erie Bay.

April 24, 1941, I saw a fine adult on the bar at the foot of Leek Island, and again on October 23 on a swimming and diving float anchored in the middle of the river at Grunderville Eddy. Off Jackson's Island I saw one in fall plumage. During all the years, from 1903 to 1941, I never saw or heard of one here.

May 7, 1943, I saw an adult in Grunderville Eddy. April 22, 1944, I saw a fine black adult in Grunderville Eddy. It was off the foot of Meade Island.

Original Allegheny River Toll Bridge at Glade Run, built by Warren Bridge Company in 1881. Note Trolley Car addition below.

Original Warren and Sheffield Trolley Car on the Glade Bridge, about 1908, a year after the tracks were set in place across the top.

DUCKS—GEESE—SWANS

In western Pennsylvania (and in the whole state) about 25 species of ducks, not including the geese and swans, have been taken. Of this number I have personally taken 19 species in the Allegheny River at Warren. One other, the Gadwall, has been taken to my knowledge. *(RBS later notes that he took a Gadwall, October 31, 1923, making his count 20 species of ducks.)* In former years, before my time, waterfowl were abundant with many great flights occurring. As they have steadily grown less in numbers, large flights at an inland place like Warren become less frequent, and ducks in general have become much scarcer.

A few of my notes were taken prior to 1890, but mostly since. During the 1890s, also 1901-02-03 and 1904, I seldom missed being out a morning during the spring migrations in March, April, and May, and whenever there was anything like a flight I usually spent the day down the river. In this way I got very complete migration notes, especially in regards to dates of first arrivals and last seen.

The northern movement begins in March with the Black Ducks which crowd north very soon after the river is free of ice. After the Black Ducks come the Canada Geese, Mallards, and Hooded Mergansers. Then about the first of April the real flights begin and continue throughout the month. During this month we sometimes have large flights of waterfowl of various species, generally just after or during severe storms. Several very large flights have occurred during my time.

The storms that drive in flights usually begin with a south wind and rain which shifts into a strong northwest wind with the rain often turning into snow. Several very large flights of waterfowl have occurred late in April. During the early part of May many ducks are still passing, especially with the warm rains and storms that bring the warblers and small land migrants. During June, July, and August stragglers are sometimes noted.

The fall movement of ducks does not amount to much here. If the water happens to be quite low there are sometimes a few Mallards and Black Ducks about with occasionally one of some other species.

After deep winter sets in, and the river becomes ice-bound, American Mergansers appear and are found in varying numbers the rest of the winter. The more severe the winter the more common are the mergansers.

Other waterfowl are also seen at times during severe weather in winter. Goldeneyes are sometimes fairly common. I have no positive knowledge of any ducks breeding in this county since 1890. *(RBS later notes in species account 17 that the Black Duck breeds in Warren County.)* Wounded birds, stragglers, or those leftover are seen at times during the summer months, but I know of no case in which a brood was raised.

At an inland place like Warren a great variety of ducks can hardly be expected in any one season, as their abundance depends very much on the weather. During 1894 I saw 14 species of ducks, also the Canada Goose and swan. During 1899 I noted 15 species, also both the goose and swan. During 1901 I also noted 14 species of ducks and the goose.

Ducks used to be hunted considerably here, but since spring shooting has been abolished they are but little hunted. They are too scarce as a rule in the fall to pay the gunner for his time spent in looking for them. Floating by boat to Tidioute or some other point down the river, and coming back by train was one favorite way to hunt ducks, but the choice ducks, such as the mallard, would give a boat a wide berth.

Shooting over decoys was seldom practiced. Once, early in April when a few ducks were flying, I placed 3 decoys on the overflow on Meade Island. I had quite fair shooting, as I secured 16 ducks—8 Lesser Scaup, 6 Bufflehead, 1 Whistler, and a Ruddy. I have no doubt that during a big flight a person could have fine success by putting out a large flock of decoys in a good place.

In my collection I have 5 species of ducks taken at Erie—Shoveller, Canvas-back, King Eider, Surf, and American Scoters—that I have never met with here, but any of which might occur here. It is quite certain that in the spring of 1888, a pair of Canvas-backs was shot here *(Warren County)*, but as I did not see these birds, and have never met with this duck here, I do not include it in any list. *(RBS notes in species account 214 that he met with the Canvas-back Duck on April 20, 1929, in Warren County.)*

Once, early in April, I flushed 5 ducks from the head of the spring-gut on Meade Island. I am positive that they were Shovellers, but may have been mistaken, as they were off some distance.

Large flights of particular note include the following: April 14, 1888, a very large flight of ducks, gulls, and grebes; April 8, 1891, lots of ducks, mostly Long-tails; April 25, 1893, an immense flight of grebes with many ducks and gulls; April 12, 1899, large numbers of ducks, many grebes; April 19, 1903, large flight of Horned Grebes, also many Bufflehead and Scaup; April 22, 1903, a large flight of ducks and grebes with Bufflehead abundant; and April 7, 1914, a large flight of 50 swans. On April 15, 1917, there was the largest flight of Long-tailed Ducks I ever saw—included one flock of 100. This is the last big flight of ducks seen here.

The large flights of waterfowl—ducks, geese, and swans—that used to occur here have been over with for more than 25 years. Up to 1945 I have noted 23 species here at Warren. Since the big flights I still see practically all species at times, none fail to come at all. *(RBS notes species 24 added in 1946, occurrence of Brant. These are records appended to his original October 1, 1923, journals.)* This past season, 1944, out of the few that still pass, I noted 19 species.

American Merganser | Common Merganser
Merganser americanus | Mergus merganser

(13.) Winter visitor.

Does not occur here during the real migrations, but is found on the river in the open places during winter, its abundance depending entirely on the weather. When we have a mild, broken up winter only a few mergansers are about, but if the winter is rather severe with plenty of snow and ice, the mergansers are found all along on the stretches of open water. The females are always seen about for some time before the males put in an appearance.

They are met with singly, in pairs, and in flocks of up to 20 individuals. During very severe spells in mid-winter I have seen as many as 60 in one flock. If March is severe they may remain until the end of the month, but rarely remain into April.

Latest dates in spring on which I have seen it here are: March 26, 1892, saw 1 female; March 29, 1893, saw 7; March 3, 1894, saw one; April 2, 1895, saw 4 females; March 31, 1899, saw 10; March 15, 1901, saw 5; March 20, 1904, saw 5; and March 23, 1905, I saw 10.

The male in full plumage is surely a handsome bird and the largest wild duck found here. Once *(May 26, 1900)* while shooting buffalo suckers at Grass Flats, we saw a female American Merganser. Upon investigation it proved to be a wounded bird and unable to fly.

They feed entirely on fish which they secure by diving along under the edge of the ice. Mullets, suckers, and minnows are the kinds they get mostly. Frequently I have shot specimens as they were feeding. I have found half-swallowed mullets and suckers, 6 to 8 inches long, in their throats. One fine male that I sent to my friend, A.E. Kibbe, at Mayville, New York, had a partly digested sucker 11 inches long in its throat and gullet.

A friend of mine was spearing through the ice at Meade Island one time when a merganser grabbed his decoy minnow and tried to make off with it. He was in a light colored boat which was unnoticed by the merganser as it fed along under the edge of the ice.

Although unfit for food, they used to furnish good sport to the gunners hardy enough to brave the wind and weather, and walk the long distances over the ice and through deep snow; then creep and crawl to get a shot—the American Merganser when here is a wary bird and no amount of cold and storm seems to tame them any.

This sport was rather dangerous, too, for besides contending with the snow, wind, and cold, the hunter had to watch the ice closely as he moved along or an unexpected bath in the slightly frozen air holes might result. This was no laughing matter if the temperature happened to be down around the zero mark and the victim got into a deep place—sometimes it was not easy to get out again without help. It only takes about a minute some days for the clothing to freeze stiff. I have broken through a few times myself and know all about it.

I used to hunt mergansers a great deal and got many fine specimens. Chance shots were frequently had at birds flying—when they were seen in time for me to lay low—but I found the best way was to get on land and sneak up to the open holes, then after locating the game, crawl up to the nearest ambush. If it was too far to shoot, I would wait until all or part had dived. I would then run out on the ice and get in a couple of shots as soon as they came up.

The 1928 spring season was cold and late, and the Americans were here, quite common with Black Ducks and others, as late as April 22, on which date I saw 10 or 12 still about.

Measurements:

January 18, 1893, adult female, 23 1/4–31–9 3/4–5, Wt. 3 lbs.

March 23, 1905, adult male, 27–37–10 3/4–6, Wt. 3 lbs., 12 oz.

March 23, 1905, adult male, 26–36–10 3/4–5 1/2, Wt. 3 lbs., 8 oz.

Red-breasted Merganser
Merganser serrator / Mergus serrator

(14.) Regular migrant. Not at all common.

Very erratic in its occurrence, some seasons quite a few are noted and again some seasons it is scarce. At Erie it is very common.

I have seen it here as early as March 15 *(1901)*, but usually it is after April 1 that it is first noted. So irregular is it that it is hard to get good dates of its first occurrence. I have seen it as late as May 4, 1891; May 15, 1901; May 5, 1902; and May 31, 1917. My only summer record is of 1 female that I saw in the Conewango Creek on June 11, 1903. It is occasionally seen in October and November. On December 26, 1896, I shot a female—my only winter record. The weather was rather mild at the time.

Usually seen here singly. I have never seen flocks except on days in April when large flights of waterfowl occurred. On such days I have seen flocks numbering as many as 20 individuals. For some reason adult male birds are scarce. I believe I have seen 20 females here for every adult male.

This duck prefers the open river and running water and does not often go into ponds and bayous. Feeds entirely on fish here and is unfit for table use.

Measurements:

November 13, 1903, female, 22–34–9 1/4–3 1/2

Hooded Merganser
Lophodytes cucullatus

(15). Regular migrant.

One of the earliest arrivals among the ducks in the spring: March 18, 1893; March 12, 1894; March 25, 1895; and March 11, 1899. About the first week in April their flight is at its best, and it is met with at times throughout the rest of April.

Strangely enough I have different dates of its occurrence here in mid-summer: June 22, 1891, saw 1; July 12, 1892, saw 2; August 6, 1893, saw 2; June 28, 1895, saw 2 and shot 1, this one a young of the year; May 25, 1901, saw 1; May 30, 1905, saw 1; and August 11, 1908, saw 1. These summer records were all either females or young of the year. These frequent occurrences lead me to wonder if this duck does not frequently nest somewhere here in western Pennsylvania.

Occasionally, but not regularly met with in fall—October, November, and early December. December 4 and 5, 1899, during a heavy, wet snow storm, a small flight came this way. Several of the flocks contained upwards of 20 birds each. I have no winter records. *(RBS later notes that he saw an adult male on January 25, 1947.)* In the spring it is met with singly, in pairs, and little parties of up to 5 or 6 individuals.

This species is a pond duck and prefers coves, bayous, ponds, overflows, and quiet places along shore. When found here this duck is cunning, wary, and vigilant. The big bayou at Grass Flats is a favorite resort of this species. I have taken some fine specimens there.

At Erie this species is known as "Pond Fisher" to distinguish it from the Red-breasted which is called "Fisher." The gunners up there claim it is good eating. Whether this is true I do not know, as I never tried to eat one.

Measurements:

April 3, 1895, adult male, 17 3/4–26–7 1/2–4 1/4

Mallard
Anas boschas / Anas platyrhynchos

(16.) Regular migrant spring and fall. Occasional during mild winter weather.

It is frequently met with during the latter part of March and early April. As it is frequently met with during open weather in winter, dates of supposed first arrivals in spring are open to doubt. I have seen it as late as April 11, 1892; April 25, 1893; and April 20, 1905. On this latter date I shot an adult male with very rusty colored under parts.

I have no summer records.

In the fall I have noted it here as early as September 11 *(1907)*—also several times during the last week of September. In October and November usually quite a few pass, especially during the first snow storms.

In the spring it is found singly, in pairs, small parties of 5 or 6, and often in company with Black Ducks. In the fall it is much more common. When the storms come just right, quite a good number pass. Many times flocks of 40 or 50 pass over and sometimes I have seen flocks numbering 75 to 100. These large flocks though do not stop, but like the geese that are migrating at about that same time, they pass right along.

If the river is rather high in the fall there is but little duck shooting. If the river happens to be quite low, and the snow storms come along on schedule in late October and early November, quite a few Mallards stop. Flocks of up to 20 or 25 are often met with.

The Mallard and Black Duck are found associated together freely in mixed flocks in the fall. This species does not like deep or running water, but prefers quiet places along shore, coves, bayous, and overflowed meadows where it can get into the grass and reeds.

The Mallard is a very wary bird and it is no easy matter to get a shot. They are hard to see when amongst the bushes or grass, and they are always on the lookout for danger. They do not linger when a suspicious object is sighted, but climb right out and are apt to leave for good.

I know the best haunts and feeding grounds of this species and just where to look the closest for them. I have had very good success in hunting them by keeping back from the water, where a hunter is a conspicuous object, and by crawling up on the most likely spots and then looking for them.

I once got into a fine mess of trouble while crawling onto a bunch of Mallards. I had been squirrel hunting with fine success one nice day in early October in the big woods back of the Grass Flats. I was coming back to the river during the middle of the day when I saw five Mallards feeding. I circled around and crawled out and up behind a big log. Under this log was a large yellow jacket nest and right up into this I crawled.

They fairly swarmed onto me before I saw them, so intent was I watching the ducks. I had to jump up and beat it through the thickest brush. I couldn't seem to shake them off. As it was I got stung no less than 6 times—good and proper. I never saw the ducks again.

This is a fine duck for the table and tastes just as good to me as did the Redhead and Canvas-back at Erie.

Black Duck | American Black Duck
Anas rubripes

(17.) A regular migrant in the spring and fall, often noted during mild winters. I have seen it every month of the year.

Like the Mallard this species is frequently met with in winter, sometimes during quite severe weather, so that it is a difficult matter to say just when they do arrive in spring. Just as soon as the ice leaves in February or March they are apt to appear, and during late March and early April they are often seen. Specimens have been taken as late as May 3 *(1891)*, but usually by April 20 the flight is past.

What I have said about the Mallards' occurrences in the fall applies equally well with the Black Duck. The two species associate together, except that the Black Duck does not appear much until well into October.

During mild winters this duck *(Black Duck)* is frequently noted and I have seen and taken it here when the river was ice-bound. During the winter of 1898-99, I shot specimens of both the Black Duck and Mallard—the Mallards all through the winter.

During June, July, August, and part of September 1893, a Black Duck spent the summer about the mouth of the Conewango Creek. This bird could fly well, but had no mate. I have seen the Black Duck in the swamp about the Clarendon Pond on Tionesta Creek in mid-summer. In July of 1922, I saw a pair about the bayous at Grass Flats; however, I never saw a brood of young.

Old timers along the river claim this duck used to breed regularly. One party who used to live near the Grass Flats tells me he often would see the old with their young. He says he is certain they bred there up until or later than 1880. However, since 1890, I know of none breeding here.

They prefer the same places as the Mallard with which they associate freely. They are often seen in company with other species also. I consider this species a little bit of the smoothest of anything found here in the way of a duck. It is very clever at keeping hidden in brush, reeds, and high grass. If the river is high it keeps out of range on the big overflows, or else skulks and feeds quietly amongst the overflowed trees and brush, where it is a difficult matter to see it at first.

Usually the first warning the gunner has is a splashing followed by a few loud "quack quacks" just as the flock jumps up a little out of range. The spring-gut on Meade Island, the big bayou, and the long wooded swamp at Grass Flats have always been famous feeding grounds.

In this wooded swamp I discovered just how foxy this duck really is. Several times I had apparently dead ones disappear while I was out of sight for a few moments—getting around or across to them. One day I shot and apparently killed one. It lay with outstretched neck—to all appearances dead. While looking for a good way to get to it I thought I detected a slight motion. Looking closely, I saw that it was shamming and was slowly paddling toward a clump of thick brush. I then started for it, and on getting close, it made a rush for shelter. This explained the mysterious disappearance of several former "kills."

During the seasons of 1925 and 1926 a brood of Black Ducks was raised each year around Grass Flats. Unfortunately, I did not know about this in time in either case to observe them myself, but they were seen and watched by several parties at different times until they were able to fly. There is no question as to the truth of this statement.

This past season *(1928)* Black Ducks were unusually common during April down there *(Grass Flats),* and Harry and I kept close watch. However, an unfortunate double drowning late in April sent a number of men down the river looking for the bodies, and the shores and islands were ransacked day after day. By the time both victims had been found the ducks had either left of their own accord or had been driven away.

Season of 1935—I have it on good authority that this duck nested again this spring at Grass Flats and was seen with its young still too small to fly.

Season of 1938—a pair of Black Ducks raised a brood at Bachops Eddy up the Conewango Creek. This brood was seen and watched by different campers. This pair returned the spring of 1939—an illegal frog hunter, who was arrested and fined, shot one.

Measurement:

March 26, 1891, adult female, 21 1/2–34 1/2–10 1/4–3, Wt. 2 1/2 lbs.

January 17, 1899, adult male, 23–36 1/2–10 1/2–3 1/4, Wt. 3 lbs.

Gadwall

Chaulelasmus streperus / Anas strepera

(18.) Straggler.

Dr. Warren in his book, *Birds of Pennsylvania,* speaks of the Gadwall as occurring frequently or regularly at Erie. Of late years such is not the case as the Gadwall is by far the rarest of the ducks occurring at Erie or anywhere else in western Pennsylvania. *(Dr. B.H. Warren was the state ornithologist for the Pennsylvania State Board of Agriculture. His revised* Report on the Birds of Pennsylvania *was authorized by an Act of the Senate and House of Representatives of the Commonwealth of Pennsylvania and approved May 4, 1889. Nineteen thousand copies were printed in 1890 and distributed throughout the state.)*

The species has been taken here at Warren but once to my knowledge. On March 20, 1890, a muskrat trapper saw 5 ducks in the spring-gut on Meade Island and, creeping up, shot 3. These he sold to a restaurant here in town where

I saw, examined, and identified them. I could easily have purchased them, but as I was rather new at the business, and ducks were quite plentiful, I did not realize their rarity.

March 12, 1894, I flushed a Black Duck from Grass Flats Island and with it was what I am positive was a Gadwall. Again April 15, 1894, two ducks flew past me a little out of range and I am very sure they were a pair of Gadwall. I might of course be mistaken about these last two records, as the birds were not secured in either case.

At Erie on November 18, 1902, I saw a specimen that was shot by a gunner in one of the ponds on the Peninsula. It had been wounded. It tried to escape into the rushes and cattails, whereupon the hunter had shot its head off, ruining it, of course, for a specimen.

October 31, 1923, while hunting ducks at Grass Flats, I flushed and shot a fine female Gadwall from along Leek Island. The bird was in fine plumage, and I secured it without mussing a feather. October 20, 1930, at Grass Flats, I found a flock of 15 ducks feeding. There was a pair of Green-winged Teal, 1 Gadwall, and the rest Black Ducks and Mallards. I shot the Gadwall, a fine specimen, and 3 Mallards. This is only the second Gadwall I have shot here.

Measurements:

October 31, 1923, female, 20–34 5/8–10 1/8–3 3/4, Wt. 1 lb, 10 oz.

October 20, 1930, male, 20–35–10 1/2–3 1/2

WATERFOWL.

18.

GADWALL.

CHAULELASMUS STREPERUS.

Straggler. = Dr Warren in his book on the "Birds of Penna" speaks of the Gadwall as occuring frequently or regularly at Erie. Of late years such is not the case as the Gadwall is, by far the rarest of the ducks occuring at Erie or anywhere else in western Penna. This species has been taken here at Warren but once to my knowledge.

On Mar. 20th 1890 a muskrat trapper saw 5 ducks in the spring-gut on Meade Is. and, creeping up, shot 3. These he sold to a restaurant here in town where I saw, examined and identified them. I could easily have purchased them but as I was rather new at the business and ducks were quite plentiful I did not realize their rarity.

Mar. 12th 1894 I flushed a Black Duck from Grass Flats Is. and with it was what I am positive was a Gadwall.

Again April 15th 1894 two ducks flew past me a little out of range and I am very sure they were a pair of Gadwall.

I might of course be mistaken about these last two records as the birds were not secured in either case.

At Erie on Nov. 18th 1902 I saw a specimen that was shot by a gunner in one of the ponds on the "Peninsula". It had been

Simpson's species account for the Gadwall.

Widgeon | American Widgeon
Mareca americana | Anas americana

(19.) Rare visitor.

The first time I met with this duck was October 11, 1894. There had been quite a storm the night before and it had snowed some. While looking around about the mouth of the Conewango Creek, I flushed 2 ducks that were strangers to me. After some circling they alighted in a little pond at the head of the island. By crawling up through the mud and weeds, I bagged both with a single shot. I found that I had a pair of Widgeon, old birds in fine plumage.

March 14, 1901, a friend and I fired at a strange looking duck in the middle of Reese's Eddy. It arose, but being hard hit, alighted in the grove where we secured it. We found it to be a fine male Widgeon.

April 20, 1903, at the foot of Grass Flats Island I saw 2 Black Ducks and a smaller, lighter colored duck. Crawling up I bagged one of the Black Ducks and this odd one, which proved to be a female Widgeon.

May 2, 1909, we had very high water. On the overflowed meadows just below town on the South Side, I saw 7 Lesser Scaup with a male Widgeon. I have also taken this duck at Erie on some of my trips there.

Of recent years, scarce as waterfowl are, as compared to 30 and more years ago, I see more of some species than I used to see. Of recent years I have noted at times a single or a pair or two of this species. This past fall, in early November of 1941, I saw a very nice flock of twenty. This is the only real flock I ever saw here.

Green-winged Teal
Nettion carolinensis | Anas crecca

(20.) Rare visitor.

The first Green-winged Teal I ever saw here was on November 20, 1899, while poling a boat along shore below Meade Island. I first saw it under some reeds along shore—not twenty feet away. It sat very still and I kept on for 60 or 70 feet, and then I reached for my gun. The Teal at once arose, but fell at my first shot. It was a young male.

January 17, 1901, at Grass Flats during a mild spell of weather, I flushed a small duck from the brush along shore. On shooting it, I found it to be a male Green-wing in very nice plumage.

April 24, 1901, we had very high water and the day was stormy and rainy. I spent the morning on Meade Island and found a little flight of ducks. On the overflowed meadows I crawled up through mud and water to find a small duck.

As it started to fly I tried a long shot, and I got a beautiful adult male Green-wing in the most perfect plumage.

I have seen small ducks on several occasions that I think were this species, but these are my only positive records, so the bird is certainly quite rare here. I have taken it at Erie where I have found it to be not uncommon.

October 21, 1930, I saw 3 here at town, 2 at Grass Flats. April 8, 1944, I saw a nice pair at Ittel's Cove.

Measurements:

April 24, 1901, adult male, 15–25–7 1/4–3

Blue-winged Teal

Querquedula discors / Anas discors

(21.) Irregular migrant.

The Blue-wing is very irregular in its appearance here and as a rule is scarce. I have taken specimens on the following dates in the spring: April 20, 1892, shot a pair; April 29, 1892, shot a female; April 22, 1893, shot a female; April 25, 1893, shot a male; April 17, 1894, shot a pair; April 24, 1894, shot 1 male and 2 females; and March 27, 1913, shot a male. They are found singly and in pairs. I have never seen over 6 in a flock.

I have but 2 fall records: September 25, 1897, shot a female; and September 25, 1900, saw 3 and shot one.

The Blue-wing is a pond duck, and when we have high water the latter part of April it is quite apt to be seen on the overflows. It is not very wild and is rather easily taken—a very good table duck.

Measurements:

April 20, 1892, adult male, 17 3/4–25–7 1/2–3

Pintail | Northern Pintail

Dafila acuta / Anas acuta

(22.) Rare visitor.

April 8, 1892, I saw a flock of 9 flying at Meade Island. February 23, 1893, I saw an adult male at Grass Flats. April 10, 1899, at Grass Flats, I shot a fine adult male in full dress. It was with 2 Black Ducks.

March 23, 1905, Carl Marsh shot an adult female on the overflow just below town. The river was very high—the ice having left several days before.

February 15, 1912, I saw a pair of Pintails in company with 2 Black Ducks. March 7, 1915, I saw an adult male sitting on the ice at the head of Highhouse's Eddy. November 6, 1927, I saw a flock of 5 at Highhouse's Eddy.

During the spring season of 1941 I saw Pintails on several occasions. On March 24 of this year I saw a fine flock of 15 Pintails—the largest bunch by far I ever met here. March 16, 1944, I saw 4 in Grunderville Eddy.

Wood Duck
Aix sponsa

(23.) Regular migrant.

This beautiful duck, never common here, seems to be getting scarcer each year. Rather uncertain of its occurrence here, I find from my notes that April is the month during which it is most likely to be seen.

During April of the years 1891, 1892, and 1893, I took several nice specimens each year. May 14, 1892, I saw a pair. During April, 1894, I found it more often than any other year and got some beautiful specimens. The first were seen on April 2 and the last on April 30.

During 1895, which was a very good year for ducks, I only noted it 4 times: March 30, saw 2; April 1, shot a pair; April 2, shot a female; and April 14, saw two.

During the entire years of 1902 and 1903 I did not see a single one. During 1904 I got 2 records: March 28, saw 3; and April 1, saw one. April 21, 1905, I mounted a fine male specimen that was shot at Grass Flats.

April 10, 1906, I mounted a fine male that was shot on the Tionesta Creek, at Barnes, this county. April 30, 1909, I saw a fine male, and April 5, 1912, I shot a very handsome male.

The only fall record I have is of a male shot from a flock of 4 at the mouth of the Conewango Creek on December 2, 1889.

When found here it is seen singly or in pairs. I have never seen over 6 in one flock. Most of my records are from Grass Flats. The two best places to look for this species are in the big bayou and wooded swamp previously mentioned.

It is quite wary and hard to detect at first. It may breed in this county, but I have not even seen it here in summer. As long ago as 1891, I spent much time about the headwaters of the Tionesta Creek, at that time a virgin forest, and I did not even see it there.

Of recent years Wood Ducks are reported as seen in summer about the larger beaver dams. It may breed here; although up to 1944 I have heard of no broods of young being seen.

Measurements:

April 10, 1890, adult male, 18–30–8 3/4–5, Wt. 1 lb., 10 oz.

April 4, 1894, adult male, 18–30–8 3/4–5

April 5, 1912, adult male, 18 1/4–30–8 3/4–5

Redhead Duck | Redhead
Marila americana / Aythya americana

(24.) Rare visitor.

The following list is a record of all the occurrences of this duck in Warren County of which I am aware. October 24, 1891, I saw a pair of Redheads at Meade Island. May 2, 1892, I saw a very fine male. It seems to me this is a very late date, but the bird was a beauty and there could be no mistake.

March 25, 1895, was a stormy, snowy day following a bad night, and the first little spring flight of ducks put in an appearance. Among them 2 or 3 Redheads were seen, and I shot a fine male near the upper railroad bridge at town.

March 18, 1899, while lying in ambush in a boat in the brush at the foot of Meade Island, I shot an adult female. March 20, 1905, with the river very high, 13 1/2 feet, and the ice recently left, I saw 4 Redheads on the overflow on Meade Island.

April 1, 1942, I saw 4 Redheads in Grunderville Eddy. April 8, 1944, I saw a beautiful adult male in Ittel's Cove.

Measurements:

April 10, 1906, Erie, Pennsylvania, adult male, 20 1/2–34 1/2–9 1/4–3

(RBS notes at this point in his species accounts that he omitted the Canvas-back Duck from his 1890 to 1923 list, but it appears in his post-1923 list.)

American Scaup | Greater Scaup
Marila marila / Aythya marila

(25.) Irregular migrant. Rather rare.

I have seen and taken specimens here on dates ranging from March 17, 1894, to April 24, 1903. When found here it is usually a single female. I have frequently found 1 or 2 specimens with flocks of the Lesser Scaup. Several times I have found two Scaup together, one of each species.

Only once, on April 24, 1903, have I seen a flock. This was a flock of 6 and rather a late record. From this flock I shot 3 fine specimens, about the finest examples of the Greater Scaup that I ever took. All were large, heavy, and in perfect plumage. The finest male was 20 inches in length, fully 4 inches longer than an ordinary male Lesser.

April 29, 1944, I saw a fine pair close-up in Grunderville Eddy. April 8, 1946, I saw a very large fine male along the shore of Grunderville Eddy.

Measurements:

April 17, 1903, adult female, 17 1/2–x–x–x

April 24, 1903, adult male, 20–x–x–x

Lesser Scaup
Marila affinis / Aythya affinis

(26.) Regular spring migrant. Rare in fall.

This is the most common wild duck found here. Arrives: March 20, 1891; March 22, 1892; March 21, 1893; March 19, 1894; March 24, 1895; March 23, 1899; March 23, 1901; March 29, 1902; and March 27, 1904.

I have noted it as late as: May 10, 1890, flock of 28; May 24, 1891, saw 1; May 25, 1892, saw 1; May 16, 1893, saw 1; May 11, 1894, saw 1; May 17, 1895, saw 1; May 31, 1901, saw 1; May 11, 1902, saw 2; May 30, 1903, saw 1; May 22, 1904, saw 1; May 30, 1905, saw 1; and May 27, 1907, saw 1.

I saw a wanderer one summer—June 10, 1910, a female. It is very rare in fall, noted several times in November. One winter record—I saw a male at town, January 1, 1890, during a mild spell of weather. The Lesser Scaup is met with singly, in pairs, and in flocks. During large flights of waterfowl in April I have seen flocks numbering up to 60 individuals. Flocks of 10 to 30 are not uncommon.

As previously mentioned, Greater Scaups are sometimes found with flocks of Lesser; otherwise, they seem to stick together pretty well and do not seem to mix much with the other species. This species arrives each spring at pretty much the same time from year to year, and usually makes its first appearance in the form of a small flight with some southern storm.

The Lesser Scaup is by far the commonest duck found here and is liable to be met with anywhere on the river, on the overflows, ponds, and small streams. I once shot one in a run in the mountains. Another time, when on my way to a Goshawk's nest, I shot 5 on the Morrison Run Reservoir, 2 miles from the river, back in the mountains. It is not at all wild and quite a few used to be shot here every season—commonly know here as Blue-bill, Butterball, and Canvas-back.

Measurements:

April 22, 1891, adult male, 17–30–8–3

March 27, 1904, adult female, 16 1/2–27 1/4–7 3/4–2 3/4

Ring-necked Duck
Marila collaris / Aythya collaris

(27.) Rare visitor. I have but a few records.

I never saw one until the spring of 1895, which was an exceptionally good season for waterfowl. On March 30, 1895, we had a nice little flight of ducks following a stormy night. While hunting along the big flats just below town I shot a pair of ducks feeding along shore, which proved to be Ring-necks in fine plumage.

April 6, 1895, while hunting along the eddy below Meade Island, some gunners in a boat flushed a duck from along shore on the other side. It circled out and around, and as it passed me, I dropped it—a female Ring-neck.

March 26, 1904, we had very high water. On the overflowed meadows about the mouth of Sill Run I saw a lone duck, which I shot—after a long crawl flat on my stomach. It was a fine adult male Ring-neck.

November 25, 1914, at the head of Highhouse's Eddy, I shot an immature male Ring-neck. It was alone. April 11, 1930, I saw a nice adult about town. March 6, 1943, I saw several.

American Goldeneye | Common Goldeneye
Clangula clangula | Bucephala clangula

(28.) Regular migrant and a winter visitor.

During severe winters this species is found more or less all winter in the open places on the river. Sometimes when March is cold and stormy the "Whistler" is quite common. In view of these circumstances it is rather difficult to give any dates as to first spring arrivals.

It is not uncommon in April. When we have large flights of waterfowl it is usually quite well represented by flocks. I have noted it in spring as late as May 6, 1892; May 6, 1901; and May 5, 1902.

During the third week of June, 1911, a fine male was around the eddy at town all week. In the fall it is frequently met with in November.

It is found singly, in pairs, and small flocks numbering up to a dozen. During large April flights of waterfowl and during severe winters I have seen flocks of 35 to 40 individuals. In winter it is found in company with the American Merganser.

It is usually quite wary and not easily approached. It feeds on fish and is poor eating.

Measurements:

April 16, 1892, adult female, 16–29–8 1/2–3 3/4

April 1, 1907, adult male, 19 3/4–32–9–4

April 1, 1907, adult male, 19 1/2–32–9–4

Bufflehead
Charitonetta albeola | Bucephala albeola

(29.) Regular spring migrant. Rare in fall.

Arrives: April 2, 1892; March 24, 1893; March 21, 1894; March 30, 1895; March 27, 1899; March 19, 1901; March 29, 1902; and March 26, 1904.

I have seen it as late as: May 6, 1891, saw 5; May 6, 1892, saw 4 or 5; May 7, 1893, saw 3; April 18, 1894, saw 1; May 6, 1901, saw 16; May 5, 1902, saw 1; April 30, 1903; and May 2, 1904.

Occasional in fall: October 29 and December 14, 1890; November 11, 1898; December 20, 1898; December 1, 1899; and November 28, 1900.

No summer or winter records.

Next to the Lesser Scaup this is the most common duck found here. It is seen singly, in pairs, and in flocks numbering up to 20 birds. During large flights I have seen flocks of Bufflehead numbering 40.

On several occasions quite large flights of mostly Bufflehead occurred. April 22, 1903, a large flight of them came in. The wind was high, northwesterly with snow flurries, and they were in all day. At Grass Flats I saw a great many flocks of 5 and 6 and up to 40. With this flight was also a very few Red-breasted Mergansers, a number of Horned Grebes, 4 Lesser Scaup, 4 Goldeneyes, 8 or 10 Long-tails, and 1 Herring Gull.

The Bufflehead is rather tame and quite easily approached. It is not particular about alighting and will drop into ponds, overflows, or swift water alike. The Bufflehead is known locally as "Butterball." Quite a few were taken each season before spring shooting was abolished. The male in full dress is a very handsome duck.

October 22, 1930, I saw 4 Bufflehead—1 male and 3 females. February 4, 1941, I saw 3 here—2 males and 1 female—my first winter record here. This was no open winter either, as the river was well frozen up. On October 27, 1943, I saw 3; April 17, 1944, saw a flock of 15 in Grunderville Eddy, the first real flock I have seen in years. On February 1, 1947, I saw one. *(RBS says he had no winter records in the original 1890 to 1923 record, but notes a February 1941 record here. Note: any post-1923 recordings are added to include a more comprehensive record—this allows the original journal notes to stand as written, but also provides a more comprehensive overall record.)*

Measurements:

Adult male, 15–24–7–3

Long-tailed Duck

Harelda hyemalis / Clangula hyemalis

(30.) Regular migrant in spring. Occasional in fall and winter.

This species occurs at times in winter, and it is sometimes found during March. It is sometimes plentiful throughout April. Other years it is scarce, except the latter part of April. It is a rather difficult task to get dates of first spring arrivals.

I have seen it here as late as May 2, 1894; May 5, 1901; and May 20, 1893. This latter date is a very late one. This bird I shot in the spring-gut on Meade Island. It was a male in full black and brown breeding plumage.

In the fall it is little more than a straggler. The only dates I have are October 29, 1890; December 12, 1898; and November 27, 1900. In the spring it is usually found in small parties and flocks. On a big duck day when a large flight of ducks would occur there would always be from a few to a great many Long-tails. Sometimes there has occurred a large flight of mostly Long-tails. At such times many flocks numbered up to 40. On April 15, 1917, there occurred a large flight. On this day I saw one flock of over 100, the largest single flock of ducks of any kind that I ever saw here.

They are not wary and quite a few used to be taken each season. They are often found in ponds or coves, but usually are seen floating down in mid-stream.

I never think of this species but what I recall to mind windy April mornings with wet snow falling. I can almost hear the well known "er er a lee" of the males as the flock floats down stream.

Most of those found here are in the black and white plumage, but late in April many females are mixed with much red and brown. Males in full black and brown breeding dress are frequently taken.

During the latter part of April, 1907, Long-tails were common and a number were taken in full summer dress. They are known locally as Pintail, Sprig-tail, and Pigeon-tail. During ordinary winters they are not found here, but during severe winters they are met with.

During the severe blizzard of February 4 to 11, 1895, zero temperatures prevailed—at one time reaching 25 degrees below zero. There was a high northwesterly wind with fine snow most of the time. The river was ice-bound and snow lay deep. Toward the end of the blizzard American Mergansers and Goldeneyes appeared in numbers in the open places and with them a few Long-tails.

Again in 1899, from February 8 to 15, we had a blizzard that, if anything, was worse than the one in 1895. At this time Long-tails also appeared. Some had their back and wings so coated with ice as to be unable to fly.

The Long-tail seems to be getting rare here now. Looking over my records from 1890 on to the present time, 1940, I find that during the period from 1890 to 1905 Long-tails were always here during the spring migrations—abundant at times. In 1905 and 1906 they were scarce; 1907, plentiful; 1908, common; 1909 to 1912, scarce; 1913 to 1916, I was absent; and 1917, plentiful. The largest flight of Long-tails I ever saw occurred here April 15, 1917. From 1917 to 1930 only a few were seen each season. On March 29, 1932, I saw several flocks at Erie. On March 2, 1933, I saw one male; April 8, 1934, several at Erie; 1935, none; April 16, 1936, saw several at Erie; April 27, 1937, saw 3 or 4 at Erie; 1938 to 1942, saw none; April 13 and 27, 1943, saw 1 male on each date.

In the 1944 season I saw it in Grunderville Eddy on three occasions. The first was a fine male on April 21. On April 23 I found a flock of 12 to 15. This was the first flock I saw for a number of years, and the first time in years I heard the formerly well known call, "er er a lee." The third occurrence was a nice pair on April 26.

In 1946 I saw 2 on April 5 and 2 on April 8. In 1947 I saw a nice flock of 12 on April 20. I saw 3 on April 22.

Measurements:

April 29, 1890, adult male, 19 1/2–30–9–7 1/4

April 8, 1891, adult male, W, 21 3/4–30–8 1/4–8 1/2 *("W" indicates winter plumage)*

April 8, 1891, adult female, 16–28–8 1/2–8

May 1, 1903, adult male, S, 22–30–9 1/4–8 1/2 *("S" indicates summer plumage)*

White-winged Scoter
Oidemia deglandi | Melanitta fusca deglandi

(31.) Irregular migrant.

The scoters, nicknamed "Boobies" wherever commonly found, are sea ducks and prefer large bodies of water, hence, they are scarce at inland places like Warren. At Erie I have taken all three of the scoters, but here at Warren so far I have met with the White-wing only, although a stray Surf or American might occur.

The first I ever saw was shot at town by a friend, Harry Parks, on May 27, 1891. It was a male in full breeding dress. I secured it for my collection.

During the great flight of grebes on April 25, 1893, I saw several of this species. May 20 of the same year I saw a pair at town. Several females have been shot at town in May of recent years. On December 6, 1900, I shot a female at Grass Flats.

Whenever large flights of waterfowl occur in April several of these scoters are usually noted. It is seen frequently late in May. I never saw over 2 together here, and it is seldom taken.

May 14 and 15, 1917, a fine adult male was about the eddy at town, and again on June 5 a fine male was along shore above the bridge all day. October 30, 1923, at Grass Flats I shot an adult male White-winged Scoter in nearly full spring plumage. The bird was alone. On March 22, winter of 1941, a female appeared in Grunderville Eddy. May 10, 1943, I saw an adult in Grunderville Eddy.

Ruddy Duck
Erismatura jamaicensis | Oxyura jamaicensis

(32.) Irregular migrant.

Some seasons a few are about, and others it is very rare or not seen at all. Since 1890 I have it recorded as follows: 1892, two adult males taken during April at town; 1893, April 25 saw 3, May 1 saw 4. On February 23, 1894, I saw a female in an open place in the river at the Glade Bridge. This is my only winter record. In 1895, March 25 saw 4, April 4 saw 1, April 13 saw 1; 1899, April 12 saw 2; 1901, April 24 saw 10 or 12; 1904, April 2 saw 2, April 12 saw 1. On April 19, 1904, at Meade Island and Grass Flats I found a little flight scattered along. I saw about 25 Ruddies altogether, and I secured some fine specimens in perfect plumage.

In 1906, October 30 I saw 1; 1907, April 26 saw 1, May 1 saw 3; 1909, May 10 saw a pair. On May 30, 1910, I found a female lying in the grass along the river on the South Side at town—the bird evidently having struck the wires. I kept her overnight and next morning found that she was lively and apparently alright. I took her back to the river and let her go. On May 14 of 1917, I saw a nice female Ruddy with a White-winged Scoter all day.

The Ruddy seems to be quite sociable and is very often seen in the company of ducks of other species, and often with a flock of grebes along shore. It is not very wild and is quite easily taken.

April 21, 1929, I saw several nice flocks of 8 to 10 at town. April 22, 1944, I saw a nice male.

Measurements:

April 12, 1904, adult male, 15–23–5 3/4–2 1/2

Canada Goose
Branta canadensis

(33.) Regular migrant spring and fall.

It arrives March 20, 1890; March 7, 1894; March 12, 1895; March 10, 1899; March 23, 1901; March 28, 1902; March 5, 1903; March 26, 1904; March 28, 1906; and March 16, 1907.

Latest dates of flocks seen are: April 9, 1895; April 11, 1899; and April 17, 1907. In the fall I have noted it as early as September 30, 1895, snowing, saw 25; October 4, 1903, saw 20; October 11, 1904, saw 28; October 14, 1905, saw 2 large flocks; October 14, 1907, saw 9; and October 9, 1910, saw a large flock. Latest fall record is November 16, 1900.

Each spring and fall a few flocks of geese, numbering from a half-dozen up to 100 birds per flock, are seen passing over. More are seen passing in the fall than in the spring. They never alight in this vicinity unless bewildered by fog or a storm. Then they are just as apt to alight on land as in the water. When they are compelled to alight here they are very wild and alert. Few gunners have ever been fortunate enough to get a shot at one.

I have known flights to alight on gravel bars, especially about the Grass Flats. They come in about dark, but these flocks would leave at the break of day.

According to the old settlers they used to alight often, but I have seen but very few in the water.

On May 20, 1890, I saw 25 in mid-stream above the upper railroad bridge. They only stayed a few minutes. On April 4, 1894, during a flight of ducks, 2 geese alighted at Grass Flats. They were on the opposite side, but were very uneasy and left very soon.

April 3, 1901, during a blinding storm of wind and snow, a lone goose alighted at Grass Flats and was shot. April 4, 1906, I found a dead goose floating in the river. It was too badly decomposed to save. February 25, 1905, during severe winter weather, a flock of geese flew about at night for some time. Their voices sounded weak, but they were certainly geese of some kind.

On April 7, 1914, during a severe storm of wind, rain, sleet, and snow a flight of ducks, geese, and swans was driven in. During the day 4 or 5 flocks of geese alighted near and at town. One flock of fully 200 passed right through town along the river. There were also a few pairs and singles scattered about.

This was the first year of closed spring shooting or else a big kill of geese and swans would have taken place here. As it was, some illegal shooting was done—for on the following morning I found a very fine specimen, floating along shore dead. It was fresh and in fine shape, so I saved it and mounted it.

March 4, 1924, I saw 4 on the beach at the head of Highhouse's Eddy. This was a very early record as there was much snow and ice. Many passed the spring of 1926 and flocks alighted. On March 4, 1928, a large flock of about 100 alighted in the river at the Outing Club—close to a great flock of swans. About this time a number of geese passed by in flocks.

Late in March of 1930 a flock of 37 spent the day at the foot of the little island, back of the McIntosh farm along Meade Island. I had a fine chance to watch them all morning at close range.

Measurements:

April 7, 1914, female, 32–60–17 3/4–6, Wt. 7 lbs, stomach empty, not fat.

(RBS notes here that the Brant was added to his waterfowl species accounts after October 1, 1923.)

Whistling Swan | Tundra Swan
Olor columbianus | Cygnus columbianus

(34.) Rare visitor.

Old residents say that swans used to be seen in the river every spring, years ago. That must have been many years ago for it has certainly been a long time since swans have occurred here except as unwilling visitors. Practically all the swans that have occurred here in my time have been driven in by storms, usually storms of wind accompanied by sleet, snow, or rain.

Swans no doubt pass north each year, in March and early April, along the Allegheny River route, and happening to get caught sometimes by a bad storm, are compelled to alight. Late in March, 1879, before my collecting days had begun, a storm of wind, rain, and sleet caught the swans on their way north and, becoming overburdened with ice, they alighted in many places throughout western Pennsylvania. Here at Warren a number were shot on the Allegheny River and Conewango Creek.

In late March of 1884 a similar storm drove down a large flock, and 4 or 5 swans were shot. In late March of 1887 two swans alighted in the eddy below Meade Island and one was killed. September, 1894, after a windy, rainy night, a swan was shot in Highhouse's Eddy just below town. It was a young one.

April 12, 1899, a good flight of waterfowl occurred and with it a lone swan. I was in a boat in ambush at the foot of Meade Island and saw the old fellow coming, but he passed too far off.

March 29, 1905, was an unusually warm day. At noon I saw 3 swans flying at a good height. These 3 alighted several times between here and Tidioute and were shot at, but escaped. Later on I learned that these 3 were all shot at Tionesta.

March 28, 1907, four passed going up the river, but they did not alight. Later on, April 5, two alighted at Tidioute, were fired upon, but escaped. During the summer of 1907, I learned that a lone swan was living near Corydon, up the river. I wrote to Mr. J.A. Waldo of Corydon, and he informed me that a swan had lived about an island in the river near Corydon from early in the season up to about July 1, when it was killed by someone. It is strange that a swan should summer here, but then it may have been wounded on its way north.

March 20, 1910, a flock estimated at 100 alighted in the river near Tidioute, and a fine one was shot and sent up here to Greenlund to be mounted. March 22, 1912, during a snow storm two flocks of 10 or 12 each passed here quite low, but did not alight.

April 7, 1914, during the storm mentioned as having driven in so many geese, quite a few swans were also compelled to alight. A flock of fully 50 alighted above the upper railroad bridge early in the morning—late in the afternoon 12 swans and 2 geese came in above the suspension bridge. Other flocks and singles were seen nearby in the river by other parties during the day. Only the new federal law saved a number of geese and swans from being killed in this vicinity.

On April 1, 1915, a lone swan was seen flying at Meade Island. April 6, 1924, I saw a fine swan in the river along the island about the Glade Bridge—a pair was there all day the day before.

About the first of April, 1925, a very large flock of swans, estimated to number fully 100, passed here early one morning. They were quite low and noisy. Late in the morning of April 8 and early morning of April 9, two swans came into the river at town above the new bridge. One was slightly gray on the neck and head. At one time one got up in the mill race back of the Exchange Hotel. They attracted considerable attention.

March 24, 1928, a great flock alighted in the river at the Outing Club. Parties who tried to count them estimated the flock to contain from 135 to 150. They were there most of the afternoon. Several stragglers were seen in the river at other places, and one was taken alive by Warden Nelson and sent to the Game Commission at Harrisburg. This one had alighted in a settling pond at Roystone—getting into a lot of oil, it was unable to fly. This same day several flocks of 100 each were seen at Jamestown and Chautauqua Lake. On March 27, during a high wind and blinding snow, 12 swans alighted just above the Glade Bridge and spent the day on the overflow of the island.

October, 20, 1930, following a severe storm of high wind and heavy snow along Lake Erie, two flocks of swans alighted. One flock of about a dozen came into the Conewango Creek at Akeley and another flock on the Allegheny River at Dunn's Eddy.

At Erie, Pennsylvania, from sometime in November, 1931, to March 5, 1932, a large number of swans, at one time estimated to number from 1200 to 1500, wintered in the bay. On February 22 and March 1, on my visits there, I estimated 800 birds. It was a wonderful sight.

November 8, 1932, I saw a flock of 17 swans in the river at Grunderville. It was snowing and had snowed 5 or 6 inches during the night. They left about 9:30 in the morning, going up the river.

March 17, 1935, six swans were driven in by a hard storm last night. They spent the day in the river at the head of Highhouse's Eddy and left toward evening. On April 11, 12, and 13, 1940, a fine large swan stayed about Meade Island and its overflow—it probably got lost from a flock.

March 28, 1942, I saw 10 in the river at Daly's Island; March 26, 1943, saw 2 flying; March 30, 1943, saw a flock of 15 in Grunderville Eddy; and April 7, 1943, saw 1 feeding off the foot of Leek Island.

On the morning of March 16, 1944, I saw 7 in the river at the head of Leek Island—a pretty sight. March 19, 1945, I saw a nice flock of 16 at Grunderville Eddy; March 9, 1946, saw 6 in Grunderville Eddy. In 1947, I saw a flock of 17 on March 20, and on March 29 a flock of 7—both flocks at Grunderville Eddy.

Measurements:

March 24, 1890, adult female, 51–79–21 1/2–8, Wt. 11 lbs., 8 oz.

(above) Lumber rafts going to market, near Grunder Run.

(below, Simpson) Lunch in the woods near head of Long Run, Feb. 22, 1921.

THE WADERS

Nine or ten species of herons and bitterns have been known to occur in recent years in this state, but only 4 or 5 occur regularly at large throughout the Commonwealth—the others being stragglers from the south and more apt to occur in the southeastern part of the state than elsewhere.

This class of birds prefers swamps, marshes, and lakes. It is for this reason Warren, being an inland place and in a mountainous region, is a rather poor place for waders. Five of the most common species found in the state occur here. *(RBS margin note indicates that his list includes a sixth species, the American Egret, August 15, 1929.)*

No rarities have yet been recorded. Only two species breed here.

The Least Bittern, smallest of all, is quite tame, while the largest, the Great Blue Heron, is wild and wary. Both of these bitterns might possibly nest in the county, but up to date I have no records.

American Bittern
Botaurus lentiginosus

(35.) Irregular migrant, spring and fall.

It is noted at times in the spring on dates ranging from March 31 to May 1. On June 23, 1891, I saw 2 at the mouth of the Conewango Creek. I saw one at Grass Flats on May 30, 1907. It is occasionally noted during September. I have never seen but 1 or 2 at a time and on the whole it is quite scarce.

The American Bittern is found along the river in brushy and weedy places along shore—also swampy places on the mainland. Once, September 21, 1894, at one of the small ponds on the island at the mouth of the Conewango Creek, I walked up to within 25 feet of one before I saw it. It stood straight as a stick, even its bill pointed up, and at first I did take it to be a piece of wood. It may possibly nest somewhere in the county.

Least Bittern
Ixobrychus exilis

(36.) Rare visitor.

This little fellow is only occasionally noted, but it might occur regularly, as it is easily overlooked. In 1892 I first noted it—taking specimens at the ponds about the mouth of the Conewango Creek on May 3 and 14, and a male at Grass Flats on May 16. I have occasionally seen it during the May migrations.

In the fall I have several times met it in September and once in August—August 12, 1910. They are quite tame and allow a close approach, and for this reason it might be easily overlooked. I never saw more than a pair together. It is possible that this species may nest in this county.

Great Blue Heron
Ardea herodias herodias

(37.) Summer resident. Breeds.

Arrives: March 22, 1890; April 2, 1892; March 14, 1894; March 23, 1899; April 3, 1901; March 22, 1902; and March 28, 1904.

Every day during April, the Great Blue can be seen along the river, singly or in pairs, and once in April of 1901, I saw a flock of 5 along Grass Flats Island. During the summer a few are scattered along the river. These summer residents nest back in the mountains. In late summer the family, old and young, are found along the islands and little-frequented spots. Remains quite late, but after September 1 is usually seen singly, the old and young having parted company.

I have noted single ones as late as October 22, 1890; November 20, 1899; and November 14, 1900. For many years there was a heronry on the Middle Fork of Hickory Creek. Ten to fifteen pairs of birds bred there annually in the tallest trees in virgin timber. One big hemlock tree always contained 5 or 6 nests. Since 1916 or 1917 the birds have not nested there, but as they are still found along the river, they must have a heronry back in the mountains somewhere, but just where I cannot find out.

It is known along the river as "Crane." The Great Blue is a wild and wary bird. It is ever vigilant and at the first sign of danger gets right up and leaves. If pursued it leaves the river and flies back into the woods, where it can sit in some tall tree or stub and keep a sharp lookout. When in the brush along shore it is a hard bird to detect.

I have taken some fine specimens in the spring when ducking at Meade Island and Grass Flats, but at this season they are hard to get a shot at. Later on, when old and young are together and the foliage is all out, it is not so difficult to sneak up on them, but at this time they are not in full dress. Several years ago I mounted a nice one that had been caught in a muskrat trap along the Tionesta Creek near Sheffield.

Although they are very wild, I once, while sitting quietly in the brush near shore at Grass Flats, had one alight close by and feed along to within 20 feet of me. It was comical to see him grab at the minnows that played about his legs. When he was hardly 20 feet away I suddenly leaped out at him, letting out a fiendish yell, and firing my gun into the air. The "Crane" was almost scared to death. It flapped, kicked, and squawked as it frantically climbed out of there. It was still squawking when it got out of sight around the bend.

During the winter of 1940-41, which was a good solid winter, I saw a Great Blue about some open water at Leek Island on January 29 and again on January 31—a real winter record. During the spring of 1941 a small heronry was discovered breeding near a branch of the Kinzua Creek. This was across the county line in McKean County. Since then, owing to the war, I have not been able to investigate, but there is no question of the 1941 nesting. I also saw one about Leek Island several times in January, 1941.

Measurements:

May 28, 1895, adult male, 42–72–18 1/4–7 1/4

August 16, 1900, young, 42–72–18 1/4–7 1/4

April 13, 1901, adult female, 47–76–18 3/4–7 1/2

(RGB notes in his journal that the American Egret was added to his list of waders after October 1, 1923.)

37.

GREAT BLUE HERON.

ARDEA HERODIAS HERODIAS.

Summer Resident. Breeds.
Arrives (April 2nd 1892 - March 22nd 1890 - March 14th 1894 - March 23d 1899 - April 3d 1901 March 22nd 1902 - March 28th 1904.
Every day during April the Great Blue can be seen along the river singly or in pairs, and once in April 1901 I saw a flock of 5 along Grass Flat Is.
During the summer a few are scattered along the river. These summer residents nest back in the mountains.
In late summer the family, old and young, are found along the islands and little frequented spots.
Remains quite late but after Sept 1st is usually seen singly, the old and young having parted company.
I have noted single ones as late as Oct 22nd 1890 - Nov. 20th 1899 - Nov. 14th 1900.
For many years there was a herony on the Middle Fork of Hickory Creek. Ten to Fifteen pairs of birds bred there annually in the tallest trees in virgin timber. One big hemlock tree always contained 5 or 6 nests. Since 1916 or 1917 the birds have not nested there but as they are still found along the river they must have a herony back in the mountains somewhere but just where I cant find out.

Simpson's species account for the Great Blue Heron.

Green Heron
Butorides virescens

(38.) Summer resident. Breeds.

Arrives: May 2, 1892; April 20, 1899; and April 30, 1901. After the first week of May it is not uncommon along the river and larger streams.

It is seen singly and in pairs. After the young have left the nest the family is found together the rest of the summer. I have noted it as late as October 10, 1900; October 5, 1902; and October 31, 1923.

It nests near the river in most any tree that it takes a fancy to—from a thorn or wild crabapple to a young pine. The nests are from 10 to 40 feet up and are a loose platform of sticks. Eggs number 4 to 5. Nesting dates: June 3, 1912, 5 eggs, fresh; May 22, 1932, 5 eggs, fresh; June 3, 1932, two nests, 4 eggs in one and the second nest 1 egg; and June 14, 1932, five eggs, incubation advanced.

Measurements:

April 30, 1906, adult male, 18–26 3/4–7 1/4–3

April 30, 1906, adult female, 18–26–7 1/4–3

Black-crowned Night Heron
Nyctanassa nycticorax

(39.) Irregular migrant in summer.

This heron occurs here at times during June, July, and August. The earliest date I have seen it is June 23, 1891. I have a number of dates ranging from this date up to September first. I have never seen or heard of an adult bird. All have been in the young of the year plumage. In spite of the fact that I have never seen an adult, these birds must nest somewhere not so very far away or the young would hardly reach here so soon.

It is found about coves and bayous where there is good cover. It is rather wild when found here. Several years ago one was taken alive with a tipped wing. It was put in a box and placed on exhibition in a store window with a placard telling its supposed name and that it was a rare Puerto Rican bird.

April 14, 1937, in the bayou at the head of Highhouse's Eddy, I saw a fine adult bird. This is the only one I have seen here in the spring season, and the first I have ever seen here in full plumage. April 27, 1944, I saw an adult in full plumage in the swamp back of Ittel's house—the second time I have seen an adult here.

Measurements:

August 31, 1894, young, 24–44–11–5

RAILS—Etc.

Virginia Rail
Rallus virginianus | Rallus limicola

(40.) Irregular migrant.

Rails are rather scarce near Warren. Birds of this family want swamps and marshes. As suitable places are scarce in the immediate vicinity of Warren, rails are only occasionally met with here. They are also rather hard to flush and are easily passed by or overlooked.

The first Virginia I ever saw here was on May 5, 1903, at Grass Flats. In the long wooded swamp I saw a snapping turtle on a log. I tossed a stick to scare it and to see it tumble in. When the stick struck the water a bird arose and flew about 25 feet—alighting on another log. I at once recognized a Virginia and secured it with a light load of number 10 shot.

May 23, 1903, a friend shot one in a wet meadow down the river. He sent it up to me. I have noted the Virginia several times in May.

September 2, 1916, while after butterflies on Meade Island, I flushed one quite a ways from water, along the edge of a buckwheat patch and a rank growth of weeds and grass. It flew but a little distance and dropped into the buckwheat. There may be places in this county where this rail breeds.

May 11, 1932, I saw one; May 14, 1945, saw one.

Sora Rail | Sora
Porzana carolina

(41.) Irregular migrant, spring and fall.

It is rather scarce and not often noted. They do not flush very easily and are usually in such places that they would be passed by. I have seen it taken in May and again in September and October.

On April 21, 1909, a neighbor saw one fly across his backyard and instantly kill itself by striking a wire clothes line. It was a fine male.

Measurements:

April 21, 1909, adult male, 8 1/4–15 5/8–4–8 1/4

Florida Gallinule | Common Moorhen
Gallinula galeata | Gallinula chloropus

(42.) Straggler.

I have seen but one specimen up to date. On May 18, 1891, a friend informed me that he had just seen a queer bird while fishing at the mouth of the Conewango Creek. He said it looked like a Banty rooster with a red top-knot.

Taking my gun, I went down and soon found the bird skulking along shore in some bushes. I easily secured it and found that I had a fine male Gallinule.

Measurements:

May 18, 1891, adult male, 14 3/8–23 3/4–7 1/4–3

American Coot
Fulica americana

(43.) Irregular migrant.

I have taken specimens here on the following dates: May 17, 1889; May 22, 1891; April 27, 1894; April 6, 1895; and April 7, 1908. I have noted it several times in October.

It is seen singly or in pairs in some cove or quiet place along shore. It is not very wild, but it is quite a good diver. It is rather rare here and not often seen—even in a good duck season.

I shot one on Grass Flats Island on October 30, 1923.

SHORE BIRDS

Fully 30 species of shore birds have been taken in western Pennsylvania. This fine showing is accounted for from the fact that the northwestern corner of the state borders on Lake Erie, where large numbers of shore birds and waterfowl occur during migrations. Of this number, four, possibly five, species remain to breed. The rest pass on to the far north to spend the summer.

Warren is not a very good place for shore birds. The shores of the river are too much gravel—not enough sand and mud-bars. As the lake shore is not much over 50 miles away in air miles, and the general course of the Allegheny River is north to south through the state, it is more or less a migration route for shore birds, as well as waterfowl. Shore birds are never met with here in any number, and when they do occur, it is usually during storms.

Almost every year late in May, if the water is not too high, there is usually some of this class of birds to be found. I have some very good records from here for late May.

Up to date I have noted but 14 species of shore birds here and only three of these breed. At Erie, Pennsylvania, on the Peninsula, I have personally taken 21 species, and on several of my trips have seen species that I did not identify.

Where shore birds are common they are found in flocks, sometimes quite large and containing different species. At Erie great flights used to occur; they are still very common at times.

As a rule shore birds are not hard to shoot, as most of them are not very wary; however, I have found some of the larger species to be quite wary and difficult to approach. Most of the shore birds, though small, are quite good for the table. Several species, Woodcock and Snipe especially, are highly prized game birds, and for this reason they are rather scarce at present. Shore birds are strong and swift fliers.

American Woodcock
Philohela minor / Scolopax minor

(44.) Summer resident. Breeds.

It arrives in spring on dates ranging from March 19, 1894, to April 8, 1904. If the weather is mild in fall it is seen sometimes well through November—being a hardy bird and not leaving until the ground freezes, thus shutting off the food supply.

When I first began collecting I thought nothing of flushing a Woodcock as they were quite common. Grass Flats was a great place for them as were other islands along the river and larger streams. They have gradually become scarcer, and I only occasionally flush one now.

Its favorite haunts are brushy places or open woodland where there are, more or less, moist or swampy spots for feeding. During dry summers it gathers along the river and larger streams in the brushy, swampy, willowy places. It is often found back in the mountains, along the streams, sometimes in virgin forest.

As soon as it arrives in spring it begins its peculiar performance at dusk. The bird sits about, frequently uttering a loud coarse note that sounds like "beeb." At intervals the performer leaves the ground and towers upward to some height with whistling wings, soon descending in circles to again alight, sometimes quite a distance from the starting point. The whole performance is again repeated. It nests in April with sets usually being completed by April 10.

Once while sitting quietly I saw an old Woodcock walking along with 4 young. They were in a row and with their bills pointing downwards, a pretty sight. Rushing at them, the young simply vanished, and I was unable to find a single one. I sat down again and waited. Soon the old lady returned and walked about, when from apparently nowhere the young appeared and the procession moved along. I rushed out and again the young vanished. I looked hard and hunted about, but not a little one could I find, so I gave it up as a bad job and went on my way.

They are hunted a great deal with trained dogs and to this method can be charged the cause of their becoming rare.

May 12, 1946, I flushed a female Woodcock from her nest by nearly stepping on her. It was well hidden in thick, tall, dead weeds on top of a bank along a swamp. The nest held four eggs. When I returned 2 days later to photograph the old lady on the nest I found the eggs had hatched. They still lay where the young had burst them open and emerged. I got a very fine photograph of the nest and eggs.

Measurements:

October 1, 1908, adult male, 11 1/4–18 1/2–5 1/2–2 3/4, Wt. 7 1/2 oz.

Wilson's Snipe | Common Snipe
Gallinago delicate | Gallinago gallinago delicata

(45.) Regular migrant spring and fall. Not at all common.

I have met with it in spring on dates ranging from May 14, 1902, to April 12, 1904. In the fall I have noted it at different times from late in September up to November in 1889. There are few suitable places in the vicinity of Warren for snipe, and when it is met with here it is singly or in pairs. I have never seen a flock or flight. I occasionally find one along the river shores in muddy, grassy flats.

May 30, 1925, S.S. Dickey and I flushed one from the cattails in the swamp at the head of the Clarendon Pond. During the 1928 and 1929 nesting seasons a pair were about the swamp near the brickyard. They showed every sign of nesting and having young; however, we could not find the nest or young. 1935 produced the first positive nesting record. On April 14, I flushed a snipe from this swamp. I visited this place frequently from then on, and soon found that a pair was located there. About the second week in May I began quite a close watch. I became convinced after watching the birds, especially early morning, by their actions—calling, circling, winnowing flight—that they were nesting or going to soon. I spent 3 or 4 mornings searching for the nest, but as I had never seen one, I was handicapped by not knowing what kind of situation to look for—or whether the female would sit close or slip off and skulk away through the heavy grass and cover. I started to comb the swamp thoroughly by sections.

On the morning of May 16, while closely and thoroughly threshing and searching over a section, I flushed the bird off her nest at my very feet. She wobbled and fluttered along, acting as if she were about to somersault or roll over any moment. There on top a large, flat, extra heavy tussock was the nest of grass. It was very well concealed from overhead by long, dead, overhanging marsh grasses. The nest contained 4 handsome, well marked eggs. The swamp was filled with water and the nest was just about surrounded by water. The following morning Harry and I went down with our cameras and secured some very nice pictures of the nest and site. While taking the pictures the old bird was quite noisy and stayed close by.

Measurements:

September 23, 1890, adult male, 11 1/2–18–5 1/2–3

Pectoral Sandpiper
Pisobia maculate | Calidris melanotos

(46.) Rare visitor.

November 11, 1898, was a cold, damp day. I was down the river that day, and in passing through an old brickyard I suddenly saw, not 25 feet away, a sandpiper in a little pool. After it arose, I shot. As I did not drop a pair of Bufflehead ducks that I carried with me, the result was a nice, clean miss.

At the time I was positive it was a Pectoral. Since then I have become better acquainted with the various sandpipers—their habits, haunts, and calls—through my trips to Erie. Now I know the bird was a Pectoral.

On April 10, 1905, Carl Marsh shot one along a grassy pond below town. The bird was made up into a skin by Professor Homer, at that time a teacher at the high school here.

During April, 1912, I saw three—two at Grass Flats on April 9, and the other near town on April 14. I have, on at least two or three occasions, seen a sandpiper in the fall that I took to be of this species.

On August 25, 1932, I saw one, and August 10, 1935, I saw one. During September of 1933, I saw this species on the bars at the head of Highhouse's Eddy at different times.

Least Sandpiper
Pisobia minutilla | Calidris minutilla

(47.) Irregular migrant spring and fall.

I have taken several in May about overflowed meadows during high water. A fine male in my collection I took May 23, 1893.

In the fall it occasionally occurs on the beaches along the river, frequently in company with the Semipalmated. I have specimens taken on August 8, 1893; August 16, 1900; September 10, 1909; and August 19, 1910.

When the river is low in the fall very few shore birds are about. At such times a few shore birds are often met with on the bars and beaches at Grass Flats. This little fellow may occur more often than I think. It is rather hard to pick out from among the Semipalmated, with which it is very likely to be found.

I saw two on August 12, 1912, and one each on August 30, 1932, and July 20, 1934.

Red-backed Sandpiper | Dunlin
Pelidna alpina sakhalina | Calidris alpina

(48.) Straggler.

At Erie, Pennsylvania, this Sandpiper is quite common in the fall. It also occurs in late May and early June. I am quite familiar with this sandpiper from my Erie experiences, but I have identified it in Warren County only twice.

On the night of May 26, 1904, we had a continuous performance of severe thunder storms accompanied with high winds. Late afternoon, May 27, while going home along the river bank just below the upper railroad bridge, I saw 2 Sandpipers standing on a piece of driftwood at the water's edge.

At first glance I took them to be Solitaries. At thirty feet I glanced at them again and saw my mistake. I sheered off hoping to pass around them without flushing them. I had walked too close though and they jumped in the air uttering their soft cry. The sun shone on their red backs, and as they turned I saw the black under parts. I secured my gun and followed on down the river. I hunted until almost dusk, but never saw them again.

On May 20, 1919, while going along the river at the head of Highhouse's Eddy, I saw on the beach near the water's edge a dead bird. It had drifted in and had been left by the receding water. At first glance I took it to be a Tip-up, but on picking it up I found it to be an adult Dunlin in full spring plumage.

The bird was fresh and had been dead but a short time. It was considerably bruised on one side of the head. It had no doubt struck a wire in town. It had fallen into the stream, drifted, and lodged where I was so lucky to have found it.

Measurements:

May 20, 1919, adult male, 8 1/8–15 1/8–4 5/8–2

Semipalmated Sandpiper
Ereunetes pusillus | Calidris pusilla

(49.) Regular migrant during spring and fall.

I have met this species here as early as April 22 in 1901, on which date I shot a fine adult on some overflowed meadow down the river. During May it is occasionally met about overflowed meadows and along the shores of the river. I have noted it quite frequently up to May 30 and 31.

In autumn I have noted it on dates ranging from August 17, 1893; September 3, 1894; September 25, 1909; July 20, 1934; August 13, 1936; and July 18, 1939. It is usually seen singly or in pairs—only rarely in small parties. I have never seen more than 6 in one flock here. It is very often seen in company with other shore birds.

At Erie I have found this species to be common.

Measurements:

May 31, 1906, female, 6 1/8–12 1/4–3 3/4–1 3/4

Greater Yellow-legs
Totanus melanoleucus / Tringa melanoleuca

(50.) Regular migrant spring and fall.

My earliest spring record is April 12, 1904, and the latest spring record is May 19, 1917. It is rather uncertain in its appearance in spring, some seasons I see a few and other years it is scarce.

On June 6, 1911, I saw a pair at Grass Flats, but this date is very late and unusual. In the fall I have many dates ranging from September 4, 1891, to as late as November 15, 1902.

It is found on the gravel bars and shores of the river, and is also seen on overflowed meadows during high water. It is usually seen singly or in pairs.

April 24, 1902, I saw a flock of 5, and on October 28, 1914, I saw a fine flock of 25 birds on a bar at the head of Highhouse's Eddy just below town. With this flock was a single, small piper that I think was a Dunlin, but I did not positively identify it. After rising, this large flock circled about for some time—keeping up a great whistling. It was a great sight to me, as this is the only real flock of Yellow-legs I ever saw.

They are a swift and strong flier. Their call or whistle reminds me of the Osprey. When found they are usually rather wild and wary and not easy to approach.

Lesser Yellow-legs
Totanus flavipes

(51.) Irregular migrant. Rather scarce.

Among my notes I find the following dates on which I have met this species: May 8, 1891, saw one with 3 or 4 Solitaries on the bars at the mouth of the Conewango Creek; May 11, 1891, saw one at a puddle of water along the river road; August 26, 1895, saw one in the gutter behind Stonaker's Island at the mouth of the Conewango; July 11, 1909, saw one along the river at town;

September 11, 1913, saw a pair at the head of Highhouse's Eddy; and on May 18, 1917, I saw one in company with 2 Greater Yellow-legs at the head of Highhouse's Eddy.

I have found this species much easier to approach than the Greater Yellow-legs.

Measurements:

Fall, 10 1/4–20–6–2 1/2

Solitary Sandpiper
Helodromus solitarius / Tringo solitaria

(52.) Regular migrant spring and fall.

Arrives: May 2, 1891; April 30, 1892; April 28, 1894; and occurs up to May 20, 1890; May 21, 1891; May 18, 1903; and May 22, 1904. It returns again the first week in August. I have noted it as late as September 27, 1890—at Grass Flats on October 1, 1908. *(RBS post-1923 journal notes indicate that a single bird stayed about the bayou at the sand pits October 20-24, 1929.)*

I have several summer records for this species, but so far no nesting records. I have seen single birds in summer: July 13, 1894; July 23, 1895; and July 17, 1903. During the summer of 1905 a pair was about Sechrist's Flats, but there were no young. The following summer a lone Solitary was about the same place all through June and July. July 27, 1923, I saw one at the old Bucher Mill site on the Tionesta Creek.

Next to the Spotted this species was until recently the most common piper found here. I have seen as many as 8 at once scattered about on the bars at the mouth of the Conewango. At Grass Flats I have seen 6 or 7 at a time scattered about the ponds in the woods on the lower flat. I once flushed a pair in May at a little puddle along an old roadway, back near the head of the Tionesta in the wilderness.

Of late years it has become much scarcer and I don't see near as many as I used to.

Measurements:

May 10, 1901, adult, 8 3/4–16 1/2–5 1/2–2 1/2

Spotted Sandpiper
Actitis macularia

(53.) Summer resident. Quite common. Breeds.

Arrives: April 18, 1894; April 20, 1899; April 18, 1901; April 24, 1902; April 16, 1904; and April 22, 1907.

From the day of their arrival they are common all along the river in pairs and small parties of 6 to 8. As a summer resident they are found in pairs all along the larger streams.

It nests in late May and June. I have at hand the following dates on which fresh eggs were found: May 21, 1891, 4 eggs; June 1, 1912, 4 eggs; June 14, 1912, 4 eggs; and June 1, 1923, 4 eggs. *(RBS post-1923 journal notes indicate 4 eggs on June 11, 1925, and 4 eggs May 29, 1928.)*

It nests on the ground in meadows and fields near the water and on the islands and bars along the river. It nests in a hollow lined with grass, usually placed where there is a cover of weeds or grass—sometimes the nests are very well concealed.

As soon as the young are hatched the old birds lead them to the water where they can feed and hide amongst the grasses and weeds. They are common in little flocks or family groups during July and August.

In September they seem to separate and become scattered and begin moving south. By the middle of September most of them have departed. My latest fall record is of one seen at Grass Flats on September 29, 1908.

Black-bellied Plover
Squatarola squatarola / Pluvialis squatarola

(54.) Straggler.

At Erie this plover is a regular fall migrant. During my different trips to Erie, I took a number of specimens of this species—also the Golden. I have a beautiful, adult, male Black-bellied in full breeding plumage that I took at Erie in the spring—late May. I became familiar with their calls and appearances from my experience with these plovers at Erie.

I have 2 records from Warren. On the morning of August 24, 1901, while on my way to work, a Black-bellied in fall plumage flew past quite low and calling loudly. I easily recognized it from my Erie experiences. On October 24, 1907, George Warner of Garland shot one at that place *(Garland)* and sent it to me to be mounted. This is the only one I know of that has been taken in this county.

Measurements:

October 5, 1904, 11–24–7 1/4–2 3/4

October 24, 1907, 11–24–7 1/4–2 3/4

Killdeer Plover | Killdeer
Oxyechus vociferous / Charadrius vociferus

(55.) Summer resident. Breeds.

Arrives: March 26, 1892; March 19, 1894; March 20, 1899; March 19, 1901; and March 28, 1904. It is found singly, in pairs, and flocks of 4 or 5—up to 30—along the shores and bars of the river and in the fields. It is usually rather wild and wary when found here.

As a summer resident it is not at all common, only an occasional pair nesting here and there in old fields in the river valley. It nests in a slight hollow on a little hump or tussock, with but little lining, if any. Eggs always 4. Eggs laid late in April: April 24, 1916, 4 eggs, fresh; May 3, 1923, 4 eggs, fresh.

Nests are not easy to find as the female keeps a sharp lookout and runs off on the ground at the approach of anyone. After the young are full grown the families are found along the river on the bars and shores. It is only occasionally met with after the first of October, but I have seen single birds up to November 17 in 1890.

The winter of 1889-90 was a very bad one. On February 8, 1890, I found a Killdeer about the mouth of the Conewango Creek. There was 8 inches of fresh fallen snow on the ground. It was snowing hard, but it was not cold and the stream was open.

May 30, 1926, I found a nest of 3 eggs on the big gravel bar at the head of Highhouse's Eddy—probably a second laying.

Measurements:

April 4, 1890, female, 10 1/2–20 1/2–6 1/2–4 1/4, Wt. 3 oz.

Semipalmated Plover
Egialitis semipalmata | Charadrius semipalmatus

(56.) Regular migrant, spring and fall—rather scarce.

The first time I ever met this little plover here was on May 21, 1891, when I found a fine flock of 25 at the mouth of the Conewango Creek. Since that time I have not seen a flock of over 5 or 6.

Usually seen here singly or in pairs, very often in company with other pipers. Other dates of its occurrences here that I have are August 27, 1894; June 5, 1895; August 14, 1904; May 31, 1906; September 11, 1907; September 10, 1909; August 19, 1910; August 31, 1910; and on August 9, 1912, I saw two.

It is tame and easily approached. I found them to be common at Erie. They associate freely with Semipalmated Sandpipers, Dunlins, Killdeer, Sanderlings, and the Piping Plover.

Turnstone | Ruddy Turnstone
Arenaria interpres

(57.) Straggler.

Of course, stragglers amongst the water birds are occurring almost every season, if not every season, owing to the fact that Lake Erie is but a little over 50 air miles away. However, I never expected the Turnstone here, as it is rather uncommon in either spring or fall at Erie.

On May 30, 1907, I started at daylight for Grass Flats. I took an old flat-boat and floated down. The morning was cool and a heavy fog hung on the river. When I reached the big bar at the head of Highhouse's Eddy I floated along between it and the shore.

As the bar gradually appeared out of the fog I saw a wader along the water's edge. It looked strange, but I took it to be a Killdeer. As I drew closer through the fog I saw that the bird had a mottled appearance. By this time I had seen enough to know that I was gazing at a rarity. I lost no more time, but gathered it in and found it to be a fine, adult, female Turnstone.

I have a beautiful adult male in my collection that I took at Erie in early June. At this time I saw a few adult Turnstones, including one flock of ten.

May 24, 1925, was a cold, windy, rainy day. It followed a very hot day that wound up in high winds and thunderstorms. Down about the head of the eddy at the sand pits I found a large wave of birds had arrived. On the bars I found 8 or 10 Tip-ups, several Killdeer, and a beautiful, adult, male Turnstone. I got up to within 40 feet of it. With the Turnstone were 2 small Sandpipers, Least or Semipalmated, I couldn't tell which. This is the second one I have seen here and this was surely a beauty.

At Erie, May 29, 1932, Harry and I saw 8 or 10 Turnstone in full dress on the outside beach. On June 10, I saw 5 more at this same place.

Measurements:

May 30, 1907, adult, female, 9–18 1/2–5 3/4–2 3/8

June 3, 1911, adult male, 9 1/4–18 1/2–5 3/4–2 1/2

QUAIL—GROUSE

This family of birds is rather poorly represented in Pennsylvania. In Warren County only two species are found—the Common Quail and the Ruffed Grouse. The Gray Grouse that appeared here a few years ago seems to have left.

The wild turkey may have been found here many years ago, but I can find no hunters or woodsmen, even old men, who ever saw it in this county. It hardly seems that they would be exterminated before the elk, wolves, and panthers became a thing of the past. It is quite likely that the turkey has been nothing much more than a straggler in this county for many years.

A quail called the Hungarian Quail was released here several years ago, but the little flock perished during the winter in spite of the fact that they were watched over and cared for. Ring-neck Pheasants have been released at different times, but do not seem to increase any. Birds of this class are most highly prized game birds and are very much hunted, especially with trained dogs.

Quail | Northern Bobwhite
Colinus virginianus

(58.) Summer resident. Breeds.

Warren County is too mountainous or else the winters are too severe to suit Mr. Bob-white. The Bobwhite must be classed as a summer resident—they occur here sometimes in summer. I have at least one positive breeding record. The truth is that the Quail is quite a rare bird, at least in the immediate vicinity of Warren.

During the summer of 1902, there was a nice little bunch near here and it was good to hear their cheery calls. Long before snow fell they disappeared—having been spotted by woodcock hunters, so I am told.

June 28, 1911, I found a whole covey of young Quail in an old brush field along the Conewango Creek above North Warren. The birds were quite young and could hardly fly 10 feet.

I have always found the Quail tame and easily approached. In my opinion the Quail is a fine, cheery, sociable bird, and I fail to see any pleasure or sport in killing them.

In the spring of 1934 a pair appeared about the head of Highhouse's Eddy in the fields and brush lands. That fall this pair had increased to a flock of about 15. This covey evidently had good luck wintering, for during the season of 1935 they scattered, and could be heard whistling in different localities along the river flats and up the Conewango Valley.

July 13, 1935, I took photos of a Quail's nest containing 14 eggs. This is the only nest actually found that I have heard of. While a farmer was picking his strawberries the nest was found amongst weeds and old strawberry vines. The nest was very well hidden, in fact, almost concealed from overhead.

Ruffed Grouse
Bonasa umbellus

(59.) Resident. Breeds.

It is more common some years than others—their abundance depending on the severity of the previous winter and the weather conditions of the breeding season. The Grouse, known to everyone here as "Partridge" and "Pheasant," holds its own well in spite of its numerous enemies.

During the winter the Grouse gets into good cover where it can keep well hidden, but when spring arrives it spreads out. The male drums more or less all through the spring and fall.

The nest, a hollow in the leaves at the base of some tree or under cover of brush, is usually filled with its full compliment of eggs early in May, and about the first of June the young broods are encountered. Nests that I have found have contained from 9 to 13 eggs. I have heard of nests containing over 13 eggs, but I have never personally seen one.

The old bird is a very close sitter. Several times while gathering wild flowers I have almost tramped on one before she flushed. The young leave the nest as soon as hatched. Several times I have come across a brood so young that they hardly knew enough to hide. They learn to conceal themselves very soon however and are hard to find.

Many times I have come unexpectedly upon an old Grouse and her little brood. In such cases the little chicks, with plaintive peeps, quickly scatter and hide—while the mother bird, with dragging wings and apparently badly injured, drags herself along trying to lead the intruder away—or else, with feathers all fluffed out and hissing viciously, she rushes at the intruder in an attempt to frighten him away.

Some people claim that the old bird gives off no scent while incubating and therefore cannot be located by foxes and other predators. How true this is I do not know, but I do know that a good bird dog can readily point a Woodcock on her nest. I rather think the same holds true of the Grouse.

In October the Grouse seems to migrate a little by spreading out and appearing in the most unexpected places. At this time of the year they are often seen in town and are frequently killed by striking wires or flying through windows.

Even during the warm months the Grouse has its enemies, as I have frequently found where one had been devoured on the ground—no doubt, by cats or foxes. As soon as the hunting season opens the real slaughter begins. By the time the season closes the Grouse is sadly depleted in numbers—the flocks are scattered and it is wild and wary.

As the leaves disappear they forsake the open woods and take to heavy cover of low hemlocks and brush where they have some shelter against their numerous enemies. They roost in Hemlocks, and when the snow is deep they plunge into it and down out of sight. Several times I have found where a fox had killed and eaten one that had gone under the snow. They are not safe in the Hemlocks either for there the old Horned Owls pick them off at night. Besides foxes, cats, owls, and hawks, the Grouse has to also reckon with the mink. I have seen where the mink has killed a grouse in heavy low cover in daytime. Even after a good fall season only a small proportion of their numbers remain the following spring.

Wintergreen berries and squaw-berries are favorite food for the Grouse—also favored are wild grapes, thorn-berries, acorns, beech nuts, various seeds, and small leaves. After deep snow has fallen and food is hard to get at on the ground, the Grouse eat the buds on the trees—the buds of the Birch tree being a special favorite.

Hunting the Grouse with trained dogs is the favorite method. When the dog points the game, the hunter knows exactly where it is. He can go in and flush it and usually secure a good shot. Still hunting is a much more difficult proposition. The still hunter never knows when or where the bird will get up. He cannot flush the bird to suit himself and still be ready to fire. At the first whirr of wings the hunter must often whirl half the way around and shoot quickly at the bird. The bird usually manages to get a small, thick Hemlock or two behind it and in the way of a successful shot.

Disease sometimes takes a heavy toll and sadly depletes their numbers. This happened in 1907 and was a statewide occurrence. It happened again in 1917. During the fall of 1912 Grouse were very plentiful, and amongst my victims I got several very large birds with beautiful, large, silvery tails—instead of the usual brown.

Some nesting dates are May 31, 1908, 9 eggs; May 7, 1924, 11 eggs; May 26, 1929, 11 eggs; May 22, 1932, 13 eggs; and May 13, 1934, 8 eggs.

Measurements:

November, 1921, old male, 19–25–7 1/2–7, Wt. 1 1/2 lbs.

Gray Ruffed Grouse | Ruffed Grouse (gray morph)
Bonasa umbellus

(60.) Straggler.

During the fall of 1901, I heard of a Gray Grouse being taken up the Conewango Creek and across the line into New York State. That same fall, on November 2, two gunners from here bagged 12 Grouse near Kinzua with the aid of trained dogs. One of these birds was all gray instead of red.

In early April, 1903, I flushed one over along Ott Run. This was a beautiful Gray. One was shot each season in 1903 and 1904 near here. I heard of others being in nearby counties during this period also. I have not seen or heard of it since 1904. *(Ott Run is a stream entering the Allegheny River from the south, a short distance above Warren. Ring-neck Pheasant was added in post-1923 list.)*

PIGEONS

Passenger Pigeon
Ectopistes migratorius

(61.) In bygone days when northwestern Pennsylvania was great primeval forest and game was abundant, there was a great flight of pigeons. According to old-timers they came by the millions and fairly darkened the sky.

They nested in the beech and hardwood ridges by the countless thousands. It was then that the netters got after them and slaughtered them all through the breeding season. From the moment of their first appearance they were an object of constant persecution.

It did not seem to occur to anybody that this constant slaughter of the Passenger Pigeon would result in extermination or even that the bird would become scarce. They must have thought in those days that they could eat their cake and still have it too.

This slaughter did result in the pigeon changing its plans as it became scarce—it shunned the region where it met only death and destruction. But the netters followed them and soon finished the job. Now the Passenger Pigeon is a thing of the past.

As near as I can find out, there has been no large flight since about 1870. A good many continued to come. I have been reliably informed that they bred here at least until 1885. Possibly a few nested in this county at a later date.

April 15, 1889, I shot a beautiful adult male from a flock of 10 birds that I found feeding on the ground in a beech woods. They were the first living ones I ever saw and recognized. They were very wild. This bird is now in my collection. I prize it very highly. *(This Passenger Pigeon is on display at the Jamestown Audubon Society's Nature Center, Jamestown, New York.)*

September 21, 1890, I saw and fully recognized 3 pigeons. August 8, 1891, near Kinzua, a pigeon flew past me very close and was fully recognized.

May 20, 1893, while hunting down the river I saw a fine large pigeon feeding in an old field with 4 or 5 Mourning Doves. It was very wild, eluding all efforts to capture it. It soon left. This is the last one I have personally seen. (*The last Passenger Pigeon, the famous Martha, died September 1, 1914, in the Cincinnati Zoological Garden.)*

I have heard many reports of pigeons, but I think these birds are simply Mourning Doves. The old-timers, who knew them well, do not report seeing any of late years. As to their habits and enemies I know nothing from my experience as they were nearly gone when I started my career.

Measurement:

April 15, 1899, adult male, 17–24–8 1/2–8 3/4

DOVES

Mourning Dove
Zenaidura macroura

(62.) Summer resident. Breeds.

Arrives: April 16, 1892; April 4, 1895; April 1, 1899; April 5, 1901; and April 12, 1904. It is not at all common here. I never saw over 10 in a flock. It is usually seen singly or 2 to 3 together. They are found about fields and the edges of woods, but not in heavy or extensive woods. Only a few nest in this close vicinity, in fact, it is rather a rare breeder. I have seen it back in the mountains in the barrens and slashings. It is quite wild and wary when found.

Recent nesting dates are May 10, 1937, and May 20, 1939. On each date there were 2 eggs in each low nest—5 feet up in thick spruce trees at Woodcrest. May 29, 1940, in these same spruce trees, I found a nest and 2 eggs apparently well incubated. Later on, September 1, in this same nest there were 2 large young doves about ready to fly. It must have been that the same pair raised 2 broods that season.

On June 5, 1943, I found a nest and 2 eggs only 3 feet from the ground in a clump of thorn brush. I stood on the ground and photographed this nest.

Measurements:

August 13, 1890, young female, 12–17 3/4–6–5

August 14, 1890, young male, 12–17 1/2–5 3/4–5 1/2

BIRDS OF PREY

In the state of Pennsylvania about 30 species of birds of prey have been known to occur. Of these species two are vultures, 16 or 17 are hawks, and the rest are owls. About 17 species have been known to breed. In Warren County I have known 22 of these species to occur: 1 vulture; 14 hawks and eagles; and 7 owls. Others of course are likely to occur at any time. Of these 22 species that have occurred here, I have known 11 to breed. *(RBS later records two additional breeding birds of prey: the Marsh Hawk and the Long-eared Owl.)*

Birds of prey have become much scarcer of late years. Gunners everywhere never miss a chance to kill one. I do not see but one or two raptors now—where formerly I used to see a dozen.

Crows often raise a great hubbub and fuss over birds of prey. They sit about and dive at the object of their wrath, be it hawk, eagle, or owl—all the time making a great racket. In the case of a hawk or eagle the victim of the mob usually soon takes to flight and escapes. In the case of a large owl the mob increases in numbers, as the owl will not rise up and leave, but sits about.

Turkey Vulture
Cathartes aura

(63.) Straggler.

I have been told of this vulture being seen in this county on one or two occasions, but as they were not taken, such records are open to doubt. They might have been eagles or ospreys. The only authentic occurrence of this bird here that I know of was in early July, 1903.

F.L. Hartley, a farmer and stockman, residing on Smith Hill near Youngsville, 9 miles from Warren, captured a specimen in a trap. Having heard about it, I succeeded in buying the bird and now have it mounted in my collection.

A calf had died for Hartley, and not having time to bury it that day, it was dragged off into a field some distance away—out of sight of the house. On going out the next day to bury the calf, 4 large birds were found feeding on the remains.

A steel trap was set and left until next morning when, on again visiting the carcass, a flock of 9 vultures were found about it. One was fast in the trap. The flock left and did not return—nor was it again seen.

For a week the captive was confined in a pen 16 feet square. This bird was an old male in perfect full plumage. Mr. Hartley had lived there many years and had stock die occasionally, but never had a vulture visited a carcass before. It seems strange that such a flock should appear so unexpectedly.

In late October, 1927, a flock of 8 hung about near Sugar Grove feeding on a carcass. September 4, 1933, I saw one at Starbrick and was told that several were about. During 1934 to 1937 vultures were about all summer. They were supposed to have been attracted early in the spring by dead deer lying about—winter killed in the woods. I have seen one occasionally each summer since. April 11, 1943, I saw one up Morse Run. On May 21, 1944, I saw one.

Measurements:

September 23, 1893, young, 28–60–20 1/2–11 3/4

Marsh Hawk | Northern Harrier
Circus hudsonius | Circus cyaneus

(64.) Regular migrant, spring and fall.

One of the rarer hawks here and is not often seen. I have picked out the following dates from my notebooks: May 3, 1891, adult male; April 18, 1901, an adult pair; April 5, 1906, a female; April 8, 1907, adult male; April 17, 1907, a female; and April 7, 1908, an adult male.

On August 17, 1900, I a shot a young Marsh Hawk just after it had caught a frog along the river below Meade Island. I have also seen it on June 7, 1900, an adult male; August 4, 1901, a young one; October 25, 1903, an adult; and October 28, 1910, a young one.

It is possible this hawk may nest in the county. It does nest in northwestern Pennsylvania, as I have personally found a nest on the Peninsula at Erie. It is never common here—it is decreasing in numbers as are all the hawks.

July 9, 1930, Harry Granquist and I photographed a nest near Clarendon. This is the first positive record I have of this hawk nesting here, although it is certain they do about the swamps near Columbus and Bear Lake. This nest was found by a farmer after the old female hawk had stolen a chicken. It was in the center of a cattail swamp about one-half acre in extent. No doubt this was a second laying.

May 11, 1932, I found and photographed a nest of this hawk in the swamp near Highhouse's brickyard. It held 4 eggs, next morning 5 eggs, which I then took. A week later this bird laid a set of 3 more in the same nest. The first set of 5 is slightly spotted. A pair also nested on Meade Island this season.

Measurements:

September 22, 1893, young male, 18 1/2–40 1/2–12 3/4–8 3/4

October 21, 1898, adult male, 18–44–14 1/4–9

August 17, 1900, young, 18–40–12 3/4–8 3/4

August 17, 1900, adult female, 21–48 1/2–15 1/4–10

Sharp-shinned Hawk
Accipiter velox / Accipiter striatus

(65.) Summer resident. Breeds.

This little accipiter I have found here at all seasons. It is most common during migrations, when it is found mostly in open country and about the edges of woods. I have seen it frequently in winter, even during very severe weather. In winter they frequently come into town after sparrows, and at such times are quite fearless. It is a fearless and daring little fellow anyway and often raids the poultry yard in search of young chicks.

As regards their food habits the following adventures with "Sharpy" show that he will tackle almost anything that he has a chance to overpower. Once I was watching one flying low across a field. As he hustled along, a Mourning Dove sprang up just to one side. "Sharpy" turned instantly, and before the dove could get under full headway, he had grabbed it. Both fell to the ground, and I walked up to within 50 feet before the hawk could loosen its hold. The dove flew off and did not seem badly hurt—although it might have been.

On another occasion I noticed a Sharp-shin flying along the river just below Meade Island. As it passed a large sycamore it suddenly turned and dashed into the tree. It grabbed a Red Squirrel off a limb, and flew heavily away with its struggling victim.

One day in May, while at Grass Flats looking up the small migrants, I was peering closely into a large thorn bush or tree in which there was a whole bunch of warblers of various kinds. Suddenly there was a rush right past my head as a "Sharpy" dashed into the tree. As the startled birds flew out in all directions "Sharpy" grabbed one and kept on going. He ran into a charge of 6 shot that I sent in ahead of him, and he came down. When the hawk fell, the victim got loose. It flew away before I could see what it was.

Still another time I heard a Pileated Woodpecker making a great racket. Hurrying that way I found a "Sharpy" making a desperate attempt to get his claws into the Log-cock's anatomy. The big woodpecker was on the trunk of a large tree, and its only hope seemed to be in keeping the trunk of the tree between itself and the enemy.

Every time the hawk rushed, the Pileated moved around the tree. All this time the Pileated made the woods ring with its distressed cries. Just how this fracas would have ended is hard to say, but this old Pileated and its mate were old acquaintances of mine. They were residents of this area, and I had always found it a convenient place to go and spy on their movements. I didn't wish to see harm befall them, so I therefore took a hand in the game. With my old "Parker" I knocked-out Mr. Hawk for good for fear he might return. *(Simpson's old "Parker" was a double barrel shotgun made in 1878 by a manufacturer of the same name.)*

A few pairs are scattered about in summer and nest. When I first began collecting the Sharp-shin was quite common. Any day during migrations the bird could be noted. In summer quite a few pairs were scattered about nesting in suitable places.

This hawk, as well as all other hawks, has become scarcer from year to year until at the present time it is only occasionally seen during migrations. It requires a large amount of observation and considerable time spent in the woods to locate a nest.

In the breeding season they retire into the woods, sometimes into far out-of-the-way places back in the mountains. At this season they are rather quiet and not often seen unless the nest site is approached too close. All of the nests I have personally found have been in second-growth pine and hemlock, but I know of one nest being found in a beech.

If robbed of their first set they will nest again, but not in the same nest. I have frequently found the nests by the actions of the birds. Before the set is complete the female spends most of her time nearby and makes quite a fuss when an intruder gets into the vicinity of the nest. I have found nests a month before the eggs were laid by noticing the birds hanging about the vicinity.

If anyone happens to pass near the nest after the female has begun incubation—and the male is about, as he is much of the time—he at once gets very excited, flying about and calling. In late May I came upon such a case, looking carefully through the second-growth conifers, I soon found the nest.

Nest range from 20 to 50 feet up—usually 30 to 40 feet. Number of eggs is 4 or 5, in one case, 6 eggs. A new nest is sometimes built and in some cases an old nest is fixed-up and used. The female usually sits tight and sometimes considerable hard jarring is necessary to start her off the nest. *(By "hard jarring" RBS refers to striking the base of a tree with a rock to discover what bird is occupying the nest, if any.)*

I have the following nesting records in my notebooks. May 18, 1899, a friend of mine found a nest 25 feet up in a beech in large woods. From this nest he secured a set of 6 eggs. This is the only set of 6 eggs that has been found here to my knowledge. It is the only nest found here that I know of that was not in an evergreen—pine or hemlock.

May 13, 1893, I took a heavily marked set of 3 eggs, incubation begun, at the head of a precipice on the big hill below Meade Island. It was in a heavy clump of young hemlock and was 40 feet up. The set was complete and is the only full set of 3 I have ever taken—other sets all being sets of 4 or 5. The female was very pugnacious and repeatedly dashed within a few feet of my head.

June 17 of the same year I found a nest 35 feet up in a hemlock deep in big woods. I had sat down near the nest to rest a few minutes and the male bird, happening to return, started at once to make quite a fuss. Looking about I soon saw the nest. This nest was old and bulky and evidently an old nest fixed-up. It held 4 eggs. Both birds were very noisy, but did not come closer than 50 feet. Incubation was well advanced, and even at that, it is a late date for eggs.

May 26, 1907, in Ott Run hollow while prowling around, a "Sharpy" began flying about and calling. A good look around revealed the nest only 20 feet up a hemlock. Limbs began within 5 feet of the ground, and it was like going up a ladder to reach the nest. This was a new nest, a flat flimsy affair, but held 5 beautiful eggs. The old birds were very noisy but not at all bold.

May 30, 1909, in the big woods of Morrison Run, I saw a nest in a large second-growth hemlock, and after a hard bumping with a heavy rock a female Sharp-shin left. This nest was a new one, flat and flimsy, and was 40 feet from the ground. It held 5 very handsome eggs.

The spring of 1911 I found 2 nests. I located both late in April by the actions of the females. Both nests were new nests in hemlocks. One was up 25 feet and the other 40 feet. One bird began incubating May 16 and the other May 21. Both birds laid sets of four. Both of these pairs of hawks were bold and noisy.

May 28, 1914, I found a nest 40 feet up in a little pine on the Brown Run ridges. This nest was large and had been fixed-up by the Sharp-shins. This nest held a set of 5 eggs. The female was very bold. Next season this nest was used by a Cooper's Hawk.

Late in June, 1915, I found a nest 50 feet up in a hemlock in Ott Run hollow. It held 5 young.

June 7, 1917, I found a nest in Ott Run hollow. It was a new nest 35 feet up in a hemlock and held 5 eggs, well incubated. The female was not very bold.

May 17, 1921, Harry Granquist and I found a nest 30 feet up in a hemlock in the virgin timber of the Four Mile creek. It was in the valley and close to the stream. It held a very pretty set of 4, and we secured some very good photos of this outfit. The female was quite bold and noisy.

During the 1924 season Harry Granquist and I found 2 nests of Sharp-shins in the Four Mile. One nest in the hemlock swamp held a full set of 4 fresh eggs on June 1, and later on the other nest held young. This second nest was 65 or 70 feet up in a large hemlock along the Pennsylvania Gas Company right-of-way in Goshawk Basin. This is by far the highest up I ever saw a nest of the "Sharpy."

On May 29, 1934, I found a nest containing 4 eggs, well incubated by the looks. It was 30 feet up in a hemlock near Ott Run.

Measurements:

October 24, 1890, young, 13 3/4–24 1/2–8–7

May 2, 1891, adult female, 13 3/4–26–8–6

December 17, 1892, adult male, 11–22–7–5 3/4

December 17, 1892, adult female, 13–26 1/2–7 3/4–6 1/4

Harry Granquist
Giant White Pine in the Four Mile Creek Region, Warren County.
Tree is 18 feet in circumference.
April 10, 1921.

Cooper's Hawk
Accipiter cooperi

(66.) Summer resident. Breeds.

Occasionally seen during the migrations and on several occasions in winter. In summer this hawk retires into deep woods to nest. Nests in this region are sometimes built new, but often old nests are repaired and used. Nests are almost always lined with small pieces of beech bark. Nests are from 40 to 60 feet up. Eggs are 4 or 5—only once did I find 3.

I have never found the Cooper's very bold when the nest was being pilfered, examined, or photographed. It nests in May: May 16, 1909, 5 eggs; May 8, 1920, 5 eggs; May 10, 1921, 5 eggs; May 26, 1923, 4 eggs; and May 16, 1927, four eggs, fresh. After the young leave the nest the whole family stays around in the vicinity for the rest of the summer.

This hawk often raids the poultry yard. One day in August several years ago while spending a Sunday with my wife's folks on the farm, I went over to have a chat with a neighbor who lived nearby. His house stood on quite a high bank along a small stream and close to the woods. Along the stream he had a large chicken yard in which were several hundred chickens.

He was telling me how the hawks were getting them. While he was talking, a Cooper's suddenly dashed out of the woods, dove among the chicks, and fastened onto a half-grown one. After rolling about on the ground a few seconds, the raider arose and quickly disappeared into the woods with its struggling victim.

Measurements:

July 31, 1889, young, 19–33 1/2–10 1/2–9 1/2
July 31, 1889, young, 17–29 1/2–9 1/4–8 1/2
August 1, 1889, young, 19–34–10 1/2–9
August 1, 1889, young, 17–29 1/2–9 1/4–8 1/2

American Goshawk | Northern Goshawk
Astur atricapillus | Accipiter gentilis

(67.) Summer resident. Breeds.

In bygone days when the pigeon was here and nested in countless numbers, the Goshawk, according to old hunters and woodsmen, was quite common all summer, nested commonly, and preyed on the pigeons. Since my time, though, the pigeon has been practically a thing of the past, and it was a number of years before I even suspected the Goshawk nested here anymore.

Every winter I saw several and had them classed as a winter visitor. Ordinarily the Goshawk is wild and wary and not easily taken, but when in pursuit of game he seems to lose his wildness and becomes quite bold. One of this hawks principal items of food here is the Red Squirrel, but Grouse, poultry, and rabbits also fall prey to him.

In my collection I have a large female Goshawk that I shot May 25, 1906, far back in the heavy timber about the head of Sanders Run, a branch of Laurel Run in Clearfield County. I was trout fishing at the time, and while fishing through a heavy patch of laurel heard quite a racket. I saw a very large Goshawk trying to drive a Grouse out from the heavy cover. I had my gun along and bagged the hawk. From what I have since learned about this hawk, there is little or no doubt that this bird had a nest nearby of good sized young.

January 2, 1912, along the edge of virgin timber and second growth on Meade Run, a branch of Elk Run, I came upon a Goshawk in pursuit of a bunch of Grouse. There were considerable low hemlocks and the Grouse came flying out in all directions and flying low. The hawk screamed loudly, and as he dashed past low down, I shot and secured him. This one was a male in blue plumage with a small patch of brown on each wing.

Early in December, 1914, an old male Goshawk met his death in a very peculiar manner at the Hertzel farm in Pleasant Township. At that time they were raising English and Golden Pheasants, which were kept in an enclosure covered on top and sides with wire netting, such as is commonly used on chicken coops and yards. An old Goshawk passing overhead saw the Pheasants, but not the wire. Plunging down for his dinner he crashed through the top netting—completely severing his head from his body. Otherwise there did not seem to be a mark on his body.

In early December of 1914, while my brother-in-law and I were hunting hares near virgin timber, Barnes, Pennsylvania, this county, we found where a weasel had been in pursuit of a rabbit. Up and down an old log road the tracks were fresh, so we slowly followed the old road toward the timber. While going along, an adult Goshawk arose ahead and a little off the road in the brush. On investigation we found that the hawk had killed the rabbit as it fled from the weasel. The rabbit was partly eaten. The following fall I saw and also heard Goshawks about this same timber and I think a pair nested there.

November 25, 1916, an adult Goshawk made a raid on the Ingram farm on Six Mile Creek. Pouncing, right behind the barn, upon one of the largest and finest hens, the hawk proceeded to kill and eat the chicken on the spot. Ingram, taking his shotgun, slipped up to the barn, and killed the bird. This was a large adult and no doubt one of the Four Mile hawks whose nest I later found—as the spot of this raid was not far from the hang-out across the mountains in the virgin timber of the Four Mile.

I am of the opinion that several pairs of Goshawks have nested in this region for many years. No doubt one of the old birds, of these different pairs, frequently meets with disaster, and the survivor gets another mate. In this way they have continued to nest year after year in the same vicinity. From my experience with nests, this shows that they do nest each year in the same place, and often in the same nest.

During early June, 1905, two friends of mine, while fishing Elk Run in the virgin timber, were attacked by a Goshawk that tried to drive them out to the woods. From their description, the bird must have been a Goshawk, but at the time their story sounded fishy. My own experience since then convinces me that their story was absolutely true—also that the reason for the attack was that the hawk had large young nearby.

I was over there one day in April the following year, but saw no signs of hawks or nests. Of course, I might easily have missed it as I have since found that the old bird would have been incubating at that time, and would very likely have been quiet and sitting tight.

May 10, 1908, I saw an old Goshawk in the big forests of the Four Mile. This record and the Elk Run instance, also the Clearfield County experience, causes me to believe that this fine hawk was still a rare breeder in the wild and out of the way places in this general region.

I now know that for many years a pair has nested in the Morrison Run region not far from town. As early as October 8, 1892, while on a squirrel hunt in that region, I saw an adult, and found a fine adult dead on the ground where it had been left by some hunters who had shot it.

At other times, during the late fall and winter months, I have noted the Goshawk in that vicinity. On December 31, 1898, while hunting hares there, I was standing on a fallen tree, waiting for the dog to bring a hare around. I happened to glance around behind me, and saw a Goshawk coming. I partly turned and fired, lost my balance, and flopped off into the deep snow, but I saw the hawk come down. On reaching the spot I found a very handsome adult Goshawk—in its talons was a Red Squirrel—just killed.

Two days later, one in the young of the year plumage was shot in the same vicinity by a friend, George Lauffer, while hunting foxes. He gave me the bird for my collection.

Although I did considerable thinking and figuring on a possible nesting site, it was not until February 22, 1909, that I got a real clue. On this day, Washington's Birthday, I had a holiday and as it was a lovely winter day—clear, calm, sunny, and not at all cold—I took a long hike with my gun for company.

During the course of the day I got into the heavy woods of the Morrison Run country. In the basin, about the head of Picnic Run, the timber was very large. It consisted of many virgin, giant White Pines with considerable hemlock and hardwoods. While going along slowly, I heard the loud screams of a hawk just ahead. The calls or screams were on the Sharp-shin order, only much louder and stronger—more of a "kak-kak" repeated rapidly.

Looking that direction I saw a Goshawk alight in a pine. Thinking to obtain a shot, I got the big pine in line, and tried to slip up near. I had gone but a few feet when she arose screaming, but again she alighted after flying 8 or 10 rods. I started slowly forward, and again she arose, and after a short flight alighted. About this time I noticed she was not flying away, but was circling around me.

Her actions reminded me of a Sharp-shin when the nest is approached. If it had been later in the season I would have suspected a nest. As it was, I suspected she had made a kill, which was no doubt close by on the ground. Going back to where she first flew from, I looked about on the snow, but saw nothing. Then on looking all around, I saw a very large nest well up in a big pine. I was gazing at it and wondering if it could possibly be her nest, when she came screaming right up and alighted within range. That settled matters, and I concluded very quickly that I did not want to shoot her; instead, I lost no time getting away from that vicinity. I looked through various bird books and magazines, but I could get no definite idea as when to expect eggs.

I kept strictly away from that immediate locality until March 9, when I paid a visit. As I was carefully approaching the nest, the old hawk flew from the pines. She alighted close by, and screamed loudly. I was now convinced that I had really found a Goshawk's nest. I left at once.

Visits on March 14 and 19 found her still on guard, but not sitting. I did not see anything of the male. On March 20, I was again on the spot, and as usual found her doing guard duty.

I now concluded that it was high time to see the inside of that nest. Shedding all loose duds, I started up. It was a hard climb and especially so as it was the first of the season. While I was going up the old hawk sat close by and screamed continually. Twice she dove at me, coming within 3 or 4 feet, before sheering off. I found the nest all finished, lined, and ready for eggs.

April 2, my friend, Norman Spencer, and I started for the nest. We were prepared to do business. Several inches of snow lay on the ground. It was a rather dark and dreary morning, and at times snowed quite hard. Getting in sight of the nest, we found everything quiet—no hawk in sight.

Going quietly up to the tree, I bumped it hard with a heavy rock. Off went Mrs. Goshawk to the nearby pines where she was soon joined by her mate. All the time we were there, both birds sat nearby and screamed, but did not come very near.

Norm climbed to the nest and found a fine set of 3 eggs. Lowering the hand line, I tied on the camera, and Norm photographed the outfit. Owing to the weather condition, this photo was not a very good one. After the camera and eggs had been safely lowered, we measured the line and found the nest to be 60 feet from the ground.

The nest was a large and rather flat affair—three feet across one way and two and one-half feet the other way—built of sticks and twigs. The nest cavity was snugly lined with old leaves and small pieces of beech bark. A few fresh sprigs of hemlock lay about on top of the nest on the rim. The 3 pale-bluish or greenish-blue unmarked eggs were fresh.

Two days later I was up there again. As I approached the nest the female left the nest tree with a scream. On looking it over I saw that some fresh hemlock sprigs had been added to the rim of the nest, so I left at once, thinking she might try it over again.

April 20, I paid the nest a visit, but saw no sign of the birds. Nearby in this basin were two other very large nests, so I took a look at these. On bumping one tree hard, I was surprised to see Mrs. Goshawk dash off.

It was May 21 before I got up there again. Spencer was with me, and when we got near the tree the old bird began screaming. On making the climb we were surprised to find the remains of 2 broken eggs. What had broken this set would be hard to say. The old female seemed to always be around her nest. I can't imagine what could have had a chance to get at the eggs without a fight. Possibly a crow happened to come along when the old hawk was absent for a short time.

Meanwhile the old bird continued to fly about nearby and was very noisy. Norm went up a large and slightly leaning maple, and on getting high enough to look over into the nest, he found it contained 2 eggs.

I sent the camera up and he photographed it. Measuring the line we found the camera was exactly 84 feet and 4 inches from the ground when this photo was taken. On May 25 I went up and found her incubating.

We planned a final visit about June 20, but it was July 2 before we got up again. It was a beautiful day and we started early. All was quiet as we drew near the nest. We began to wonder if something had happened to her housekeeping plans again. We had just got in sight of the nest, when suddenly from up amongst the limbs of the trees ahead of us, the old hawk appeared.

She did not utter a sound, but came straight at our heads with wings almost closed. So close did she come that I ducked, and Spencer struck at her with his climbing irons. He didn't come far from hitting her. The instant she had passed us she began to scream fiercely. She was at once answered by her mate who was nearby. We sat down awhile on a fallen tree to give them a chance to cool off a little.

Both old birds were very bold. They screamed continually and often alighted within 30 feet of us, so close we could almost see every mark of their plumage. Both were in very good feather.

The male was the smaller and his voice was not as strong as the female's. Their calls were a "kak-kak-kak" and they seemed to say "get out, get out, get out"—this call having two notes to each call. Repeatedly they dove at us as we sat there, passing sometimes not 6 feet overhead. So hot was the reception that we sat there awhile until they quieted down. Then we withdrew a little.

Spencer then went up the maple. He used his safety belt so as to have his hands free in case of an attack. He also took along a stout stick. While on his way up the tree, the old lady made 4 or 5 vicious dives at him. I warned him each time. It was comical to see him thrash about with his club and yell "shoo" at her.

A photo was taken of the young in the nest. I then sent up a long pole with which he poked them out one at a time—as they fell, I caught them. They were husky little cusses. About the time I grabbed the largest one; he grabbed my hand and brought blood.

I shipped these 2 youngsters to T.H. Jackson of West Chester, Pennsylvania, who raised and photographed them at various stages of their development. He then sent them to the zoo in New York City.

March 20, 1910, I paid my first visit to the nesting site. After prowling about awhile, I heard the call of a Goshawk. Going in that direction I saw her fly from a new nest in a rather small beech tree. April 3, Spencer and I went up. We flushed the female from the nest. We secured several photos and a set of 2 eggs without difficulty—the female not coming very close. This nest was fully three-quarters of a mile from last year's nest, but in the same valley, and in a part of the woods composed mostly of beech. It was 45 feet up in a beech. It was a large, coarse affair of various sized limbs with practically no lining except small twigs. It was a new nest.

I did not bother them again until June 9, when I went up through that region. I was going along, and got close to the first nest used last season in the big pine, when I heard something coming from behind and overhead. I ducked and a female Goshawk dashed past. Then the music began and both old birds appeared.

The female was the braver, as usual, and fearless. She sat around close by, screaming continually. At times she dove at me, and coming so close, I really believe I could have killed her with the club I carried. She and the female last year, probably the same one, were certainly the most fearless and vicious birds I have yet encountered.

The cause of the rumpus was 2 big husky youngsters sitting up in the nest and taking it all in. I left them alone and did not bother them again that season.

In 1911, I visited the nesting site early in March and found a Great Horned Owl at home on 2 eggs in the nest in the big pine. I looked about the other nests, but saw no hawks. I could not get a trace of them that season.

From then on until 1920, I found no nests. I did however see a bird at times in summer in the Morrison Run region, as well as in the Four Mile region, and out near Barnes. I was sure the Goshawk was still nesting, but couldn't seem to find the place.

In 1920, I had better success. On March 28 I saw a fine pair of Goshawks near the forks of Ott Run. A thorough search of the Ott Run hollow during the following week failed to reveal any trace of them. They were not about any of the large nests that I knew of, nor could I see or hear a bird. I then extended my search of the ridge to the Morrison Run side. This meant a lot of territory to look over, but I knew they must be there somewhere.

On April 25, I was successful. I found the nest near the head of a hollow that was well wooded. The nest was 40 feet up in a beech. It was a very large, bulky affair of sticks, some quite large. This nest was an old one fixed up from the previous season.

It was lined with fine twigs and pieces of beech bark with several sprigs of hemlock—very much like my first nest in the big pine. In this nest I beheld a fine set of 4 big eggs. I was afraid that they could not be saved, but an investigation showed that they could. So I returned richer by a set of 4. I easily saved them by going to a little trouble and taking my time.

The female made several dives at me, but was not very ugly, contenting herself by making a big fuss. In this same vicinity I found a couple more big nests. I now think that these hawks had used this locality for several years, maybe ever since having to leave the other locality because of the lumbering operations started there in 1913.

In 1921, I was again successful in finding a nest. In late January, while in the Four Mile country, I was going through a basin at the head of a small tributary of the Four Mile when I heard a Goshawk calling. This basin is large and is in a virgin forest of mostly large hemlock with considerable beech and other hardwoods. It was an out-of-the-way place and previous experience caused me to investigate, as I knew the Goshawk was located somewhere in that country, and this place looked good. I looked around awhile and found several very large nests.

On Washington's Birthday, Harry Granquist and I went over for the day and during the course of our ramble went through this basin. We found the female there and were certain one of the nests would be used. April 5, the female was sitting on 4 eggs. She was quite bold and ugly. Some good photos were obtained of the nest and eggs. We then left them until May 9, when we again paid a visit. This time we found 4 husky little white youngsters; we secured excellent photos of the little fellows in the nest *(Goshawk photo follows)*.

The old birds where very ugly on this second visit, and we got a hot reception. Both old birds dove at us repeatedly. The female, being especially ugly, just missed us at times by a couple of feet as we were going up. This nest was 60 feet up in a large hemlock. It was a very large, flat nest—fully 3 feet across, and as usual built of coarse sticks. It was lined with finer sticks, and the nest cavity was completely covered or lined with pieces of beech bark, some quite large. Around the rim on top were quite a few sprigs and small pieces of fresh hemlock limbs. The young were pure white.

In 1922, I looked up both pairs of birds. I found both at their old nesting sites. H.W. Brandt, Harry Granquist, and I visited the Four Mile pair on April 9. We found them at home in a very large and evidently much used nest in a big beech—eggs 2 this time. We did not get a good photo, as the weather conditions were very bad. *(H.W. Brandt, millionaire and nature lover, Cleveland, Ohio, organized a scientific expedition for an extended trip into the isolated sections of western Alaska—with the main objective the study of birds and wild fowl and the possible relation of their habits to agriculture and plant life. Professor S.S. Dickey, naturalist and nature writer, assisted him. c.1921)*

H.W. Brandt and I visited the Morrison Run pair on April 10. They were using the same nest in the beech from which I secured my set of 4 on April 25, 1920. This time she had begun incubating a set of 3. Neither pair was ugly this season. We got a fine photo of the nest and eggs of the Morrison Run pair, as it was a very nice day.

Later on in middle May, I went through the basin in the Four Mile. I found this pair had fixed up a large old nest in a big dead tree. The female was incubating. I did not bother her again.

Mr. S.S. Dickey of Waynesburg, Pennsylvania, spent a few days with me in 1923. One of our trips took us to the Four Mile, and we visited the basin. We found the old Goshawk at home this time in a large, old, fixed-over nest about 50 feet up in a big beech. We visited this nest several times. The last time in late May, we found large young sitting up in the nest—I think 3 in number. The old bird was quite ugly the last time we visited her. I looked up the Morrison Run pair in March, but did not see them.

I found them at the head of Ott Run on April 6. I was hunting for a Barred Owl's nest when I discovered the hawk. The nest was only 30 feet up in a small beech, although there was plenty of big timber there.

The nest was large, flat, new, and built of coarse limbs—several fully 4 feet long. The nest cavity was lined with the usual pieces of beech bark. It held a fine set of 3. This nest was altogether too close to civilization to leave. It was certain to be found, in which case the old female would have been shot—so I took this set for my collection. I did not locate their second nest.

July 27, 1923, I saw a Goshawk while trout fishing at the old Biecher *(Bucher?)* Mill dam just below the game preserve on the Tionesta Creek. During the 1923 season Mr. Dickey found the nest of another pair near the Forest County line, and from this nest secured a young bird to raise. This makes 3 pairs that nested near here that I know of.

During the 1924 season we failed to find the Morrison Run pair, but found the Four Mile pair with a nest full of young on May 11. We missed it earlier in the season, as the birds had built a new nest in a large beech off to one side of the old nests.

In 1925, Harry and I spent 2 full days and 3 or 4 half-days looking up our two pairs of Goshawks. The Four Mile pair we had no trouble in locating. They used last year's nest. On March 29 we went over, and Harry went up and secured a swell set of 4 eggs. This nest was fully 65 feet from the ground in a large beech. The nest was large, deep, and bulky. It was well lined with chips of beech bark and sprigs of hemlock.

On March 22 we found the Morrison Run pair again. This time they had built in a new place. This nest was 40 feet up in a beech. As usual it was a large, bulky affair of sticks. This nest was well lined with chips of beech and hemlock bark and the usual sprigs of hemlock. It held 3 eggs, and on March 29 still held 3 eggs. This nest was complete on March 22 and is my earliest nesting record. The female was not at all bold and kept well away, contenting herself with angry calls. This set seems to be slightly spotted.

On March 29 we visited the Morrison Run pair. They used the same nest that they used last year. It is now a huge affair and was lined with pieces of beech bark and hemlock sprigs. It held 4 very fine eggs. The old female made several dives and was very noisy.

1926 was a late, cold, backward season. No Goshawks seen—all hawks scarce.

In 1927, the Four Mile Goshawks returned and built a large, bulky, new nest within a stone throw of their 1925 nest. We secured a fine set of 4 eggs from this nest on March 29. With Mr. George H. Stuart of Philadelphia, we visited this nest on April 3. We took a fine set of 4 eggs. It had snowed all night the night before and about 3 inches of snow lay on the ground. Every twig and limb was loaded, and Harry, who made the climb, found it to be a wet, slippery, cold job. The nest was 72 feet from the ground.

The season of 1928 we did not find the Goshawks about their old nesting sites.

During 1933, a nest with young, together with the old bird, was collected by bounty hunters, sent in, and bounty secured. This one was taken near Brookston, Pennsylvania, but in Warren County.

I saw an adult near Barnes on August 5, 1934. Also saw an adult, January 9, 1938, in the woods back of where I now reside at Starbrick, just below Warren.

Measurements:

December 31, 1898, adult female, 23–48–14 1/4–10 1/4

May 26, 1906, adult female, 24 1/2–48–14 1/4–12

January 2, 1912, adult male, 21 1/2–42–12 1/2–9 ½

Four young Goshawk
1921, Four Mile Run,
Warren County.

This very large nest was located 60 feet up a large hemlock tree. The nest was 3 feet across and the young were pure white.

Red-tailed Hawk
Buteo borealis / Buteo jamaicensis

(68.) Summer resident. Breeds.

Sometimes seen in mid-winter: December 1, 1899; November 22, 1900; January 22, 1901; February 18, 1906; January 5, 1907; and February 28, 1907.

Arrives in March. Very few pairs nest in this region. It is not at all common and always was rather scarce.

Nests in April; eggs laid second week in April. Nests high in large trees, both conifers and hardwoods are used. Nests are large and bulky, and are used year after year if not disturbed—eggs usually 2 here, rarely 3.

It nests in rather out of the way places back in the mountains, but after the young are flying, both old and young, during July and August, are found together. They come out to the edges of the woods and old fields, and they are quite noisy. Later on the birds separate, and in the fall the Red-tail is usually found alone.

The Red-tail is wary and hard to stalk. When climbing to a nest I have never found them to be very bold—usually keeping out of gun shot range.

Measurements:

August 12, 1890, young, 22 1/2–51–15 1/4–10 3/4, stomach: chicken
August 16, 1892, young, 21 1/2–47–14 1/2–9 1/4, stomach: empty
October 22, 1898, adult male, 20 1/2–49–15–9, stomach: rabbit
March 25, 1899, adult male, 20 1/2–48–14 3/4–8 3/4, stomach: empty
November 5, 1915, young, 22–52–15 1/2–10 1/2, stomach: empty

Red-shouldered Hawk
Buteo lineatus

(69.) Summer resident. Breeds.

Arrives: March 22, 1890; March 24, 1891; March 26, 1892; March 16, 1893; March 30, 1895; March 9, 1899; March 19, 1901; March 20, 1902; March 20, 1903; and March 17, 1907. It is generally common from the day of its arrival.

This has always been the most common hawk here, but of late years it has become much scarcer. In early April it used to be not uncommon to see 7 or 8 in the air at once, all "killaying" loudly, but of late years it is rather unusual to see more than 3 at once during the mating season.

It is quite generally distributed throughout the county. I have seen this hawk far back in deep woods, but it is more apt to be found about the outskirts of big woods and the more cleared farming districts.

It nests in April, usually about 40 feet up, sometimes high in a big tree. It uses the same nest year after year unless disturbed. Nests, used each season, soon become large and bulky. Nests are built of sticks and lined with twigs and often dried leaves—usually also lined and rimmed with sprigs of hemlock, sometimes quite thickly. Eggs usually 3, often only 2, and occasionally 4—I have never found a set of 5.

I examined nests on the following dates in 1890: May 5, 2 eggs, incubation far advanced; April 26, 2 eggs, incubation begun; April 25, 3 eggs, incubation just begun; April 7, 2 eggs, fresh; and April 6, 2 eggs, fresh.

In 1909, on April 13, at Grass Flats, I located 2 nests—one set of 3, the other of 4, both fresh; May 2, 2 eggs, advanced; and May 15, 2 eggs, incubation begun, second laying.

In 1910, I examined a nest on April 10, 3 eggs, fresh; April 17, 2 eggs, fresh; April 26, 4 eggs, incubated a few days. Other examinations of nests include May 2, 1911, 3 eggs, incubation far along; April 21, 1913, 3 eggs, fresh; May 8, 1913, 3 eggs, incubation advanced; April 26, 1914, 4 eggs, incubation a few days; April 22, 1915, 4 eggs, fresh; May 3, 1923, 4 eggs, fresh; and May 4, 1923, 3 eggs, fresh—a late season.

They are generally quite noisy and rather bold when the nest is being examined or pilfered, but as a rule are not bold enough to be dangerous. One time however, May 24, 1893, I climbed to a nest in a beech tree in which I found good sized young. The female did not seem to be particularly ugly so I did not pay much attention to her. When within 5 feet of the nest, she landed unexpectedly square on my head, and almost caused me to fall from the tree.

My hat, a soft felt, stuck to her talons, and she carried it 25 or 30 feet before shaking it loose. She left 3 or 4 nasty scratches in my scalp that, before healing, got quite sore. This is the only hawk of any kind that ever actually landed on me while going up to a nest.

After leaving the nest, both old and young, hang about the vicinity until well along toward September when they seem to separate—probably to shift for themselves.

They are seldom noted after the first of October. My latest fall dates are October 10, 1900, and October 5, 1902. I have no winter records.

I have never found any traces of poultry in any that I have examined. I have frequently seen this species flying with a snake in its talons. It is not as wild and wary as the Red-tail, but usually manages to keep well out of gunshot.

(Post-1923 note follows. Simpson was not certain what year it occurred.)

It once was the commonest large hawk found here, but now almost extinct. I have seen little or nothing of it for several years. This year I found a nest on June

4 in Crawford County. This nest contained young. Although not in Warren County it is worth recording as still being found in this part of the world.

Measurements:

March 24, 1889, adult male, 18 1/2–40–13–7 3/4

July 29, 1889, young, 19 1/2–42–12 1/2–9

March 31, 1890, adult male, 19–41–13–9, stomach: sparrow

July 31, 1894, young, 19 1/2–42–13–9

Broad-winged Hawk
Buteo platypterus

(70.) Summer resident. Breeds.

This hawk was formerly of rare occurrence here. The first I ever saw was an adult shot in early May, 1890, in the woods back of the cemetery. It was shot by a friend of mine and given to me. I mounted this specimen, but while drying in my workshop it was torn to pieces by a cat or dog—probably a dog that got into the place when I was absent.

In spite of all my hunting for birds and nests I never saw another to recognize for 11 years. On May 18, 1901, in the heavy woods on the Grass Flats, I heard a bunch of jays making a great fuss. Going carefully over that way, I suddenly saw, in easy range, a hawk sitting on a limb about 20 feet from the ground. It was gazing quietly at me. I knew it at once and lost no time gathering it in. This bird was a male, but still I did not meet again with this hawk until May 31, 1912. On this day, while in company with R.C. Harlow, we found a nest of this hawk on the river side of the mountain between Brown Run and the river. *(Richard C. Harlow wrote primarily of the birds of central Pennsylvania, specifically Huntingdon County, 1909–1918.)*

This nest was 30 feet up in a yellow birch, and it was not very large. It was built of sticks and twigs, and it was well lined with fresh birch leaves. It held a very pretty set of 4. The female stayed close by, but was not at all aggressive. The male did not appear at all.

During the 1913 season I found 2 nests—one on May 12, near Brown Run, and the other May 18, on the river hills below town. Upon bumping the trees I flushed the birds. I did not know either pair was about until I found the nests.

One was 45 feet up in a hickory. This nest was lined with fine twigs and a few fresh, green leaves on top of the 3 fresh eggs. The other nest was 50 feet up in a basswood and very inconspicuous. It was lined with a few pieces of fine bark—no fresh leaves—eggs 3, fresh. The birds in both cases sat close by and called. The call is much on the order of the Red-tail's "squeal," but weaker.

From this time on I occasionally see or hear this hawk in deep woods. I would not be surprised if the bird was more common of late than I suppose, as its quiet, retiring ways cause it to be easily overlooked.

June 6, 1917, I found a nest in Ott Run hollow 35 feet up in a beech. It held 3 eggs. This nest was an old one, and had been used in other seasons by raptors. I intended to get a photo of the young at this nest, but did not get around to doing so.

May 30, 1921, I found a nest in the Ott Run hollow and secured several very nice photos. This nest was 30 feet up in a cherry tree. It was a new, small, easily overlooked affair of sticks lined with a few leaves. It contained 3 eggs. On the eggs were several fresh green leaves. While the photo was being taken the female kept away and contented herself by whistling or squealing

May 28, 1923, two friends and I found 2 nests in the Ott Run valley, both about 35 feet up in beeches. One held 3 eggs, the other 4 eggs, both of course quite badly incubated at this date.

These hawks seem to be rather tame. They sit quite close when incubating. They seem to prefer rather deep and extensive woods and are easily overlooked. They are certainly becoming commoner of late.

Measurements:

Immature male, 14 3/4–32–10 1/4–6 1/4

Adult female, 15 1/2–35 1/2–10 7/8–6 1/2

American Rough-legged Hawk | Rough-legged Hawk
Archibuteo lagopus

(71.) Regular migrant in late fall, winter, and early spring.

Earliest dates I have noted it here in the fall are one on November 27, 1899, and two on November 22, 1900. It is seen, more or less, at times all through the winter. During the winters of 1898-99 and 1900-01, it could be seen almost any day, possibly the same birds spending the winter season here.

I have seen 3 in black plumage: March 22, 1899; January 31, 1901; and March 15, 1901. During 1899 I saw birds here on April 4, (one); April 5, (two); April 7, (two); and April 22, (one). During 1901 I saw birds here on April 1, (one); April 11, (one); April 15, (one); April 18, (one); and April 26, (one). On March 18, 1899, I saw 3 at once, on all other occasions, singles or pairs.

This large, fine hawk is met with here only along the river valley. I never saw it back in the country or in the mountains. Meade Island, the largest island in the Allegheny River, is the principal hang-out when here.

They must feed mostly on mice and small stuff, as they always seem to be found about old fields, brushy and marshy places. On Meade Island I tried various ways to get a specimen, but owing to the lack of hemlock or heavy cover on the island at the season of the year when this hawk occurs, I found it impossible to stalk them, as they are wild and wary.

February 1, 1899, during severe weather and deep snow, I set a steel trap for them on Meade Island. I took the skin of a Black Mallard that I had shot a few days before, and laid it out on the snow, close to a lone tree on which the Rough-legs had a habit of sitting. On top of the skin I partly concealed a trap amongst the feathers. In a short time a fine, female adult pounced on it and got fast in the trap.

This is the only one of these hawks I ever saw taken here. This is about the only way to get one—a person needs a little time to watch the traps.

Measurements:

February 1, 1899, adult female, 22–54–21–9

The Allegheny River, August 19, 1928.
(above) Looking upstream from Meade Island.
Meade Island is 1 mile in length and contains about 300 acres.
It is located opposite Starbrick, Warren County.
(below) Looking downstream from Meade Island

Golden Eagle
Aquila chrysaetos

(72.) Straggler.

Late in November, 1891, while going up the road on top of the mountain just this side of the Reig farm, overlooking the river valley, I saw a large Golden Eagle soaring about. He got quite low at times so I could look down on him. This is the first one I noted here. On two trips to Kansas in the fall, I saw this eagle very often and became quite familiar with it.

December 4, 1891, a fine one was caught in a trap at Tidioute and sent up to Greenlund to be mounted. December, 18, 1891, I saw a fine one in a big sycamore tree at Highhouse's Eddy. It was very wild and left at once on being pursued.

All three of these records occurring in late November and December of 1891 make it appear that a few of these birds may have migrated through this part of the country that fall. Since then I have but one record. April 1, 1899, while ducking at Grass Flats I saw a very large and fine Golden Eagle. He was on the ground at the foot of Leek Island. I was quite close and had a fine look at him, but not close enough for a shot. I have several times seen eagles at a distance at a time of the year when they might have been Golden, but couldn't tell for sure which species they were.

Measurements:

October 16, 1898, adult male, 33–6 feet, 8 1/2 inches

Bald Eagle
Haliaeetus leucocephalus

(73.) Irregular migrant.

The Bald Eagle is a rather scarce bird here. Occasionally during the warmer months, one or two are seen along the river. At Grass Flats and Meade Island I have seen it more than anywhere else. Most of those seen here are immature, but occasionally a fine adult is noted.

May 23, 1893, just below town along the river I stalked and shot a large Gray Eagle sitting in a big elm tree. In May, 1900, two Gray lived about the Grass Flats. One of these was trapped and kept alive here in an amusement park for some time.

May 25, 1910, at the head of Highhouse's Eddy just below town, I shot a very large eagle that was turning into an adult. This bird was feasting on a dead dog. It stunk worse than a buzzard. Other dates that I find in my notes are September, 21, 1890, a gray; May 7, 1892, a gray; September 1, 1893, a gray; July 23, 1900, a gray; July 25, 1900, an adult; September 4, 1900, a gray; September 19, 1901, an adult; September 1, 1902, a gray; May 1, 1903, two grays; April 12, 1904, a gray; May 5, 1905, a gray; April 30, 1901, an adult; June 6, 1912, an adult; and June 5, 1917, a gray.

It would seem that they ought to occur here more often, as at Erie along the lake, they are of regular occurrence and breed. On the Peninsula near Erie I have seen 6 or 7 at once, and I have a fine adult that I took there. It is a wild and wary bird and not easily taken.

On August 9, 1928, I saw a gray and an adult around Meade Island. On August 15, 1928, Harry saw 3, and on August 19, 1928, we saw one.

In the spring of 1932, at Erie, I found eagles nesting on the Peninsula. On March 29 the female was sitting on her eggs in a huge nest in a tree—in the interior of the Peninsula, back of Big Pond. This is the first eagle's nest I have ever seen.

March 16, 1934, an adult female was sitting on her nest on the Peninsula. September 9, 1941, I saw an adult, and March 6, 1941, I saw a Gray—both at Grass Flats. March 20, 1947, I saw an eagle (immature plumage) feeding on a dead fish on the ice in Grunderville Eddy.

Measurements:

August 8, 1888, gray, 33–6 feet, 6 inches
May 23, 1893, gray, 34–6 feet, 9 inches
August 11, 1900, adult male, 31 1/2–6 feet, 7 inches
May 20, 1905, adult male, 33–6 feet, 9 inches
May 25, 1910, gray, 35–7 feet, 1/2 inch–22 1/2–12 3/4

Duck Hawk | Peregrine Falcon
Falco peregrinus

(74.) Straggler.

This hawk must be of very rare occurrence here. For some reason, in spite of all my hunting trips covering a number of years, and in spite of all the time I have spent along the river, I have never seen it but once to recognize it. I have never known of one being taken here.

The one I did see, I met when I least expected to. June 6, 1912, at Grass Flats, I was going along the river bank when I noticed a large hawk flying out over the middle of the river. It had a small bird in its talons, and stopping in the air, it reached down under with its bill, and seemed to peck at or change its grasp on its victim.

Four or five swallows were in pursuit when I first saw it, and a passing crow dove down at it with loud "caws." At the crow's attack the hawk came down closer to the water. It turned and came in over the land below me. As it came past it uttered a cry, a sort of rapidly repeated "kak, kak, kak, kak"—repeated 4 or 5 times.

As it passed within easy range, I saw all its colors and markings. I had no difficulty in recognizing a fine adult Duck Hawk. How I wished for my old reliable

"Parker" duck gun—for here within easy range was something I had looked for in vain for many years. I was down again 2 days in succession with my artillery, but never saw it again.

Pigeon Hawk | Merlin
Falco columbarius

(75.) Irregular migrant. Rather rare and not often met with.

I have the following dates at hand from my notebooks: September 8, 1887, shot a young one; April 17, 1889, saw 2 adults; April 25, 1889, saw an adult; April 23, 1891, saw an adult; November 14, 1892, shot a young one; April 11, 1893, saw an adult; October 5, 1893, saw a young one; September 24, 1900, saw a young one; September 28, 1900, shot an adult male at the mouth of the Conewango Creek. It was sitting in a dead tree and feasting on a small bird. Several of those seen had small birds in their talons at the time, and I shot one that was in pursuit of several Flickers.

September 20, 1936, I saw one below town—first one I have seen to recognize for several years.

Sparrow Hawk | American Kestrel
Falco sparverius

(76.) Summer resident. Breeds.

It arrives early in April, but it is frequently seen in winter. I have seen one or two about town all winter. They preyed on English Sparrows about the factories on the East Side.

It is not uncommon during migrations, but as a summer resident it is quite scarce with only a few pairs nesting in this region. Close to town I know of a couple of old Flicker holes in large trees along the river that are used every year as nesting sites by Sparrow Hawks.

They are found in broken and farming country, but are rarely seen in deep woods. They are the tamest of all the hawks.

May 6, 1930, located a nest 40 feet up in an old Flicker hole in a large stub—5 eggs, incubation well along.

Measurements:

March 31, 1899, adult male, 10 1/2–22–7 1/4–5

American Osprey | Osprey
Pandion haliaetus

(77.) Regular migrant, spring and fall.

Arrives: April 1, 1891; April 10, 1893; April 4, 1899; and April 10, 1901. Latest spring dates are May 4, 1891; May 4, 1892; May 8, 1893; May 28, 1901—one summer record, June 5, 1900. It arrives again in autumn: August 6, 1891; August 17, 1893; August 17, 1900; August 1, 1909; and I have noted it up to October 8, 1900; October 7, 1902; and October 28, 1903.

It is known here as Fish Hawk and Eagle. During their migrating season there are but few days that 1 or 2 cannot be seen about Meade Island or the Grass Flats, sitting on some dead tree or hovering Kingfisher-fashion over the water on the lookout for its finny prey.

They prey on suckers and mullets in low water on the bars and on the riffles. They secure their prey by plunging with a great splash into the water, and seizing the victim in their powerful talons. I have seen one make 5 or 6 plunges before getting its hooks into a fish. After a successful attempt the fish is carried away in the bird's talons—length-wise with the bird's body—to some big tree, there to be eaten at leisure.

Its call is a loud, short whistle repeated rapidly several times, and resembling very much the call of the Greater Yellow-legs—only, of course, much louder. The Osprey is quite wild and wary. I have taken several specimens here, spring and fall, and of course, could have taken many more.

April 18, 1899, I shot a very fine pair, both adults. One I shot on the big hill along the river at Meade Island. It was feasting on a freshly caught 15 inch sucker. The other I got on the wing at Grass Flats. The female was a very large one, and measured 2 feet long and 5 feet, 8 inches in extent.

In 1941, a pair nested on the Peninsula at Erie, which is the nearest to Warren of a nesting that I know of.

Measurements:

April 23, 1890, adult male, 21 1/2–5 feet, 5 inches–17 1/2–8

April 18, 1899, adult female, 24–5 feet, 8 inches

April 18, 1899, adult male, 22–5 feet, 4 inches

September 10, 1909, young, 21 1/2–5 feet, 2 inches–18–8

Long-eared Owl
Asio wilsonianus / Asio otus

(78.) Rare visitor.

While hunting rabbits on December 1, 1892, a friend of mine shot a Long-eared Owl in a thicket of large willows and grapevines along the river near Hemlock, six miles above Warren.

February 20, 1906, while coming down over the hill and through the woods, back of the cemetery, I found a pair in some small hemlocks. I secured both birds. *(The cemetery referred to is most likely Oakland Cemetery, Warren.)*

April 3, 1915, I saw a pair in the hemlock swamp of Grunders. These birds stayed several days before leaving. I had hopes that they would stay and nest.

February 4, 1925, I saw one in the grove at the sand pit. It was in a pine. I discovered it by the scolding of a pair of nuthatches. A look about the little pines across the road showed that this bird had been about all winter, as the ground was covered under some trees with pellets of mice.

A pair has hung about this place every winter since, but I could find no nest until May 31, 1930, when I accidentally discovered the nest a mile away. It was halfway up the mountainside in heavy, second growth hemlock. It was 25 feet up in what looked like an old crow's nest. The young were fully grown and ready to leave.

Measurements:

March 20, 1906, adult male, 14–37–11 1/4–5

March 20, 1906, adult female, 14 1/2–39–11 1/2–5 1/8

Short-eared Owl
Asio flammeus

(79.) Straggler.

As this owl is, more or less, of regular occurrence in many parts of the state, and is not at all uncommon at Erie, I have always thought it strange that it did not occur here at times.

I have but one record. April 23, 1904, I found a dead Short-eared in the marshy swamp at Highhouse's Eddy. The bird was fresh, and had not been dead long. Examination showed it to have been badly wounded. From its location when found, it had evidently escaped the gunner, but had fallen into the heavy grass and died.

November 1, 1930, one was shot by a gunner while after Ring-neck Pheasants in a swamp near Russell.

Barred Owl
Strix varia varia

(80.) Resident. Breeds.

The most common owl found here, at least the one most often seen. It is usually found in the larger and heavier woods, but it is apt to be met with in most any woodland.

It nests late in March, and fresh eggs can usually be found by March 25. I have never known an old hawk's or crow's nest to be used, but I have always found a hollow stub with an open top or a natural cavity in a living tree to be used.

Nearby is a very large maple tree with a large opening on one side—about 20 feet up. This tree has often been used during the past as a nesting site. In this tree I have found fresh sets on the following dates: March 26, 1911, 3 eggs; March 23, 1915, 3 eggs; March 31, 1920, 2 eggs; and April 10, 1922, 2 eggs, incubation advanced.

March 29, 1908, I found a set of 2 in the open top of a large 30 foot stub in deep woods near Morrison Run. April 9, 1909, at Grass Flats I found a Barred Owl sitting on 1 addled egg. It was in an opening 20 feet up in an oak.

June 1, 1912, a friend and I found a nest in virgin forest on Elk Run. This nest was only 15 feet up in a large cavity in a big, living Yellow Birch. The female was sitting on 3 addled eggs, one of which was a runt. She looked quite ragged, and no wonder for she must have been trying to hatch those eggs since late in March.

In April, 1923, I found a nest in a dead, leaning, 30 foot stub near Ott Run. Late in May I took S.S. Dickey to this stub to show him the nest site, and we found that a peculiar accident had happened. The top of this stub was split, with several cracks running down 2 or 3 feet.

On coming into the nest, the old bird had caught one wing in one of these cracks, and going on down had become fast—half of the wing sticking out on the outside of the stub. The wing was broken and twisted by her struggles. She had been dead several days. The young, who had been very large by this time, were gone. The old male, no doubt, had taken care of them as none were in sight.

Nests are hard to find here, as the woods are extensive and there are many hollow trees and stubs. This owl is not very wild. It is usually quite easily approached. A number are usually shot every fall by gunners.

From several of my experiences I have concluded that the Barred Owl gets a good many squirrels. One time in October, when squirrel hunting, I lay down in a little hollow to take a mid-day snooze. I had crawled out of bed at 3:30 a.m. so as to be in the woods at daylight. I had walked 6 or 7 miles in the dark.

It was a warm, lazy day, and along about noon I got sleepy. On coming to a little sink or hollow where I would be out of sight of any fool hunter, I lay down, and was soon dozing. Beside me lay my string of black and gray squirrels—10 in all.

I don't know how long I slept, but awakening suddenly, I saw not 10 feet over my head a Barred Owl fluttering on the air—attracted, of course, by my squirrels. When I first opened my eyes he was so close that he seemed to fill the whole atmosphere, and for an instant I thought the old boy was after me. I started up, and he flew to a nearby limb, alighted, and then faced about. After rubbering hard at me, he hurried away through the woods. I didn't shoot. I often smile to myself when I think what a scare he gave me when I opened my eyes.

Another time while hunting squirrels on the Brown Run ridges, I heard a Black Squirrel barking. On sneaking up, I saw him on a big chestnut stub. I had just gotten nicely in range when a big gray object dashed into the tree. "Blacky" ducked into a hole none too soon, and the gray object alighted on a limb. It proved to be a Barred Owl.

Another time on these same ridges I was sitting quietly on a log, when I heard a racket on the ground amongst the fallen leaves, on the mountainside below me. Very soon a Black Squirrel, hotly pursued by a Red Squirrel, raced up toward me on a fallen stub. I slowly raised my gun, and was about to shoot, when a Barred Owl dove past me from behind. In a moment the owl was right onto the squirrels.

The Black Squirrel whisked around under the log. The Red Squirrel sprang to a tree and started up it, but he was quickly and neatly picked off by a sudden, upward swoop of the owl—who kept right on going, with a good breakfast plainly in view.

I often see Barred Owls in summer. In winter when the trees are bare of leaves they keep quite well hidden in dense hemlock. In summer they have a liking for cool mountain streams in deep shady woods. I frequently flush one from such places when fishing for trout or prowling along the streams.

The Barred Owl hoots very frequently during the daytime if it is cloudy or rainy. The hoots are not deep in tone like those of the Great Horned Owl. They are about 8 in number, given in rapid succession—the last one being rather drawn out. At a distance the hooting of the Barred Owl sounds very much like a dog barking.

Small rodents, squirrels, and rabbits form their food supply, possibly also birds. I never knew of one to raid the farmers' chickens, as the Great Horned Owl does; although, they may sometimes do so.

They are often mobbed for hours by an ever increasing horde of crows, whose excited "caws" eventually bring in all the crows for a mile about.

On March 29, 1925, Harry and I examined a nest that I had found in Ott Run on March 18. This nest was in a cavity in the top of a very large tree. It was fully 65 or 70 feet from the ground. The nest was shallow—only about 4 inches deep. In it were 2 little owlets just hatched and the following supply of fodder: 1 chipmunk, 1 deer mouse, and 4 field mice.

Measurements:
October 18, 1888, adult female, 19–43–x–x
October 5, 1899, adult male, 19–42 1/2–13–9 1/4
October 25, 1900, adult male, 19–43–12 3/4–9

Acadian Owl | Northern Saw-whet Owl
Otus asio | Aegolius acadicus

(81.) Summer resident. Breeds.

This little owl seems to be strictly nocturnal in its habits. It very seldom moves about in daytime. The Acadian is seldom noted, but they are very easily passed by or overlooked. Every one I have ever seen was well hidden, and was very close when first seen. They will also allow a very close approach before taking wing. This is one of the easiest overlooked birds that I know. Instead of being rare, it may be fairly common at times.

December 17, 1892, in low, thick hemlock in Ott Run hollow, I saw an Acadian in a very thick clump of low hemlock. The bird was only 4 feet off the ground. It was not more than 8 feet from me when I first saw it. I had to go even closer to flush it.

February 25, 1895, during a hard wind, snowstorm, and cold weather, I was going home through the woods at the head of Highhouse's Eddy. Happening to glance up, I saw an Acadian sitting on a limb not 10 feet away. I had to back up to shoot it with a light load.

December 19, 1920, while in Ott Run hollow I came upon one in some low, thick hemlock. I was within 8 or 10 feet of it before I saw it. In fact, I couldn't have seen it much farther off. Picking up a stick I walked slowly up to within 5 feet of it. With the stick I knocked it off the limb and captured it. Others that I have known of being taken were all captured in pretty much the same way. They were only seen by accident and were always very tame.

This little owl breeds here. I have heard them in spring and in summer.

June 19, 1910, I was looking for warblers' nests on the river side of the mountain between Brown Run and the Allegheny River. Coming to a very thick clump of low hemlock, I parted the branches and peered in—there within a few feet of my face sat an Acadian in the brown young of the year plumage. It was the first I ever saw in that plumage.

Cutting a stout stick about 6 feet long, I swiped him off the limb, and added him to my collection. I considered this very good evidence of their breeding here, but if any further was needed it was obtained this past season *(1923)*.

June 3, 1923, two friends *(S.S. Dickey and Harry Granquist)* and I spent the morning up the Six Mile. In deep woods, near the stream in a region heavily covered with low, thick hemlock, we discovered 4 of these little owls. They were sitting close together in the small hemlocks—when first seen, 2 were sitting side by side.

We captured one with a stick, and it was kept alive by Mr. Dickey. These birds had not been out of the nest long. There were so many hollows and suitable places in the vicinity that we couldn't determine where they were raised.

Measurements:

December 17, 1892, adult male, 7–17 1/2–5–2 1/2

February 23, 1895, adult female, 7 3/4–18–5 1/2–2 3/4

December 19, 1920, adult female, 7–19–5 1/2–2 1/2, Wt., 3 oz.

Screech Owl | Eastern Screech Owl
Otus asio

(82.) Resident. Breeds.

I have seen it here all seasons of the year. It is secretive and usually well hidden during the day. As it allows a close approach before taking wing, it usually escapes observation—even if a person passes very close by.

It nests in early April, fresh sets being laid by April 5, eggs 4 to 5. All the nests I have examined have been old Flicker nests and usually 10 to 15 feet up.

I have always found the Screech Owl to sit tight and to refuse to leave its nest, in spite of hard pounding and jarring—although I have had them look out from the nest, then drop right back in. I have even reached in and lifted them up without any demonstration or injury to my hands. *(Hard pounding refers to striking the base of the tree with a rock or similar object to see if a nest is in use and to identify the occupant.)*

The young leave the nest early in June. The little silvery-gray fellows are a pretty sight as they sit about after first coming out.

They feed on mice and small birds. Once, February 22, 1907, on a cloudy, snowy day, I saw one eating a White-winged Crossbill it had just captured.

About all I have seen were in the gray plumage. I have seen only a couple in red plumage, and one of these was a female sitting on 5 eggs.

Measurements:

April 20, 1892, gray female, 9–24–6 1/2–3 1/4

May 10, 1912, red, 8 1/2–22 1/2–6 1/2–3 1/4

March 22, 1917, gray, 8 3/4–24 1/2–6 3/4–3 3/8

Great Horned Owl
Bubo virginianus

(83.) Resident. Breeds.

A few pairs are resident the year round in well timbered hollows and large tracts of woodland. The Horned Owl is a wary bird, and is a difficult bird to get a shot at. A few are killed each year by gunners, but the main cause of their becoming rare is, I think, the destruction of the heavy timber by lumbermen.

It nests early. Fresh eggs are to be found by March 1, and the young usually hatch by March 18. Old hawk nests, large natural cavities in big stubs, and living trees are used. All nests that I have seen have been high and the climbs hard.

A set of 2 eggs in my collection I took March 3, 1912, in heavy woods near Brown Run. The nest, 60 feet up in a large chestnut tree, was that of an old Red-shouldered Hawk. This nest was well lined with owl feathers. At daylight that morning the thermometer stood at zero. The snow was one foot deep and crusted hard. The old owl left the nest at the first hard bump. My friend, Spencer, was with me this trip, and we got a very good photo of this set.

This pair of birds did not use the same nest each year. Several years they used a large opening in the top of a very large, dead White Pine. This nest was 55 or 60 feet from the ground. Owing to the condition of the stub, the nest was inaccessible unless a person wished to take a chance on a bad fall.

I have known a pair that used a sycamore tree on the Grass Flats for a number of seasons. On Meade Island a huge sycamore had a pair for tenants each season for many years. Before the "Point" at the mouth of the Conewango Creek was cut off, a pair used to nest each year in a large natural cavity in the largest sycamore. All these sycamore nests were high, and the climbs were difficult and dangerous. *(The "Point" is where the Conewango Creek enters the Allegheny River at Warren. At one time there was much dredging done at this location. This activity is most likely the reason for Simpson's comment regarding the "Point being cut off." This area is also historically significant, as this is the location where Celoron, in 1749, buried a lead plate, thus claiming the region for France. The lead plate has never been found.)*

The Horned Owl seems to know when the young will hatch, and about that time food is kept on the nest in readiness. March 22, 1908, I climbed to a nest 40 feet up in a large birch. This nest was an old Red-tails, and it was a very large affair. The nest held 2 young just hatched, and the third just breaking through the shell. On the nest was a rabbit several days old and a large brown rat, fresh. March 10, 1911, I took a set of 2 from the Goshawk nest in the big pine on Picnic Run. On this nest was part of a rabbit and part of a grouse. On March 26, 1911, in a nest in the top of a stub, I found a single young a few days old. In the nest there were a few fresh grouse feathers and the hind leg of a rabbit.

The Horned Owl raids the poultry yard very frequently, and often comes to grief at it. When one starts in on the poultry he usually keeps coming back until trapped or shot.

They destroy many rabbits and grouse in winter. They are evidently not adverse to skunk, as I have handled several Horned Owls that smelled very strong of skunk.

They seem to be an object of great hatred to crows, and when one is discovered by a crow, the black fellow at once raises a great fuss. His excited "caws" bring every crow within hearing. The poor owl is mobbed by an ever increasing and noisy throng. If the owl undertakes a short flight the hubbub is terrific. I have seen fully 75 or more crows mobbing an owl, and the racket they made could be heard for a long ways.

April 27, 1941, a nest was found near the mouth of Hatch Run. It was an old hawk's nest, and in it were 2 young owls about full grown and ready to leave the nest.

Measurements:

Adult female, 23–58–15–10, stomach: chicken

Adult male, 21 1/2–54–14–8 1/2, Wt. 3 lbs., 12 oz., stomach: rabbit

Adult male, 22–56–15–9 1/2

Adult male 20 1/2–52–14 1/2–9

Snowy Owl
Nyctea nyctea / Nyctea scandiaca

(84.) Rare visitor in winter.

This fine owl occurs here rarely. I have but few records. December 4, 1890, I saw one at Meade Island. On February 25, 1893, I saw a large fine one at Grass Flats, but did not get a shot, as after a little circling it left. November 24, 1895, one was shot near here somewhere and sent to Greenlund to be mounted. On January 15, 1904, one was seen near Tiona.

January, 30, 1909, one was shot at the Gantz farm on the main road near the head of Ott Run. This bird was in quite immature plumage. It was shot off one corner of the barn. January 11, 1912, one was seen in the country nearby. It was seen again on several occasions during the following week.

February 10, 1922, one was presented to me by a friend who shot it near Garland. This bird was a very fine specimen. It is as white as any I have seen anywhere. It is almost an immaculate white—there being but a very few markings anywhere.

CUCKOOS

Yellow-billed Cuckoo
Coccyzus americanus occidentalis

(85.) Summer resident. Breeds.

It arrives the first week in May (May 5 in 1899). An occasional pair is found in suitable conditions along the valleys of the Allegheny River and large streams. I never saw it back in the mountains, in heavy woods, or in slashings. It seems to prefer the bottom woodlands.

It nests in June: June 1, 1915, 4 eggs, fresh; and June 12, 1915, 4 eggs, fresh. It nests a loose platform of twigs, 5 to 8 feet up in bushes. Eggs are usually 4, larger and lighter colored than those of the Black-billed.

Black-billed Cuckoo
Coccyzus erythrophthalmus

(86.) Summer resident. Breeds.

Arrives the middle of May—I have not seen it later than September 20.

Within 2 or 3 days of the first arrival they seem to be as common as they get here. Found anywhere in woods, brush, orchard, and thickets—both in the valley and in the mountains. I have seen this cuckoo far back in virgin timber.

It nests in June. It builds a flat nest of coarse twigs in bushes and small trees, 4 to 10 feet up, eggs 2 to 4.

My records indicate: June 13, 1909, 3 eggs; June 2, 1912, 3 eggs; June 5, 1923, 3 eggs; and June 13, 1923, 3 young, just hatched. On June 2, 1912, R.C. Harlow and I found a Black-billed sitting on 7 eggs that looked like the product of one bird.

KINGFISHERS

Belted Kingfisher
Ceryle alcyon

(87.) Summer resident. Breeds.

It arrives late in March and early in April, and is common along the Allegheny River and larger streams. I have often seen it along the trout streams in the mountains, where no doubt it gets many trout.

In October it becomes scarcer, but occasionally one is seen about until the river freezes up. I have known one to stay all winter, feeding on small fish in a warm, open pond and outlet at the Electric Light Company's plant at the West End.

I saw one about the mouth of the Conewango Creek during the fierce blizzard of February, 1895. I have also noted it occasionally during mild winters.

It nests in holes excavated by the bird itself—in banks along the river, sand banks, and railroad cuts. The holes are dug back in 6 to 10 feet. Eggs are usually about 7. Fresh eggs laid on an average date of about May 14—May 14 in 1892, and May 24 in 1901.

The Kingfisher is well known to about everyone. It is noisy, restless, and rather wild. It generally keeps out of shotgun range. It feeds on small fish of all species, also crayfish.

On June 2, 1929, I photographed one on six eggs. During the winters of 1936 to 1941, excluding the winter of 1938-39, a pair wintered here. They ranged for food from the West End of Warren down to Irvine at the mouth of the Brokenstraw Creek.

Foot bridge across the Conewango Creek, Warren, Pennsylvania. Location is near the current Third Avenue bridge.

Lower railroad bridge across the Allegheny River, Warren, Pennsylvania. c.1890

WOODPECKERS

Eight members of this family have been taken in Pennsylvania, but only seven occur regularly. All of the seven occur in Warren County. Three of these are residents the year round. Three are summer residents, and one is a straggler from the south.

Woodpeckers are found everywhere. Several species seldom wander into large and heavy woods, while one, the Pileated, is seldom seen except in deep forest. The little Downy is at home anywhere.

The woodpeckers are insectivorous, but at certain times several species feed to some extent on berries and fruit. Six of the seven species occurring here breed regularly.

Hairy Woodpecker
Dryobates villosus / Picoides villosus

(88.) Resident. Breeds.

It is more or less regularly met with at all seasons of the year in woodlands. It is occasionally seen in orchards or anywhere there are trees, but it prefers woods.

It is more of a real woodland bird than the Downy, and it is much shyer, also less common. It is found in summer in the larger tracts of timber and wild lands.

It nests in May—May 8, 1923, 3 eggs, fresh, and May 6, 1923, 4 eggs, fresh—in holes excavated by the bird itself in dead trees, stubs, and dead tops of living trees in woods and slashings. It nests from 20 to 80 feet up—usually quite high.

Downy Woodpecker
Dryobates pubescens / Picoides pubescens

(89.) Resident. Breeds.

The smallest of our woodpeckers and is much more common than the Hairy. It is quite tame and liable to be seen most anywhere in woods, slashings, groves, orchards, and frequently in shade trees about town. No troop of small birds roaming about the woods in winter is complete without a Downy or two.

Although mostly insectivorous, they also feed at times on berries and fruits. I have seen them pecking at dead carcasses in winter.

It nests in stubs and dead parts of living trees in late May—May 24, 1923, 5 eggs, fresh, and May 30, 1923, 4 eggs, incubation begun.

It nests from 10 to 50 feet up, usually 12 to 30 feet—not so high as a rule as the Hairy.

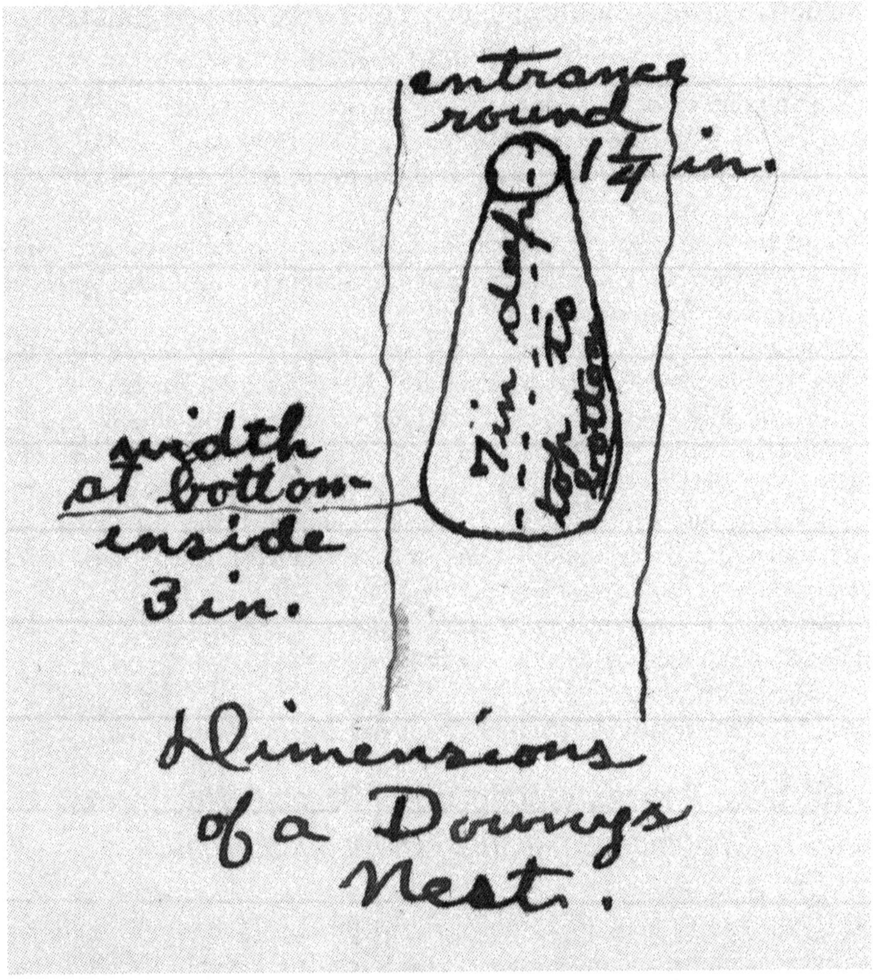

Downy Woodpecker
Nest measurements. Drawing from the Simpson journals.

"No troop of small birds roaming about the woods in winter is complete without a Downy or two." RBS

Yellow-bellied Woodpecker | Yellow-bellied Sapsucker
Sphyrapicus varius

(90.) Summer resident. Breeds.

Arrives: April 21, 1888; April 11, 1889; April 11, 1890; April 14, 1893; April 22, 1899; and April 18, 1901. It is not at all common, and is met with singly and in pairs.

During the nesting season an occasional pair can be found in the deep woods of the mountains. They are also found in the slashings where large stubs and some timber have been left standing.

By watching the old birds I have found 4 or 5 nests. All were high up in stubs, and as a rule inaccessible, unless a person feels like committing suicide.

It nests in early June. Once while camping and trouting in June we had our camp in a large shanty on Wildcat Run, a branch of the Tionesta Creek. A pair of Yellow-bellied had a nest high up in huge stub about 100 yards from our camp. Every morning just after daybreak the male would alight on the roof of our shanty and beat a lively tune for some time. We called him our alarm clock. *(Wildcat Run is a small stream entering the West Branch of the Tionesta Creek, six miles east of a point one mile south of Althom, Warren County.)*

The call of the Yellow-bellied is a hawk-like note.

Measurements:

May 14, 1890, female, 8 1/2–14 1/2–4 3/4–3 1/2

Northern Pileated Woodpecker | Pileated Woodpecker
Ceophloeus pileatus | Dryocopus pileatus

(91.) Resident. Breeds.

The Pileated, the king of our northern woodpeckers, is a bird of the forest. The larger the timber and more extensive the forests, the better he likes it. In fact, the Pileated does not seem to be found in settled or farming districts except as a straggler or visitor.

In the mountains of Warren, Forest, Elk, McKean, and several other of our northwestern counties, there are large areas of practically uninhabited wild land—at the present time the greater part of these wild lands have been lumbered over.

The deforested regions are a wilderness of briars, laurel beds, and impassable jungle with many large stubs and old trees standing about. Where the fires have not swept through too hard or not at all, a second growth forest of mostly hardwood timber is replacing the original coniferous growth.

In this general region there are still many small tracts and a few large bodies of heavy timber. In this sort of country the Pileated is still resident. Although seen in both the deforested areas and the big timber, it is more often seen in the big woods.

Their presence is to be seen in the shape of huge, old, standing, dead, hemlock stubs stripped of their outer bark from top to bottom. I have seen the ground under such stubs completely covered all around under the tree with chunks and pieces of the bark.

Large holes and excavations are also cut into logs and fallen timber in quest of ants and grubs no doubt. I have seen where they have dug holes and excavations into the very heart of standing timber that has large ant or grub infestations. I have seen excavations 2 feet long and 3 or 4 inches wide in such trees. Where these trees happen to be oak or chestnut the work must take some time.

They are great wanderers and roam about considerable territory. I often see them flying from one mountain to another across the valley at considerable height.

Their call is much like a Flicker's call, but much louder and more cackling. This cackling is uttered when in flight as well as when at rest. When at rest, though, the call is repeated rapidly as many as 15 to 20 notes in succession, but when in flight the calls are given 2 or 3 in succession, and quite slowly as compared to the way they call when at rest on a tree trunk.

The Pileated is wild, wary, and difficult to approach. When followed up it leaves the pursuer behind by taking long flights.

Being such a large and conspicuous bird the Pileated is seldom spared if it gets in range of a gunner. Squirrel hunters, sitting quietly about watching for squirrels, frequently shoot one as it comes along their way.

It has other enemies, too. I once shot a Sharp-shinned Hawk that was trying very hard to catch a Pileated on a big tree. The Pileated dared not attempt flight, but stuck to the tree trunk about which he shifted with great quickness at every rush of the hawk. The Pileated made such a great racket that I was attracted from quite a distance, and I settled the argument with my gun. I often wondered how it would have ended, but I didn't want the Pileated killed. I frequently visited that vicinity and didn't want them missing from the scenery.

Once in summer, while trout fishing in the mountains in deep, heavy woods, I came to a mossy, shady spot where a Pileated had been wrecked—having been evidently caught on the ground. A close inspection revealed the trail of a huge old Wildcat—a Bay Lynx. The following fall, close to this same spot, I trapped one of the largest Bay Lynx I ever saw—possibly the very one that had killed the Pileated.

I had a lot of trouble finding my first nest of this woodpecker. At that time I could find no account of its nesting in this state, so I was at a loss as to just when to expect fresh eggs, or where or how to go about locating the nest.

I did not know if there would be any particular sort of timber or particular situation in which to search. Inquiries of lumbermen and woodsmen failed to get me any information, as I could not find a man who had found a nest. A person can spy on the movements of many birds and find the nest, but I soon found that spying on the Pileated didn't get results, as they were so shy and moved about over so much territory.

About 5 miles below town along the river is a large tract of wild land known along the river as the "Grass Flats." This has always been a favorite hunting and collecting ground with me. In these heavy woods the Pileated could always be found. As I was down there a great deal, I made a special effort to find a nest during the season of 1909.

I noticed that on one of the flats, where there was a hemlock swamp, signs of the Pileated were unusually plentiful. I remembered that I usually saw the birds about this place in April and May.

On May 4, I spent the day down there and combed the swamp and vicinity. The result was that I found 3 large, fresh, promising looking holes in as many stubs. On the ground under each tree I found a large amount of chipping. This was very encouraging, even if I failed to flush the female from any of the tree holes.

On May 16, I went down again. At the first hole a jar on the stub with a heavy rock started out a Black Squirrel, who made a flying leap into a hemlock and disappeared. At the second and really best looking stub I pounded out into view a family of Flying Squirrels. This was not very encouraging. I went to the third stub and gave a couple of thumps, and out came a scarlet-crested head.

It took considerable pounding to make her leave the nest. As I stood there sizing up the tree, she came back and alighted directly under the opening. She changed her mind about entering, and finally flew off into the swamp. During the time I was there she stayed nearby and frequently cackled, but I saw nothing of the male.

The nest tree was a large oak. It was 3 feet in diameter and broken off 45 feet from the ground. Only one side of the tree was alive, and 25 feet from the ground this living wood branched off into a large limb a foot in diameter. The rest of the stub was bare, dead, punky, and soft.

This big limb left the stub at a right angle, then turned and grew straight up, along side of and about 4 feet from the stub itself. Where the green wood met the dead wood on the stub there was quite a bulge. By getting behind this bulge on the living side I found it made a good place to grip onto. I managed to shin and work my way up and onto the big limb.

The rest was easy. I had only to climb up the big limb to get opposite to the nest opening, which was on the opposite side of the stub from me. I could reach the stub easily, and with my heavy knife I soon cut through the wood which was punky. I opened up a large hole into the nesting cavity.

The opening or entrance was about 2 feet down from the broken off top of the stub—making it about 43 feet from the ground. The entrance was about 4 inches in diameter and not perfectly round. The cavity was 20 inches deep and fully 10 inches in diameter, being large and roomy.

The eggs, 4 in number and crystal white beauties, lay on loose chippings. They were about one-half incubated and measured 1.50 x 1.06, 1.05 x 1.00, 1.50 x 1.06, and 1.45 x 1.06.

In 1910, about the middle of April, I was in this same place again. I located a nest in the swamp by the large amount of chippings about the base of the tree. It was 50 feet up in the dead top of a large poplar.

I got down again May 14, and made the climb. Both old birds stayed close by, and were very noisy and anxious. When I reached the entrance I found that the youngsters had hatched out, so I did not break into the nest.

In 1911, I found their nest again—this time on the river flat. It was high up in a huge sycamore in a large leaning-out stub of a broken limb. Needless to say I did not bother it, as I am not taking any chances like that. Several times since then the birds have nested in this same sycamore—digging a new nest each time.

In the swamp and heavy woods about the Clarendon Pond on the Tionesta Creek these woodpeckers nested. I found a nest there on two occasions. One was high up in an enormous dead tree in the swamp. The second nest was in the woods, 30 feet up in a large, very dead, wobbly, and much leaning stub. It was not safe to fool with either of these stubs, so I left them alone.

In the vicinity of Sill Run I located 2 nests. One was in a huge dead hemlock. The other was in a large, rotten, dead oak—I did not care to risk my neck for either of these.

During the spring of 1920 I found a nest in a large, dead stub in the Ott Run hollow. In early June, after the old birds were finished feeding the young, Harry Granquist and I spent an entire morning with our cameras at this nest tree. We secured some very good photos of the old female at the entrance to the nest.

By securing our cameras to the limb of a nearby tree, the cameras were only 15 feet from the nest. We then secured a couple of close-ups of the old lady, as she alighted and clung to the tree at the entrance to the nest. In this case we operated the cameras from the ground with a stout cord.

Sometime during the winter of 1923-24, this old stub blew down. Early in the spring of 1924, when one day I happened to pass by, I found it flat on the ground. I examined and opened this nesting cavity and got measurements of the nest site.

Measurements:

Adult male, 18 1/2–29 1/2–9 3/4–x

Adult female, 17 1/2–28–9–7

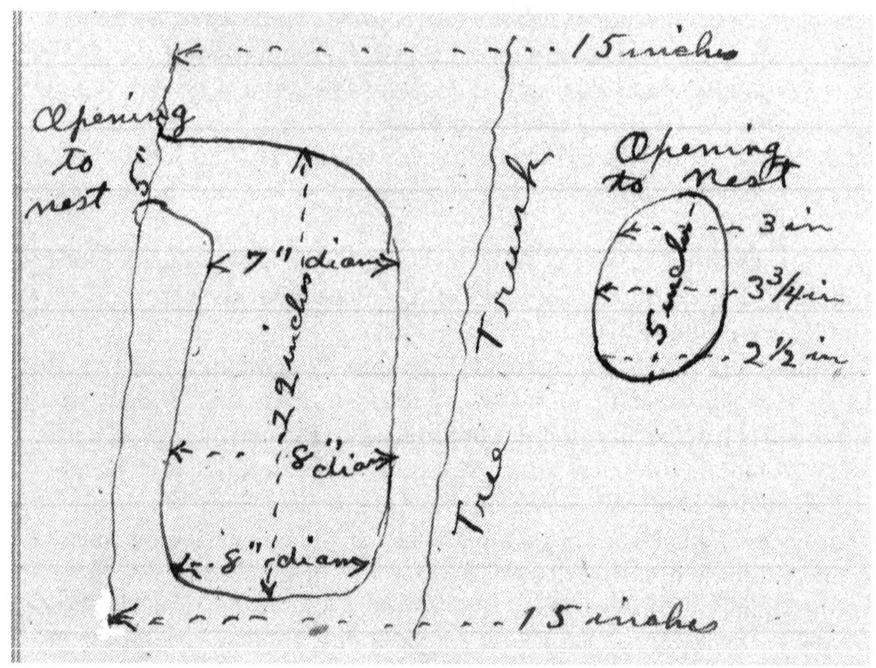

Pileated Woodpecker
Nest measurements. Drawing from the Simpson journals.

"Sometime during the winter of 1923-24, this old stub blew down. Early in the spring of 1924, when one day I happened to pass by, I found it flat on the ground. I examined and opened this nesting cavity and got measurements of the nest site." RBS

Red-headed Woodpecker
Melanerpes erythrocephalus

(92.) Summer resident. Breeds.

Arrives about the first of May, and after October first it is seldom met with. It is found about farming districts, slashings, and open country generally, but it is never found back in heavy woods. The Red-head is not very common here.

I have several winter records. At Grass Flats during severe weather in January of 1901, I saw one. During the winter of 1906-07, one lived all winter along the river here in town on the South Side.

It nests in stubs and dead tops of living trees. I have seen nests only 10 feet up, and I have seen others 50 feet up. It nests in June: June 7, 1914, five eggs, fresh.

Measurements:

Male, 9 1/4–17 1/8–5 3/4–3 3/8

Female, 9 3/4–17 1/2–5 3/8–3 1/2

Red-bellied Woodpecker
Centurus carolinus / Melanerpes carolinus

(93.) Straggler from the south.

December 11, 1888, I shot a fine one on the Point *(see photo)* at the mouth of the Conewango Creek. This bird was alone, quite noisy, and kept high up in the large trees. I have seen this woodpecker north of here in Chautauqua County, New York, but I have never met with it here except on this one occasion.

Northern Flicker
Colaptes auratus

(94.) Summer resident. Breeds.

Our commonest woodpecker—it arrives April 1, 1893; March 15, 1901; March 30, 1902; and March 26, 1904. It is common everywhere except in heavy woods. It is quite well known to most people.

It is not often seen after the middle of October, but I have seen it up to the first of December. It is fond of old meadows and pastures, where it is found in flocks with robins and field birds in summer and autumn.

It nests in late May, at all heights, in stubs and dead trees. I have seen a nest only 3 feet up, and again I have seen nests 70 to 80 feet up in huge, old stubs in the slashings. Eggs are usually 6 to 8—May 28, 1894, 8 eggs, fresh, and on May 21, 1930, 4 eggs, fresh. During the winter of 1939-40, a pair wintered at Starbrick and vicinity.

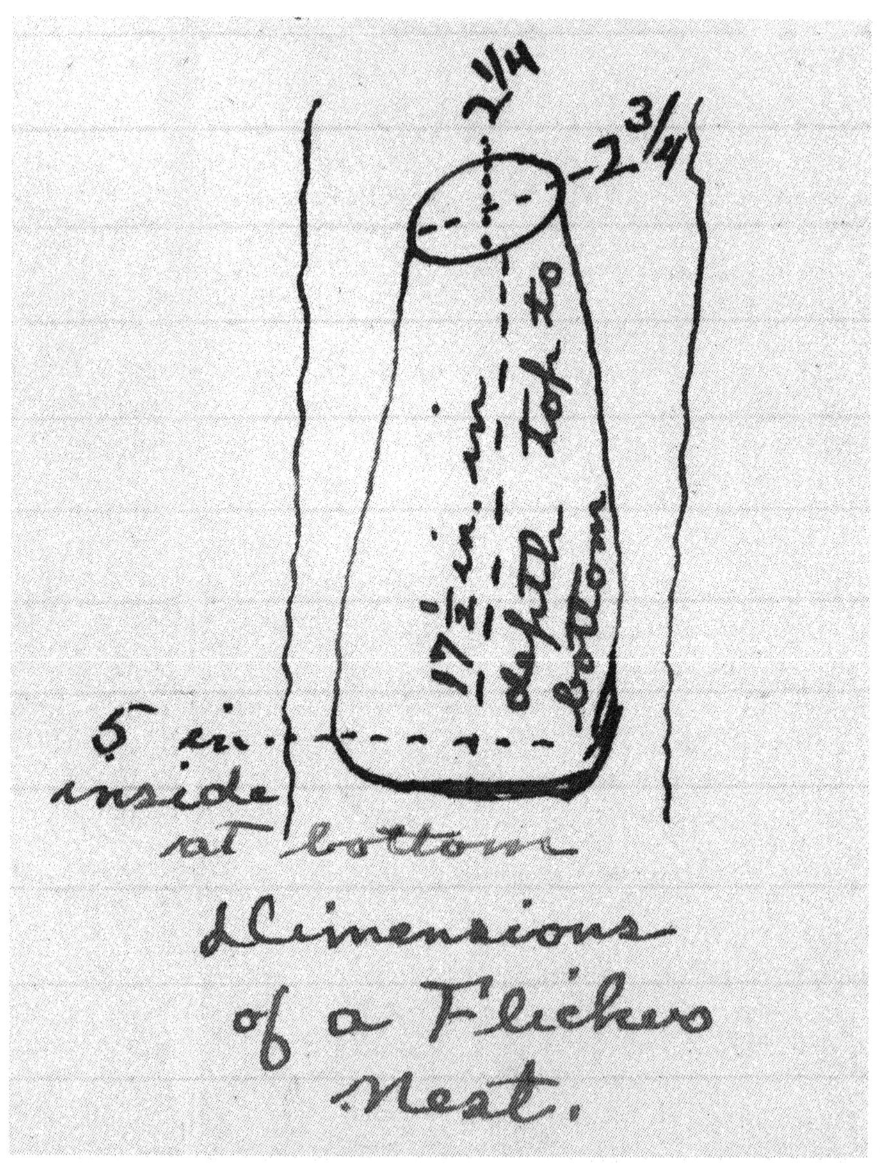

Drawing of a Flicker's nest
from the journals of Ralph Simpson.

WHIP-POOR-WILLS

Whip-poor-will
Antrostomus vociferous / Caprimulgus vociferus

(95.) Summer resident. Breeds.

Arrives: May 8, 1901; April 28, 1902; and May 3, 1906.

The Whip-poor-will is not at all a common bird in this county, and is confined almost entirely to the mountains, being seldom seen in the river valley even during migrations. They are active and about as common as they ever get from the time of their first arrival in spring. Right after sunset they call constantly, but during the night they are rather quiet—toward daylight they again become noisy.

It is very unusual to hear one calling during the day, but on several occasions, with the sun shining brightly, I have heard one calling during midday. After the nesting season is over, and during the latter part of the summer, they become quiet, and do not call much.

When close to one that is calling, a "cluck" can be heard between notes. At different times I have been very close to one when it began to call. I found that sometimes 2 or 3 of these "clucks" preceded the regular call, and again the "cluck" would only come between notes. At times, I have heard them utter a sort of deep, croaking note, when not giving their regular call. So soft and noiseless is their flight, that unless a person is looking in their direction, they will escape unseen.

It nests in late May and early June—May 30, 2 eggs, fresh, and June 2, 2 eggs, fresh. Eggs are hard to find as the female is a very close sitter. While in West Virginia I found this bird common, and I found a number of sets.

I found that one night lapses between the laying, as on several occasions where I flushed a female from a single egg, it would be 2 days before the second egg was laid. As to moving their eggs when disturbed, I had the following experience. A friend and I found a nest, and repeatedly flushed the female for several days—to see if she would move. It seemed that she did not intend to move at all. Several days after we had quit bothering her, I went that way again. I found that both bird and eggs had disappeared, and no amount of searching could locate her again.

They are very apt to return each season to the same locality, and to nest close to last year's site. The Whip-poor-will and Nighthawk are assumed to be the same bird by most of the people here.

Most recent date: June 13, 1943, 2 eggs.

NIGHTHAWKS

Nighthawk | Common Nighthawk

Chordeilus virginianus / Chordeilu minor

(96.) Summer resident. Breeds.

Arrives late May: May 15, 1890; May 17, 1901; and May 17, 1904.

It is common during migrations, especially in autumn. Often large flights pass on their way south the latter part of August. As a breeder the Nighthawk is rare. Several pairs nest about town on the flat roofs of business blocks, but they rarely nest in the fields here.

It is often seen flying about during midday. It is known to a great many people as the Whip-poor-will.

June 9, 1938, two pairs nested on the flat pebble roof of the Federal Building at Warren. On this date I photographed both of these nests—one had 1 egg, the other had 2 eggs. This was the first chance I have had to take photos of the eggs of this bird.

Measurements:

Female, 9 1/2–23 1/2–7 3/4–4 3/8

SWIFTS

Chimney Swift

Chaetura pelagica

(97.) Summer resident. Breeds.

Arrives: April 30, 1902, saw 4; April 30, 1903, saw 20; and April 24, 1904, saw a great many; April 30, 1907, saw 1; and April 19, 1910, saw 1. Although it arrives quite early, it does not stay late. It has just about disappeared by the middle of September.

They are common about town and in the country. It is not unusual to see them flying about over the slashings and open timber, back in the mountains.

Swifts may often perish early in their spring migrations. On several occasions, during snow storms, after they had first begun to arrive, I have picked one up alive, but exhausted. Otherwise, I never saw a Swift alight anywhere in daytime, and few people know what a Swift really looks like.

Their flight is swift and erratic—noisy and chattering most of the time, while they fly about. During the spring migrations in May, it is sometimes very abundant. I have, on several occasions, seen from 300 to 500 at once, flying over town.

It nests in chimneys as a rule, but I have on several occasions seen it nest on the walls of old shanties in the woods. In an old stack of boilers, left standing at a deserted sawmill on Wildcat Run, I found on July 4, 1894, a nest containing 3 eggs. I used to know of two huge broken-off stubs in slashings that were used yearly as nesting sites, but these are now blown down. No doubt there are others.

June 29, 1933, I photographed a nest and 3 eggs in a silo at the Gregory farm near Russell. In 1934, a pair again nested in this silo, but this time in such a position that it could not be photographed. Five eggs were laid this time.

I found in 1942, and again in 1943, that Swifts nested in the silo at the Greenlund farm at Starbrick. Maybe this is not unusual when a silo is open for ventilation near the top—open either by an overhanging roof, an open window, or a door.

HUMMERS

Ruby-throated Hummer
Archillochus colubris

(98.) Summer resident. Breeds.

Arrives: May 9, 1901; May 18, 1904; and June 1, 1907. It is seldom seen after the middle of September. The latest fall date I have is September 29, 1900.

It is not a common bird, but almost everyone knows the Hummingbird. It is found everywhere, except in very heavy stands of timber.

It nests in June in woods and orchards—June 11, 2 eggs, fresh, and June 28, 2 eggs, fresh. When in woodlands it usually builds its nest at an elevation of 20 to 25 feet. The nests are almost impossible to find, unless the female is watched. Nests are usually well out on a limb and hard to get at.

During 1938, two pairs nested at our place *(Starbrick home)*. One was 20 feet up in an oak; the other was 30 feet up in a maple. Both nests were way out on a long limb at a place where the limbs were about one-half inch thick. Both nests were robbed—one was by a crow. Both nests had sets laid by the middle of June. One pair nested a second time, and laid 1 egg, which hatched successfully. This nest was 10 feet up and way out on a long lower limb of an oak.

July 7, 1940, I found a nest at our place containing 2 youngsters. This nest was 15 feet from the ground. It was way out near the end of a long, drooping limb of an oak tree.

June 15, 1941, a pair finished a nest 18 feet up, and well out on an oak limb. They raised their 2 young in peace.

Measurements:

Adult male, 3 3/8–4–1 1/2–1 1/8

FLYCATCHERS

Nine species of flycatchers are found in Pennsylvania, and all breed in the Commonwealth. Of these 9, I have found 8 occurring in Warren County, and I have found 7 of these breeding here, with the chances very much in favor of the other nesting here rarely.

The only flycatcher I have not noted here is the Alder. As it is rare anywhere in this state, I may have overlooked it. It may yet be detected. The Yellow-bellied I am very sure is a rare breeder here, but up to date I have no positive records.

As flycatchers feed almost entirely on insects captured on the wing, they are, with the exception of the Phoebe, rather late arriving in the spring, and depart rather early in the fall.

Kingbird | Eastern Kingbird
Tyrannus tyrannus

(99.) Summer resident. Breeds.

Arrives: May 3, 1899; May 6, 1901; May 6, 1902; May 15, 1904; and May 7, 1907.

It departs in September. It nests in June—June 3, 1912, 3 eggs. It usually nests 10 to 20 feet up, but I have seen nests 50 feet up in sycamores along the river. I have never found a nest with 4 eggs, always 3.

It is well distributed everywhere about cleared lands, groves, orchards, and the edges of woods. A hawk or crow flying, with a fighting, scolding Kingbird pouncing at his back, is not an uncommon sight.

Measurements:

Female, 8 1/2–14–4 1/4–3 9/16

Crested Flycatcher | Great Crested Flycatcher
Myiarchus crinitus

(100.) Summer resident. Breeds.

Arrives: May 6, 1892; May 6, 1901; and May 16, 1907. It is not at all common, but if a person is out a great deal, this flycatcher will be frequently noted, singly or in pairs, during migrations, especially in May. As a summer resident they are scarce, only an occasional pair being found here and there along the river valley.

The nests I have found of this flycatcher, I have located by watching the birds building, and all have been high up in trees in natural cavities. At Meade Island and Grass Flats they nest annually—high up in large sycamores. Their voice is loud, harsh, and can be heard for some distance.

Measurements:

Adult male, 9–13 3/4–4 1/2–4

Phoebe | Eastern Phoebe
Sayornis phoebe

(101.) Summer resident. Breeds.

Arrives: March 24, 1890; March 24, 1893; March 19, 1894; March 25, 1901; March 30, 1902; March 26, 1904; and March 17, 1907.

The Phoebe is the earliest of the flycatchers to arrive in spring, being a month or more ahead of the others. It departs in October, but I have seen it here as late as November 1.

It is common everywhere, and quite well known—even in heavy woods, they are often found about a camp or shanty. It nests in May and June, in and about buildings, barns, camps, and shanties in the woods—under bridges, and sometimes on ledges of overhanging rocks.

Eggs are 4 to 6.

Measurements:

Male, 6 3/4–10 1/2–3 1/4–2 7/8

Female, 6 1/4–10 1/4–3 3/16–2 3/4

Olive-sided Flycatcher
Nuttallornis borealis | Contopus cooperi

(102.) Summer resident. Breeds.

This flycatcher, which is very rare in Pennsylvania at any season of the year, I have found to occur in this general region as a rare migrant and summer resident. For its summer home it chooses a place in some mountain valley, where the timber has not been too closely cut. Big stubs are standing about and there are scatterings of timber left, including good-sized second growth hemlock.

The birds, especially the male, spend much of their time on the top most limb of some big stub. Here they sit, uttering their call at intervals. The call is a loud, harsh whistle of 2 and often 3 syllables, which can be heard quite a distance off.

This flycatcher first came to my notice during the summers of 1891, 1892, and 1893. Each June, while camping and trouting on the Wild Cat and Shaw Runs, at the headwaters of the Tionesta Creek, I heard and saw these birds in the slashings and along the big timber near camp. During the summer of 1893, there was a pair of these birds in the Ott Run hollow.

On coming back from West Virginia in the spring of 1900, I began to look these flycatchers up. In June I located a pair in the vicinity of our old camp, at the head of the Tionesta Creek, while on a trouting trip. I wrote to Todd, of the Carnegie Museum, Pittsburgh, who had been trying for several years to get a pair from this state, and he came up. I took him over, and he secured the birds for the museum. *(W.E. Clyde Todd, curator of the bird section, Carnegie Museum, Pittsburgh, Pennsylvania.)*

In July, 1900, I spent a week trout fishing near the head of Blue Jay Creek in Forest County. I was with an old hunter, and we covered a lot of wild country, during the course of which I located 2 pairs of the Olive-sided. The old fellow had taken a shotgun into camp, as dogs were running deer. He intended to stop it by bumping off the dogs. With this gun, and a load of coarse shot, I soon secured one of the birds. I tore it up so badly that I did not shoot another.

September 18, 1900, on the Peninsula at Erie, I shot a female in very fine fall plumage. This is my only record from there.

June 3, 1901, at Grass Flats I saw a bird on top of a tall White Pine stub. After watching it perform, I concluded it was an Olive-sided. It was a long shot, but my old "Parker" brought it down, without mussing a feather. It was a fine adult male.

May 30, 1904, while crossing from Ott Run over the hill into Morrison, I heard an Olive-sided calling. I found him in the usual kind of place. I left and returned again June 5, when I found the male still there. After watching the male a few minutes, I saw the female, so I transferred my attentions to her.

I was on hand at just the right time, as the female soon got very restless—frequently uttering a call of 3 to 8 notes, repeated rapidly. Each note was much like the first note of the call of the male. It was something similar to the chatter call of a crossbill, only louder and harder. After calling a little, she would quiet down. Pulling off some lichen or fine twigs from a limb of one of the dead hemlocks standing about, she would fly directly to the nest, which was on a horizontal limb of a hemlock—up 50 feet from the ground, and 5 feet from the trunk.

June 14, at daylight, I was up that way. I found both birds in the vicinity. I climbed the tree, but to my disappointment I found that a jay or Red Squirrel had beaten me to it, and robbed the nest. I watched the old birds awhile, but they showed no signs of re-nesting. They moved about a great deal. The male often moving about, and the female frequently calling. At times they got quite spoony, sitting close together and chattering to each other.

June 16, I again watched them. I found that the female was building a new nest in the same tree—this time 15 feet lower down, and 10 feet out from the trunk. Although the punkies *(gnats)* bit fiercely, I watched her for some time. She would sit quietly at times on an old, dead stub, frequently flying out to catch some insects. Then getting restless, she would begin calling, soon making 3 or 4 trips to the nest, after which, she would again perch for a time on the stub.

June 24, I again paid a visit. I found the male perched high up, on top of a dead stub, close to the nest tree. On my jarring the nest tree, the female darted from the nest. Making the climb, I found a set of 3 eggs, that looked very much like a Wood Pewee's, except, of course, much larger.

May 26, 1906, along the edge of the heavy timber on Sanders Run in Clearfield County, I secured a pair of these flycatchers.

During the seasons of 1907, 1908, and 1909, a pair was located each season nesting in the slashing near the Morrison Run Reservoir. During the seasons of 1908 and 1909, another pair was located each season about a mile farther up the run. I spent considerable time watching these two pairs of birds during those seasons.

The season of 1908, I found the nests of both pairs, by watching the old birds—one held 3 eggs, June 14, and the other held 3 eggs, June 16. The season of 1910 was late, cold, and neither of these 2 pairs returned—on May 25, I did see 2 migrants.

In 1913, I saw 2 migrants—one on May 29, the other June 1. June 9, 1915, I heard a male calling on the big hill opposite Meade Island. I watched, and found the female building. On June 25, I found the female at home on 3 eggs. I had the pleasure of looking this outfit over. Up to date, I have had the pleasure of examining 6 nests of this flycatcher. All were found by watching the old birds.

The actions of the old birds, while building, were about the same in each case. In no case did the male carry any material to the nest. All nests were on horizontal limbs of hemlocks. The nests are rather flat and bulky. They were all built of dead hemlock sprigs, some with a little lichen on, and lined with finer sprigs, and few fine grasses. Three seems to be the full set.

When climbing to the nests, I have found the birds quite courageous. At one nest I had the birds repeatedly dart within 4 feet of my head.

Additional data on the nests that I have found is as follows: nest number 1, June 14, 1904, 50 feet up, 5 feet out, robbed by a jay or squirrel; nest number 2, June 24, 1904, second nesting, 35 feet up, 10 feet out, same tree; nest number 3, June 14, 1908, 20 feet up, 12 feet out; nest number 4, June 16, 1908, 25 feet up, 4 feet out; nest number 5, June 15, 1909, 40 feet up, 5 feet out; and nest number 6, June 25, 1915, 35 feet up, 8 feet out.

Eggs were 3 in number in each case, all fresh. The females were incubating at the time the nests were examined.

May 24, 1925, I saw and listened to a migrant in the grove at the sand pits. May 30, 1925, I saw a pair in the Cranberry Swamp near Clarendon. May 22, 1927, I saw a migrant in Ott Run hollow. In June of 1927, I saw a pair located near Morrison Run, but no nest was found. June 7, 1928, I saw a migrant.

June 13, 1937, I photographed a nest and 3 eggs in the lower part of Morrison Run valley—nest was 15 feet up in a hemlock, and 5 feet from the trunk. May 25, 1938, one spent the day at our new home at Starbrick. I saw one on May 19, 1942, and on May 18, 1943.

Measurements:

Adult male, 7–13–4 1/8–2 7/8

Adult female, 7–12 3/4–4–2 3/4

Fall, female, 6 3/4–12 1/4–4–2 3/4

Wood Pewee | Eastern Wood-Pewee

Myiochanes virens | Contopus virens

(103.) Summer resident. Breeds.

It arrives about the middle of May, being one of the late spring arrivals. It is found everywhere in woodlands of all kinds, also in orchards and in places about town. It is one of the common birds of the big woods, and one of the few birds to be heard on a hot day.

It nests in June: June 10, 1923, 3 eggs, fresh; June 16, 1923, 3 eggs, fresh; and June 4, 1928, 3 eggs. The nests are saddled on a horizontal limb, 20 to 50 feet from the ground. The nest is very often on a dead limb—three eggs in all the nests I examined.

Measurements:

Male, 6–10 1/2–3 3/8–2 9/16

Female, 5 7/8–10 1/2–3 5/16–2 5/8

Yellow-bellied Flycatcher

Empidonax flaviventris

(104.) Irregular migrant in the spring.

I have no fall record. For a number of seasons I did not meet this little fellow. After clearing up a lot of other things, I began to look up the small flycatchers that I sometimes saw in the thickets. It was then that I discovered the Yellow-bellied.

During the last week of May, and the first week of June in 1907, I saw more than during any other season. At Grass Flats, that same season, I saw quite a few. Other seasons I have found them to be rather rare. I have found them mostly about thickets—along the streams, and in the valleys.

Three times in late June, I have seen this little flycatcher in very suitable places for nesting. I feel quite positive that it breeds rarely in this vicinity; although up to date, I have no breeding record. The Yellow-bellied, as well as several of the other small flycatchers, is very easily overlooked.

Sightings: July 12, 1900, I found a pair along Blue Jay Creek in Forest County; and June 16, 1907, I found a pair at a swampy place along Morrison Run, but I could not find a nest. Recent records: May 7, 1932; May 20, 1935; May 19, 1944.

Measurements:

Adult male, 5 1/4–8 1/2–2 3/8–2 1/8

Adult female, 5–8 3/8–2 5/16–2 3/16

Acadian Flycatcher
Empidonax virescens

(105.) Summer resident. Breeds.

In West Virginia I found this flycatcher to be quite common. I have also taken it on the Peninsula, at Erie, Pennsylvania. Here at Warren, up to date, I have never met with it but once, and then strangely enough, it was nesting.

June 6, 1912, I went down the river. During the course of my rambles, I went along a little stream, well back in the woods in open hardwood timber on the Grass Flats. In a rather open place I heard an Acadian, and I recognized the notes at once. I soon saw the bird, and while watching it a few minutes, I found that it was building. I watched her make a number of trips, and then I left.

June 14, I went down again, and found her at home on 3 eggs. It seems strange that I have met this flycatcher here only once, and that it should be a breeding record, too. Maybe the Acadian will be found here more often, as is the case with several other southern species that now occur here, but formerly were never seen.

Measurements:

Male, 6–8–x–x

Least Flycatcher
Empidonax minimus

(106.) Summer resident. Breeds.

Arrives: April 30, 1890; May 3, 1892; May 2, 1901; May 3, 1902; May 6, 1903; and May 8, 1907.

It is common in groves, open woodlands, shade trees in town, and orchards. It is not found in heavy timber. It nests about the first of June: May 24, 1901, 4 eggs, fresh; and May 30, 1901, 4 eggs, fresh.

It nests usually in an upright fork of a limb, 10 to 40 feet up, sometimes out on a horizontal limb. I have seen nests in alders only 4 feet up. Once I found a nest near Morrison Run, out on a horizontal limb of a hemlock—the only nest I ever saw in an evergreen.

Eggs are 3 or 4, usually 4. It is quite a common victim of the Cowbird.

Measurements:

Male, 4 3/4–7 1/2–2 3/8–2 1/8

Male, 4 3/4–8–2 1/2–2 3/16

Male, 5–8–2 1/2–2 3/16

Female, 4 7/8–7 3/4–2 3/8–2 1/16

LARKS

Prairie Horned Lark | Horned Lark
Octocoris alpestris | Eremophila alpestris

(107.) Summer resident. Breeds.

Early in February the Horned Larks usually begin to appear. Some seasons, late in February and early in March, they are abundant in flocks. Some flocks contain up to 150 birds, and with these flocks there are sometimes a few Snowflakes and an occasional Longspur. Toward the first of April only a few pairs are left, and these usually stay and breed.

It nests early: March 24, 1913, 3 eggs, fresh; and April 5, 1914, 4 eggs, fresh—possibly two broods, as I have found nests in June—June 10, 3 eggs, fresh. It nests in old fields and pastures in the lowlands and on the mountains.

Records: April 14, 1935, a large young ready to leave the nest; and March 15, 1940, a flock of 25. In 1944, I note that for a number of years now, this bird has been scarce. No longer do I see the large flocks of late February and March as in former years. The only place where they now nest here are the large fields and pastures, on high ground and in the hills. In such places, here and there, a pair can be found. I do not know why they have changed their migration route, and now are so seldom seen in this vicinity.

Measurements:

Female, 6 1/2–12–3 3/4–2 3/8

CROWS—JAYS—Etc.

This group of birds is not very well represented in western Pennsylvania. Two of them, the Blue Jay and American Crow, are two of the best known birds in general.

Birds of this group are shy and difficult to approach. The raven is perhaps, from all accounts, one of the shyest birds found in the Commonwealth.

Owing to their pilfering habits, these birds are not protected by law.

Blue Jay
Cyanocitta cristata

(108.) Resident. Breeds.

The jay is found the year round, but is not very common. In fact, it seems to me that there are not as many as a few years ago. They are found anywhere in woods, valleys, and the mountains, but are more common in suitable situations in the mountains.

In October they seem to be most common. They nest in late May and early June. Nests are usually built in hemlocks, but often in deciduous trees. I have found several in large orchards. It builds its nests from 10 to 30 feet up, eggs 3 to 5.

The jay is a quite noisy bird and somewhat of a mimic. They often give a very close imitation of a Red-shouldered Hawk. They are continuously moving about and nosing into everything.

If a jay discovers a hawk, owl, fox, or any large animal or bird, Mr. Jay at once starts a fuss. This quickly brings in any other jays that may be within hearing distance—then they all sit about and scold. In the fall they feed a great deal on acorns, beechnuts, and chestnuts, especially beechnuts.

In winter they live in old corn shocks, and will eat most anything. They will feed on carrion and bait. I have often caught them in traps set for coon, fox, and weasel. They rob many bird nests, especially those of warblers and tanagers that are built on horizontal limbs. Jays are rather shy, and usually do not allow a very close approach.

May 27, 1900, 3 eggs; June 5, 1900, 3 eggs; May 30, 1909, 3 eggs; and May 27, 1927, 3 eggs.

Measurements:

Male, 11 3/4–17–5 1/2–5 1/2

Northern Raven | Common Raven
Corvus corax

(109.) Years ago, when this region was mostly a great virgin forest and big game was abundant, the raven was a common bird. As the forests began to disappear before the lumberman's axe, the raven also became scarcer.

Up to at least 1880, ravens were still residents about the headwaters of the Tionesta Creek and in the Four Mile and Kinzua Creek regions. In the early 1890s, I was camping at different times—winter and summer—and hunting and fishing about the headwaters of the Tionesta. As I did not see or hear anything of the raven, I think that by this time, it was gone for good as a resident. Woodsmen who used to hunt and work in these regions tell me the raven was noisy at times, and could be heard a long ways. They also say they were shy and hard to get a shot at. They would feed on carrion and carcasses of all kinds.

In the early winter of 1909-10, a raven or two were seen for several weeks about the Minister Creek in Forest County, near the Warren-Forest County line. April 24, 1910, while on top of the hill back of the cemetery, I saw 3 ravens flying about. I was in the Morrison Run region for two days in succession afterwards, but I did not see them again.

Early in May, 1910, two were around the big hill opposite Meade Island for a couple of days. They called at times, and were seen and watched by an old lumberman who lived there and was familiar with the bird. He sent word to me, but they had gone by the time I could get away for a day.

In my collection I have a full grown young of the year taken in Center County in 1909, and a fine set of 5 eggs taken at the same place March 4, 1911.

Just why the raven should have deserted this region so early I do not know. Where the raven is still found, the conditions are no better than here, as we have large areas of wild uninhabited land in this region—they ought to be able to exist here as well as where they are now found in greater numbers.

American Crow
Corvus brachyrynchos

(110.) Summer resident. Breeds.

During mild winters a crow or two sometimes stays about, but during ordinary severe winters none are seen, as their food supply is gone—so it could not be called a resident. Arrives March 1, 1893; February 23, 1895; February 19, 1899; February 26, 1901; February 28, 1902; February 14, 1904; and are soon common thereafter.

At the time of their arrival, and for sometime afterwards, the mountains are covered with snow. The fields and meadows in the valleys and lowlands are more or less bare—it is here that they look for food at first. They band together in flocks in the fall. Very few are seen after November 1.

It builds its nest in April and May: May 6, 1888, 5 eggs; April 6, 1889, 4 eggs; May 9, 1909, 5 eggs; April 14, 4 eggs; April 22, 3 eggs; April 24, 5 eggs; April 26, 2 sets of 4 eggs; and May 13, 5 eggs. Eggs in all cases were fresh, and incubation had just begun.

Nests are built 30 to 50 feet from the ground in most any kind of tree. Nests are well built, well cupped, and warmly lined—usually with grapevine, bark, and coarse grass. Eggs are 3 to 5. One nest that I found contained a runt egg no larger that a jay's.

The crow is a hardy bird. No doubt it would be a permanent resident the year round, if it could find sufficient food during the severe weather.

They are noisy and quarrelsome. When a crow discovers an owl it at once sets up an excited cawing that quickly brings all the crows in the vicinity. The owl is soon surrounded by a noisy and ever-increasing mob that dives at him, and makes a great hubbub at every move made by the owl. If it is a Great Horned that the crows are mobbing, they seem to raise an extra amount of noise.

Hawks and eagles also come in for a mobbing at times. When the mob of crows gets too noisy and numerous, they shake them off by rising and taking a long flight. I have seen crows swoop at ducks and grebes on the water. Once when I was duck hunting at Grass Flats, I saw a flock of crows mobbing something on the ground about some old logs. Upon investigating I found the cause to be a Red Fox that the crows had discovered prowling about. Mr. Fox, when he saw me, lost no time in going away from there.

In 1895, an albino crow was hatched in the vicinity of Meade Island. It hung about until August 3, when a friend of mine, Harry Jackson, who lives down that way, shot it, and gave it to me. It was very light, slate colors, which made it appear pure white at a distance.

No bird is better known to everyone than the crow. In spite of constant persecution, they seem to hold their own pretty well—as they are shy, wary, and not easily taken.

Measurements:

Female, 17 3/4–36–11 3/4–6 3/4

BLACKBIRDS—ORIOLES—Etc.

Eleven species of this family have been found in western Pennsylvania. All of these are more or less common, except the Yellow-headed Blackbird, which only occurs as a very rare straggler from the west. Of these 11, eight occur in Warren County and the Orchard Oriole is apt to occur anytime. Of the 8 occurring here I have found 7 nesting. All of the birds are found about cleared lands, farming, open country, and town. None are forest birds.

Some of this group stays near water pretty much. Some gather in large flocks in the fall.

The Blackbirds are classed as game birds, but are not hunted to any extent here. It is no particular sport, and there is but little flesh on one.

Starling | European Starling
Sturnus vulgaris

(111.) This bird first appeared here in the spring of 1923. April 15, 1923 while taking a little stroll with S.S. Dickey—along the river on the South Side and just below the brewery—we saw a pair of Starlings in the field. They were with or among a flock of Robins. They were first noticed by Mr. Dickey, who is familiar with the bird.

By May 10, 4 or 5 pairs were around. I discovered that a pair had a nest in an old Flicker's hole in a chestnut tree on the river bank—on the South Side, in front of the Arird and Conarro properties. I found this nest by detecting the old birds feeding the young.

May 27, the young left the nest. On June 18, I climbed up, as I had noticed the old bird about, and I thought they had a second set of eggs. On cutting in with a small axe, I was surprised to find that the second laying had already hatched. I found 4 young and 1 addled egg. The bird had evidently lost no time laying a second set.

In 1924, I first noticed the presence of the Starling here on March 9, when I saw 3. A few were about all summer. Several pairs nested with the sparrows under the eaves of the W.A. Works card shop. A pair also nested in a Flicker's nest in a sycamore at the head of Highhouse's Eddy. There seemed to be more birds about than during 1923.

During the 1925 season I watched Starlings a great deal. Along the river and woods at the sand pits, I found 6 pairs nesting. All were well up in natural cavities and old Flicker holes in big trees. Two of these nests were opened up by Harry Granquist and myself in late April. In each case we found a fresh set of 5 eggs. I think the birds have increased considerably since last year.

So far I don't see that they are doing any damage or bothering our native birds—maybe they aren't plentiful enough yet. During the winter of 1926–27, I shot a pair (first I had taken) and mounted them.

They were common the summer of 1927—by 1932 they are plentiful with a number wintering.

Measurements:

April 1, 1927, male, 8 1/2–15 1/4–5–3

April 1, 1927, female, 8 1/2–15–4 7/8–3

Bobolink
Dolichonyx oryzivorus

(112.) Summer resident. Breeds.

Arrives: April 29, 1893; May 3, 1899; May 6, 1901; and May 4, 1904.

The males arrives first; the females arrive a few days later. They are not at all plentiful, but a few pairs are always found in suitable meadows, both in the valleys and on the hills. It nests the first of June: June 11, 5 eggs; May 31, 1908, 2 nests, 5 eggs each; June 2, 1912, 6 eggs; May 25, 1913, 6 eggs; May 27, 1914, 3 nests, 5 eggs + 1 Cowbird, 5 eggs, and 4 eggs; and June 1, 1916, 6 eggs—eggs fresh in all cases.

Nests are well concealed and, as a rule, difficult to find. The female invariably runs off through the grass, and flushes away from the nest. To my way of thinking the male is a fine songster, and I never tire of listening to him.

In August and September the Bobolink is found in flocks, has changed his dress, and does not sing—only utters a single note. It then hardly seems like the same bird. It is not common enough here to do any particular damage.

I have tried in several ways to find nests, and I have had as much success on a windy day as on any other day. By walking briskly against a good wind, I have found that the birds flush close and almost right off the nests, evidently not hearing the approach in time to slip away.

1930 and 1931, not a Bobolink to be seen. In 1932, I saw 4 or 5 between Corry and Erie on my Erie trips. 1933, only an occasional one seen this season.

1944, the Bobolink is still very scarce in this vicinity. Why it should suddenly become so scarce here is as much of a mystery as the disappearance of the Prairie Horned Lark.

1946, a few Bobolinks were here this summer. I saw 1 flock of 15 on May 11. It is the first time since they disappeared in 1929 that they have been here in any number.

Measurements:

Adult male, 7 1/2–13 1/4–4–3 1/2

Cowbird | Brown-headed Cowbird
Molothrus ater

(113.) Summer resident. Breeds.

Arrives: April 10, 1889; April 5, 1901; April 17, 1902; April 9, 1904; and April 13, 1907.

It is quite common in all the open country. It is found about fields, pastures, and marshes—in pairs and small parties of 5 to 10. I never saw over 25 in one flock. It never strays far into deep woods. In the fall it flocks with other blackbirds. I have seen it several times in mid-winter with flocks of English Sparrows: January 14, 1889; January 1, 1901; and December 26, 1904.

The following is a list of the birds that I have found to be victims of the Cowbirds. Eggs of the Cowbird have been found personally in nests of each of the following species listed: Phoebe, Least Flycatcher, Bobolink, American Goldfinch, Pine Siskin, English Sparrow, Vesper Sparrow, Chip Sparrow, Field Sparrow, Song Sparrow, Indigo Finch, Red-eyed Vireo, Blue-headed Vireo, Yellow Warbler, Chestnut-sided Warbler, Ovenbird, Yellow-throated Blue Warbler, Hooded Warbler, Redstart, Wilson's Thrush, Bluebird, and Magnolia Warbler—22 species in all.

Measurements:

Male, 7 3/4–13 1/2–4 1/4–3 1/4

Female, 7–12–3 3/4–2 3/4

Red-winged Blackbird
Agelaius pheniceus

(114.) Summer resident. Breeds.

Arrives: March 20, 1890; March 25, 1892; March 5, 1894; March 14, 1901; and March 4, 1902. Departs in October, but I have seen it here as late as November 3, 1890, and November 28, 1900.

Being one of our early arrivals, their well known "mock-ta-lee" is a welcome sound long before the snow is gone for good. It is common along the river valley and larger streams. It is occasionally found about wet swampy places back in the hills.

It nests in rushes and willows—eggs 4. It collects in flocks in August and September with other blackbirds. I have seen flocks of 4 or 5 hundred blackbirds in the fall—a large percentage of which were Red-wings.

It nests the last week of May and the first week of June—May 27, 1927, 2 nests, 4 eggs each.

On May 17, 1941, I visited a swamp nearby where a few always breed, and here I found 8 nests in a very short time. They were from 4 to 12 feet up in thick brush. Four nests were finished and ready for eggs, and 4 nests held 4 eggs each.

The season of 1943, I visited this swamp again on May 20, and I found 10 nests ranging from 1 to 8 feet above the ground and water—3 nests just finished; 5 nests with eggs, 3 with 3 eggs, and 2 with 2 eggs; and 2 nests—one with 4 young, and the other with 3 young and 1 egg just hatching.

Meadow Lark | Eastern Meadowlark
Sturnella magna

(115.) Summer resident. Breeds.

Arrives early: March 26, 1892; March 24, 1893; March 12, 1894; March 23, 1899; March 19, 1901; and March 22, 1907—departs in October. I have noted it here twice in mid-winter: February 7, 1901, saw 1, and December 25, 1901, saw 3.

It is found in small parties at first, but soon pairs off for the nesting season—common anywhere in meadows and pastures. It flocks together in autumn and fall, and is rather shy and difficult to approach. It nests the last of May and early in June—eggs 4 or 5.

A peculiar Meadow Lark in my collection was shot by George Warner near Garland. This bird has a very light faded-out appearance, the wings being almost white.

May 30, 1909, nest with 5 eggs; December 26, 1927, saw 2; and May 22, 1929, 5 eggs, fresh.

Measurements:

Male, 9 3/4–15 3/4–5–3 1/8

Female, 9 3/4–15 1/4–4 1/2–4

Baltimore Oriole
Icterus galbula

(116.) Summer resident. Breeds.

Arrives: May 1, 1890; May 2, 1892; May 3, 1900; May 5, 1904; and May 11, 1907.

The males arrive a few days in advance of the females. It is found about shade trees and parks, in the country about small groves, about farm houses, shade trees along roads, and also in sycamores along the river.

It nests about the first of June: May 31, 1911, 5 eggs, fresh, and June 7, five eggs, fresh.

The nests are usually built rather high—30 to 50 feet up, but I have seen nests only 15 feet from the ground. Eggs are usually 5, sometimes only 4.

It departs early, being gone by the first of September. It is one of our most beautiful birds, and it is a fine songster. It is quite well known and seldom molested.

Rusty Grackle | Rusty Blackbird

Euphagus carolinus

(117.) Irregular migrant, spring and fall.

In the spring I have found this species to be very irregular in its appearance here. I have met it as early as March 28, 1888; March 28, 1904; and as late as April 30, 1890—on which date I saw 3 or 4.

It is found along the river and about ponds and swamps. It is met with singly, in pairs, and rarely in parties of 4 to 8.

If we happen to have high water in April, a few Rusties can be found about the overflows. If the water stays at a low stage, the Rusties are usually very scarce. In the fall I occasionally meet with it along the river. I have seen it in fall as late as November 8, 1890, and November 9, 1905.

Measurements:

Adult male, 9 1/4–15–4 1/2–3 1/2

Adult female, 8 1/2–13 1/2–4 3/8–3 3/8

Bronzed Grackle | Common Grackle

Quiscalus quiscula aneus

(118.) Summer resident. Breeds.

Arrives: March 20, 1890; March 12, 1894; March 7, 1899; March 28, 1901; and March 20, 1904. I have seen it here as late as November 1, 1903, and November 26, 1917.

It nests about the middle of May, usually in evergreens about town, in cemeteries, and in small pine groves. It also frequently nests in deciduous trees. I once found a nest at the mouth of the Conewango Creek. It was only 6 feet up in a willow, but this latter nest was very unusual. It usually nests in small colonies, quite high up in the trees. In the fall it gathers in large flocks, and is quite destructive to grain and gardens.

Eggs are 4 to 5: May 13, 1911, 5 eggs; June 2, 1929, 4 eggs, advanced incubation; and May 18, 1930, 2 nests with 4 eggs each, incubation 4 or 5 days.

Measurements:

Adult male, 12–17 3/4–5 1/2–5 3/4

Adult female, 10 3/8–16–5–4 5/8

SPARROWS—FINCHES—Etc.

This is the largest family of North American birds, and is represented by over 30 species in Pennsylvania. In the vicinity of Warren, I have known 29 to occur, and I have found 13 nesting. Although this is the largest North American family, it is not represented in Pennsylvania or in this vicinity by the greatest number of species. The warblers have that honor.

Of the sparrows and finches, a number are plainly colored, but some are highly colored and are beautiful birds. Almost all have pleasing songs, and some are very fine songsters.

Birds of this family usually travel in flocks when migrating, sometimes in large flocks. Species of this family are found in all sorts of country and situations.

They are largely seed eaters and, for this reason, different species can be looked for in winter. As a rule they are all rather tame and easily approached. New additions to this family are likely to be met with here at any time.

Evening Grosbeak
Coccothraustes vespertina

(119.) Straggler.

During the winters of 1889 and 1890, this species straggled east, and was a visitor in different parts of the state. At that time I was rather new at the bird business, and I was not watching closely for rarities; consequently, I did not see it. One was shot here though, and it was brought to Greenlund to be mounted. *(Greenlund was a taxidermist in Warren.)*

Dr. Warren, then State Zoologist, was here. He saw and identified the bird. The party who shot it said there were others. I have a pair of these birds taken down near Williamsport, Pennsylvania, on March 18, 1890, and April 11, 1890.

On February 27, 1910, a friend stopped while on his way to work, and described to me some birds that he had seen around the vicinity of his home for several days. I couldn't figure out what they were, so I went up. I was surprised to find a little flock of Evening Grosbeaks—6 in number, 4 males and 2 females.

They were very tame, and I walked up to within 20 feet. I watched them for some time. These birds were so tame that they attracted considerable attention. They stayed right in the one vicinity until March 17, and people learned a considerable amount about them. They fed about on bare places on lawns, and budded on maple trees. They also frequently visited some apple trees and fed on apples, which had frozen on the trees.

In March, 1942, a small flock of Grosbeaks were about town as late as March 27. In late January, 1944, several flocks were reported—I am certain of only 1 flock. This was a small flock of Evenings—other flocks may not have been Evenings.

On the late date of May 12, 1946, five Evening Grosbeaks were on and about our lawn and trees for several hours—2 males and 3 females. On May 13, a pair was also here. I did not see or hear of any the previous winter, and these seemed to be around very late for winter visitors.

Late in February, 1947, a flock of 40 or 50 were seen on the East Side in Warren. They were only around for a few days.

Pine Grosbeak
Pinicola enucleator

(120.) Rare winter visitor.

Two flights of Pine Grosbeak have occurred here during my time. The first was during the winter of 1903-04. Up to this time, I had never met this species here at all.

On November 26, 1903, (Thanksgiving Day) while hunting grouse in Ott Run hollow, I heard a bird that was new to me. It flew before I got near enough for a shot, but I saw it and suspected its identity. I was up several times later, but I did not see or hear it again.

On Christmas morning, 1903, I went up through the Ott Run side, then across the mountain, and down on the Morrison Run side. While going along on the Morrison side, I heard the same note. I stopped, and through the falling snow, I saw 3 birds flying. As they passed I shot, and secured a female Pine Grosbeak—the first I had ever taken.

Although I was out a few times during January and February, I saw no more. Early in January, 1904, a friend came upon 6 birds near here (*Warren County).* He got up very close, and he described them perfectly. February 11, 1904, a friend of mine, while hunting wildcats, came upon a flock of 12. He shot 3 (1 male, 2 females), which he sent to me. The male was not very red.

Parties, who were in the woods a great deal—lumbering or about oil leases—saw a little flock occasionally. The 1903-04 flight was small and scattered. I got little information about it.

The flight of the winter of 1906-07 was a good flight. I saw considerable of the birds and their habits, and I secured some fine specimens.

The first I saw or heard of them again was on Thanksgiving Day, November 29. *(The year uncertain, somewhere between 1908 and 1918.)* I was hunting hares near the Hood Run, a branch of Brown Run, when I heard the call of a grosbeak. Following up, I secured a male off the top of a tall, dead hemlock. I saw one more bird during the day. From then on until December 21, I saw or heard several birds on every trip.

December 21, in the big timber on the ridge between Morrison and Picnic Runs, I saw single ones flying and whistling every little while. It occurred so often that I looked about a little more. Soon I found several ash trees, on which they were feeding.

I found fully 25 birds there, but all were restless and noisy. It was a dark day, the trees tall, and I could not see the colors of the birds. I shot 3, but all were females. This was the first real flock I have seen.

December 26, 27, and 30, I was out a couple of hours each day, but on each occasion I saw only a few flying and calling. I could not find a flock.

January 5, I was out all afternoon, but failed to locate a flock and only saw 7 altogether—these all flying. On the afternoon of January 11, it was quiet outdoors. The sun shone clear and bright. I spent the afternoon in the Morrison Run and Picnic Run region. I found one flock of 8, budding in a large maple. Two of the 8 were beautiful red males, and I secured both.

On January 23, while fox hunting, I found the feeding ground that I had been looking for all winter. It was a grove of large ash trees at the base of a steep and heavily timbered mountain. Fully 75 birds were scattered about in the trees feeding, and the snow was covered with their cuttings. It was a very cold day, blowing a fine snow through the trees, so that I could tell nothing about their colors. I watched them for awhile, and then I left.

The next morning, January 24, was the coldest of the winter. At 8:00 o'clock it was still 20 degrees below zero on my porch. It was bitter cold, but as it promised to be a quiet, clear day, I started for the feeding grounds.

An impenetrable fog hung along the river, and everything was loaded with heavy frost. After an hour-and-a-half of hard walking through the deep snow and intense cold, I arrived at the place.

The trees were covered with frost, and there were frequently loud pistol-like reports from the frozen timber. It was colder up there in the woods than in town, but the air was not loaded with the river fog, so I really did not feel the cold as much as I did at first along the river.

I spent the entire morning at this place. I was compelled to move around considerably, and several times I took short runs, off a ways and back, to keep warm. In spite of the discomfort, I felt amply repaid for my cold trip. When I arrived, there must have been fully 100 birds scattered about feeding in the trees.

As the sun was out by that time, I could easily see the red males. I secured several beautiful specimens without trouble. All the time that I was there, there were always a number of birds feeding, although they were continually coming and going.

Those that were feeding sat very quiet, only moving a little to reach more seed. Those not feeding were noisy, restless, and continually calling. Flocks were coming and going all the time.

Some flocks would come around the mountain side, while others would plunge straight down from the mountain top. Before starting to feed, the flocks would almost always first alight in some big hemlock or hardwood and in a few minutes drop into the ash trees.

On the tall, dead hemlocks and large, living ones, little flocks would alight—every now and then, one would sing. I couldn't tell whether or not just the red males sang, but the song was a very nice one. About 1 out of 12 or 15 was a beautiful red male.

While visiting with these grosbeaks, I saw some large flocks of American and White-winged Crossbills. These always alighted in the hemlocks, and they fed on the little cones. They did not feed on the ash with the grosbeaks.

I was surprised to find a little bunch of 5 or 6 Crimson Finches feeding in the ash with the grosbeaks. I did not know that any of the finches were about.

I would liked to have spent the day with them, as I will probably never have another chance such as this, at least in this region, but it was so cold that when I finally did leave, I had to plough along at top speed for a long ways before the blood got to circulating right—and then I felt half frozen when I did reach home.

The last day on which I saw any was February 21, on this day I saw 9—one fine male and the rest female or immature ones. This flock was budding on a maple.

I saw no more grosbeaks until December 11, 1918, when in a slashing near Ott Run; I came upon 2 females in some tall brush. I approached to within 10 feet. I did not see these birds again, nor did I see another that winter.

May 25, 1923, I was greatly surprised to see a fine adult pair in Ott Run hollow. They were feeding on the buds of good-sized, second growth poplars. I got up close and watched awhile. They did not move about much, but kept close together—uttering a twittering note much of the time. Later visits to this vicinity failed to discover them again.

Measurements:

Adult male, 8 1/2–13 3/8–4 5/16–3 5/8
Adult male, 8 1/2–13 1/4–4 1/4–3 1/2
Adult male, 8 3/4–13 3/4–4 1/2–3 5/8
Adult male, 8 1/8–13 1/4–4 1/4–3 1/2
Adult male, 8 9/16–13 3/8–4 1/2–3 5/8
Adult female, 8 3/4–13 1/4–4 1/4–3 1/2
Adult female, 8 1/4–13–4 1/4–3 1/2
Adult female, 8 3/4–13 1/4–4 1/4–3 1/2
Adult female, 8 3/8–13 7/8–4 1/2–3 5/8

Crimson Finch | Purple Finch
Carpodacus purpureus

(121.) Summer resident. Breeds.

Arrives: March 23, 1889; April 3, 1901; April 14, 1902; March 18, 1903; and March 26, 1904. Usually all are gone by November: November 1, 1890; November 8, 1903; and November 1, 1905.

It nests in May—in evergreens about town, in small groves, and in cemeteries. I never knew it to nest in the woods. A few pairs nest about or near town annually. The nests that I found were located by watching the females, and all nests were high—40 to 60 feet up, near the top of evergreens.

During the migrations, especially in the spring, the Crimson Finch is often common in flocks about town and in the woods, but it can be irregular—both in its appearances and in numbers. Some seasons it is quite scarce, others it is quite common. I have seen it in winter, but not often—January 1, 1906, and January 24, 1907.

It has a fine song. The song often attracts the attention of people who do not know the name of the singer.

May 25, 1927, I found a nest 20 feet up in the top of a thick, pointed hemlock in the swamp above the Morrison Run reservoir. It was the first nest I ever found in the woods. It held 5 eggs. June 4, 1943, I found a nest in a spruce at Woodcrest, 4 eggs.

Measurements:

Female, 6–10 1/8–3 1/8–2 1/4

American Crossbill | Red Crossbill
Loxia curvirostra

(122.) Winter visitor and irregular migrant.

During the winter of 1887-88, when I was just getting interested in birds, there was a very large flight of crossbills. In the hemlock woods they fairly swarmed. I have not seen such a flight since.

Some winters quite a few are about and again they are scarce—being very irregular in their occurrence. During the winter of 1904-05, there was quite a flight. During the winter of 1906-07, there was also a large flight.

Crossbills are frequently seen or heard in summer. I haven no doubt that they nest here sometimes. When camping and trouting about the headwaters of the Tionesta Creek, in June and July, summers of 1891-92-93, I saw little flocks of 4 to 6 almost every day. At that time they undoubtedly were nesting in the big woods that covered that region.

September 14, 1891, at Grass Flats, I shot a mottled red and green one from a flock of a dozen. Again at Grass Flats on May 30, 1905, I saw a flock of a dozen—all of which were more or less mottled in plumage.

Crossbills are very restless birds. They are continually moving about. When flying they have a loud chipping note, which is also frequently given when feeding or resting. The males have a really fine song, which they sometimes pour forth from the top of some tall tree. In the winter they feed here on the seeds of the small cones of hemlocks.

March 3, 1932, I found a flock of 50 crossbills and siskins in Ott Run hollow—first crossbills I have seen for several years.

January, 1944, since the above date I have not seen a living crossbill here—another bird, once more or less common in season, that has disappeared from this region.

Lunch Camp with shanty is at 4 Mile, in the Spring, May 25, 1924. Harry Granquist may be seen just to the right of the camp structure.

White-winged Crossbill
Loxia leucoptera

(123.) Winter visitor and irregular migrant.

December, 12, 1904, I shot 2 White-wings from a flock of Americans. On December 26, I got a female. There was a good flight of Americans, but these were the only White-wings that I saw to identify.

The winter of 1906-07 was a great winter for northern visitors. Not only did the Pine Grosbeak appear in numbers, but there was also a very large flight of White-winged Crossbills—the only real flight that has appeared in my time.

They first appeared in late October, and were common by November 15. During December and January they were abundant. Only small flocks were seen at first, but by the middle of December many large flocks were to be found. One flock that I saw on the Four Mile must have contained over 300 birds.

Late in February they became scarcer, and I often heard flocks flying over town on their way back north. My latest winter *(1906-07)* date is March 8; no doubt I could have seen it later, if I could have been in the field every day.

Like the Americans they were restless and noisy. The males were really good songsters. A few Americans were mixed in with the flocks of White-wings. They seemed to feed entirely on the small cones of the hemlocks, though they seemed to alight more often in deciduous trees than the Americans did.

Toward the last of their stay they become rather quiet, and were then often seen on bare places in the snow, on the ground under the hemlocks and on sunny side hills. They would hop about quietly, feeding on the little cones scattered about. When they were on the ground I could easily approach within 10 or 12 feet, as they were very tame and unsuspicious.

During the winter of 1922-23, a few flocks of crossbills were around. With them were a very few White-wings. March 11, 1923, over in the Four Mile region, I walked up to 4 females feeding on a spot bare of snow. I got within a few feet. They were the last seen that season.

Measurements:

Adult male, 6–10 1/4–3 3/8–2 5/16

Adult female, 5 7/8–9 7/8–3 1/4–2 1/4

Immature female, 6–10 3/8–3 7/16–2 3/8

Adult male, 6 1/8–10 1/8–3 3/4–2 1/4

Immature male, 5 13/16–10–3 1/4–2 5/16

Redpoll | Common Redpoll
Acanthis linaria / Carduelis flammea

(124.) Winter visitor. Rare.

December 17, 1887, the year of the great crossbill flight, I secured a pair of Redpolls from a flock of 15 or 20 in an old ragweed field. These were the only ones seen that winter.

Late in the winter of 1908-09, a few small flocks of Redpolls put in an appearance. They seemed to hang about and feed in old grassy and weedy fields. Often I found them in company with Tree Sparrows. The last date on which I saw any Redpolls was April 9. They were very tame and allowed a close approach.

During the winter of 1911-12, Redpolls again appeared. I first saw them in early December, and almost every day I was out I saw a few. On several occasions I saw flocks of 40 to 50. I saw several birds as late as April 25.

During the winter of 1946-47, a small flight appeared here. The first I saw of it was February 7, 1947, when I saw one with a flock of Tree Sparrows. I saw it about in pairs and flocks up to March 25, on which date I saw 5. The largest flock I saw was on February 23, on which date I saw fully 25 in one flock.

Measurements:
Male, 5–8 1/4–2 3/4–2 1/4
Female, 5 1/8–8 1/4–2 3/4–2 1/2
Male, 4 7/8–8 3/4–3–2 3/8
Female, 4 3/4–8 1/2–2 7/8–2 1/2

American Goldfinch
Astragalinus tristis / Carduelis tristis

(125.) Summer resident. Breeds.

During summer the Goldfinch is common anywhere about groves, old fields, and roadsides—in fact, almost anywhere except in heavy timber. In winter it is sometimes seen in the woods and about old fields. Some winters, flocks are about all season, other winters it is almost, if not entirely, absent. It does not come far from being a resident.

It nests about the first of August: August 5, 1912, 6 eggs, fresh, and August 15, 1912, 5 eggs, fresh. It usually nests in a maple, well out near the end of a limb, at a height of 8 to 50 feet. Nests here are built entirely of fine vegetable fibers, and are neat and very pretty. It nests commonly in shade trees in town and along roadsides, as well as in pastures and groves, but not in woods.

The goldfinch is a pretty bird and fine songster. It is well known as "Yellow-bird" and "Wild Canary."

Measurements:
Female, 4 5/8–8 1/2–2 3/4–2

Pine Siskin
Spinus pinus / Carduelis pinus

(126.) Summer resident. Breeds.

Winter visitor in irregular numbers. Not a winter passes but a few flocks are about, and large flights occur at irregular intervals.

During the winter of 1887-88, when the crossbills were so plentiful, we also had a very large flight of siskins. They were abundant in large flocks everywhere in the mountains.

During the winter of 1891-92, a very large flight came this way. Previous to the year 1912, I had sometimes, when trout fishing in summer, seen a little bunch of siskins. Once in April, while fishing in virgin timber, I saw a siskin on the ground gathering nesting material. I dropped my fishing pole and tried to follow her, but I lost her in the hemlocks. Although I moved about and watched for over an hour, I never saw the bird again. These instances caused me to think that the siskin was a rare breeder some seasons.

When large flights occur, flocks of 200 are not uncommon. Pine Siskins seem to feed on the small hemlock cones, but sometimes they are seen budding in a deciduous tree. They are noisy and restless. Their flight and note resemble the goldfinch very much.

During the winter of 1911-12, they were very plentiful. Many large flocks of upward to 200 birds were seen—besides numerous small flocks. They first appeared in mid-November and were soon abundant. About the first of April I began to see a good many near town.

By the middle of April they were still common near town, wherever there were evergreens in cemeteries, groves, or patches of woods. April 14, I was surprised to discover a pair building in a pine in the little grove near Yaegle's barn. I then put all my spare time into visits to the nearby evergreens. I found plenty of birds. Judging by their actions, most of them mated.

At this time they were feeding on the new buds of maples, as well as on the conifers. They were very noisy and restless. Their sharp notes, very much like a goldfinch's, could be heard everywhere. The males were in full song and singing constantly.

I made one trip to the woods. Although there were birds about, I had no luck with nests. I think that in the heavy timber they probably nested high.

If I had had the time, I could, no doubt, have found a great many nests. As it was I had the pleasure of examining 10 nests.

Of the 10 nests located, I found 5 in the cemetery one morning before 10 o'clock. This first nest, found April 14, was in a White Pine 25 feet from the ground, and 10 feet out on a horizontal limb. This nest was entirely finished, but for some reason no eggs were ever laid.

Nest number 2 was 25 feet up in a hemlock, and 3 feet out on a horizontal limb. I found this nest on April 16, at which time it was just nicely started. I visited this nest frequently to watch building operations. The female did all the work, with the male frequently following her back and forth on her trips after nesting material.

The birds were constantly calling. The female often called while at the nest. The male was continually singing. On April 29, the female began to incubate a set of 3 eggs.

Nest number 3 was also 25 feet up in a hemlock, and 7 feet out near the end of a horizontal limb. This nest was completed on April 21. On April 30, I found the female sitting on 3 eggs.

Nest number 4 was a surprise. I was passing the site of a farmhouse that had burned the previous fall, when I heard a Siskin singing in the trees along the road. Just inside the gate there stood two little Yellow Pines, so small I would never have looked in them, if the male had not been singing.

In the smaller of the two little pines, I at once saw the female sitting on her nest—only 6 feet up, and 4 feet out on a limb. It was a very pretty nest, and it held 3 well marked eggs of the siskin and 1 of the Cowbird—thus adding the siskin to my list of the Cowbird's victims. This was on April 28 *(1912).*

Nest number 5 was found on April 28. It was 30 feet up. This nest was way out near the end of a long, drooping limb of a thick spruce. The female was sitting, but as it was in the cemetery I had no way of reaching it without injuring the tree, so I passed it by

Nest number 6 was found in a spruce in the cemetery on April 28. It was 8 feet up, and 8 feet out on a limb. The nest was entirely finished. Strange to say—the female lay dead amongst some thick twigs within 2 inches of the nest. There was no mark upon her to show the cause of death.

Nest number 7, found on April 28, was 10 feet up in a hemlock, and 5 feet out. This nest contained 3 young several days old. This pair must have begun house keeping quite early.

Nest number 8, also found on April 28, was 10 feet up and 4 feet out on a limb of a small, thick spruce. It held 2 eggs, badly incubated.

Nest number 9, May 2, was in a White Pine 20 feet up and 15 feet out. It held 3 young, just hatched.

Nest number 10 was found on May 3. It was in a White Pine, 15 feet up and 15 feet out on the limb. The female was busy feeding 3 young, who were just hatched.

The nests were pretty, well built, and about the size of a goldfinch's nest. They were solidly built of fine twigs of conifers, and fine strips and shreds of vegetable material. They were warmly lined with hairs and fine grass. Three seemed to be the full set.

After the young were hatched, the old birds became rather quiet. They remained so the rest of the summer. Occasionally I would hear a male sing a little or hear a little bunch flying. Frequently during the summer I came upon little groups feeding on the ground. At such times I found them to be very tame and unsuspicious, allowing me to approach within a few feet before they took flight.

During the winter of 1924-25, the siskins were quite plentiful in flocks. A large number nested here. This time they nested early, probably due to the weather being mild throughout March. On April 1, I accidentally saw a nest, 15 feet up a hemlock and 8 feet out on a limb. This nest held 2 young and 1 egg just hatching. Next day I looked about in the cemetery *(Oakland)*, and I found a nest low in a spruce. It held 3 eggs apparently far gone.

April 6, 1925, I found a nest with 3 young in Ott Run, 25 feet up in a hemlock. October 8, 1943, I saw a lone siskin, first siskin I have seen in a number of years. May 14, 1947, I was much surprised to find 6 or 8 siskins feeding about the tips of limbs on blossoms.

English Sparrow | House Sparrow
Passer domesticus

(127.) Resident. Breeds.

Abundant about town, common in the country about farm buildings, it seems to be found anywhere there are humans, except in the woods. It begins nesting in March, and keeps it up until late into the fall. It nests in all sorts of crevices and nooks about buildings and in bird houses. It often builds a large covered nest in trees and in vines on buildings—the entrance to the nest being on one side. Eggs are 4 or 5.

They are noisy and quarrelsome among themselves, but to tell the truth, I don't see where they interfere with our native birds around here. When Martins first came here the sparrows used to fight them, but did not seem to drive the Martins away, as several pairs still come. I do not see any quarreling now.

I have seen a Robin knock them right and left, keeping a whole bunch of sparrows away, while it drank and bathed at a leaky hose connection on a lawn.

It is not unusual to see a sparrow with white feathers in tail or wings. A few years ago a light creamy-white one was about the street in the business section for some time. A couple years ago in the fall I saw a real albino up at Glade Run. I had a friend watch for this bird, as I thought it might offer a chance to make a specimen, but it seemed to disappear somewhere.

I have on several occasions in winter seen a Cowbird with a flock of sparrows—the Cowbird, no doubt, having been reared by the sparrows.

(above) Hickory Street suspension bridge over the Allegheny River.
(below) Allegheny River toward Glade Run, 1898.

Snowflake | Snow Bunting
Plectrophenax nivalis

(128.) Winter visitor.

The Snowflake is very irregular in its occurrence here. Although a common bird in fall and winter along Lake Erie, we seldom see it here unless the weather is very severe. Some winters I do not see a single bird.

During January and February of 1895, there were a good many about. Some flocks numbered 40 to 50 birds. There was also a great many during the winter of 1903-04.

They are a very restless bird and are constantly on the move. When flying they utter a note very much resembling that of the Horned Lark. When the Horned Larks are migrating in numbers in early March, and the weather is cold and stormy, small bunches of Snowflakes are sometimes seen with them.

During January and February, 1936, a few flocks visited this region. On February 18, I saw a flock of about 100. March 4, 1943, I saw 5—the only ones seen that year.

Lapland Longspur
Calcarius lapponicus lapponicus

(129.) Rare visitor in winter.

During February and March of 1912, the weather was cold and stormy, and large flocks of Horned Larks were here. On February 27, in the fields below the brewery, I found a large number of larks. On looking them over, I occasionally saw what seemed to be smaller birds among them. They were quicker in their movements and wilder.

I finally became sure there was some odd bird with the larks, so I got busy and secured a couple. I found I had the Lapland Longspur. I saw it on several occasions early in March, 1912.

In 1913, I watched for the larks, and on March 8 I found larks plentiful. With them were several Longspurs and Snowflakes. March 3, 1914, I found several large flocks. Occurring as it does here, it could be easily overlooked. It may be here more often than I think.

February 18, 1935, I saw 3 Longspurs with a flock of Horned Larks.

Measurements:

February 27, 1912, 5 7/8–10 7/8–3 1/2–2 9/16

Vesper Sparrow
Poocetes gramineus

(130.) Summer resident. Breeds.

Arrives: April 5, 1901; April 9, 1902; and April 12, 1904.

It is rather common anywhere in old fields, pastures, and meadows. It feeds a great deal on plowed ground. When migrating they are often found in flocks and in the company of other sparrows.

It nests in May: May 9, 1908, 4 eggs; May 15, 1913, 4 eggs; May 25, 1914, 4 eggs; and May 7, 1928, 4 eggs. Nests are only partly concealed in the grass—a frequent victim of the Cowbird.

The Vesper Sparrow has a pleasing song.

Measurements:

Male, 5 7/8–9 3/4–3–2 3/4

Female, 6–10 1/8–3 1/8–3

Female, 6–9 3/4–3–3

Savanna Sparrow
Passerculus sandwichensis

(131.) Summer resident. Breeds.

It arrives the first of May—May 3 in 1893.

During the migrations the Savanna is rather common. As a summer resident it is quite well distributed in meadows and fields in valleys, as well as in the mountains.

It nests in late May: May 22, 1908, 5 eggs, fresh; June 5, 1908, 5 eggs, fresh; May 15, 1910, 4 eggs, fresh; May 19, 1912, 4 eggs, fresh; May 24, 1914, 4 eggs, fresh; and May 16, 1927, 4 eggs, incubation advanced. Nests are well concealed and hard to find.

The male spends much time sitting on a bunch of grass or weeds pouring forth his peculiar ditty.

Grasshopper Sparrow
Ammodramus savannarum

(132.) Irregular migrant.

This species may occur more often that I think. Owing to its habits, and the fact that all small sparrows flushed in fields look much alike, I might often overlook it. Only occasionally do I see one, and then I find it first by hearing its weak song, and then following up.

May 31, 1901, while in a grassy meadow, along the river just below town, late in the afternoon, I heard a weak song that was new to me. Going along carefully I found the singer in the short grass along an old road. A light charge of 12 shot procured the first Grasshopper Sparrow I had ever met. Since then I occasionally hear one.

June 9, 1923, one was singing on the big meadows on Sechrist's *(Sechriest's)* Flats. It is possible this one was located for the summer. June 15, 1925, I heard one singing in a meadow along the road near the John Grunder farm.

Nelson's Sparrow | Nelson's Sharp-tailed Sparrow
Passerherbulus nelsoni | Ammodramus nelsoni

(133.) Straggler.

May 27, 1904, the day that gave me my first record for the occurrence of the Dunlin here, also gave me my first—and so far only—record for the Nelson Sparrow in Warren County.

After seeing the Dunlins disappear down the river, I lost no time following up with a gun. Among the places where I looked for them was Honhart's Pond on the flats below town. At the head of this pond a sparrow flushed from the long grass in front of me.

By September, 1900, experience at Erie with the Nelsons led me to think that this was one, judging from its flight and general appearance. So I put in a light charge, followed up, flushed, and shot the bird. Sure enough I found it to be a male Nelson's Sparrow in full spring plumage.

Measurements:

At Erie, Pa., male, 5 1/4–7 3/8–2 1/8–1 7/8

At Erie, Pa., female, 5 1/8–7–2 1/16–1 13/16

White-crowned Sparrow
Zonotrichia leucophrys

(134.) Regular migrant, spring and fall.

Arrives: May 9, 1891; May 7, 1892; May 8, 1901; May 11, 1904; and May 16, 1907.

Its stay in spring is brief, my latest date being May 20, 1903, and June 1, 1907. It arrives again from the north late in September, and I have seen it until well into October.

It is usually not very common. Although on several occasions, after a night of warm southerly rains which brought a number of small migrants, I have seen flocks of fully 50 White-crowns.

Small parties of 8 to 12 are usually seen. It is generally found in company with other sparrows, about brush heaps, fences, and borders of woodlands and slashings. It does not seem to penetrate into the woods as far as the White-throated.

White-throated Sparrow
Zonotrichia albicollis

(135.) Regular migrant, spring and fall.

Arrives: April 27, 1889; May 1, 1890; April 28, 1891; May 5, 1892; and May 6, 1901.

It is common from the day of its first arrival, and it is seen in plentiful numbers for about 2 weeks. It returns again in late September, and it is common during October. I have seen it as late as November 2, 1895, and November 1, 1903.

It is found anywhere in brushy places, and it is often seen in brushy places deep in woodlands. It flocks with other sparrows. This sparrow has been found nesting in Pennsylvania, but up to date I have never met with it in this region in summer.

Measurements:

May 1, 1890, male, 6 7/8–9 1/2–2 7/8–3

May 1, 1890, female, 6 3/4–9–2 3/4–2 3/4

Tree Sparrow | American Tree Sparrow
Spizella monticola | Spizella arborea

(136.) Winter visitor—or rather a winter resident.

It arrives in November, and it is more or less common all winter in flocks about brush, old fields, and edges of woods. It is found well into April: April 11, 1892; April 11, 1894; April 18, 1901; April 20, 1904; and April 25, 1907.

Toward the latter end of its stay, it is found in flocks with Juncos and Song Sparrows.

Chip Sparrow | Chipping Sparrow
Spizella passerina

(137.) Summer resident. Breeds.

Arrives: April 12, 1895; April 18, 1901; April 24, 1902; April 21, 1904; and April 5, 1907. It is common everywhere except in heavy timber. The Chip Sparrow is common in town.

In the fall it gathers with flocks of other sparrows about brush and weed-grown fields. It is a very common breeder in June. Eggs are 3 or 4—in one instance only, 5 eggs. It is a common victim of the Cowbird.

Field Sparrow
Spizella pusilla pusilla

(138.) Summer resident. Breeds.

Arrives: April 15, 1901; April 20, 1902; April 22, 1904; and April 27, 1907. In 1903 I saw it as late as November 1.

It is abundant in the fall in flocks with others of the sparrow tribe. It nests on the ground and in low bushes. Eggs are usually 4—May 23, 1889, 4 eggs; May 23, 1889, 3 eggs; and June 8, 1909, 4 young. It is a frequent victim of the Cowbird.

Junco Sparrow | Dark-eyed Junco
Junco hyemalis

(139.) Summer resident. Breeds.

Sometimes during winter a Junco or two may be met with about barns or sheltered places, but it can hardly be called a resident. During the migrations they are abundant particularly in spring—late March or early April. At times I have seen flocks of 300 to 400 spread out all over an old weedy field.

Quite a few breed. It retires in summer to the mountains. It nests in the barrens and slashings, as well as in the woods. It nests under banks along roads, under and amongst upturned roots, under banks along streams, on mossy fern-covered rocks, in crevices in logs—in fact, most anywhere on the ground where the nest can be partly under cover.

It nests in May and June: June 11, 1910, 4 eggs; May 26, 1911, 4 eggs; June 6, 1911, 4 eggs; June 1, 1912, 4 eggs; June 5, 1915, 4 eggs; and May 24, 1916, 4 eggs—all fresh. I have seen 5 eggs or young in a nest, but 4 is the usual number.

October, the fall of 1921, while going up the Six Mile from Tiona, on my way to the Four Mile, I saw a flock of Junco—I met with a perfect albino. There was no way to secure it, as I did not have my gun.

Song Sparrow
Melospiza melodia

(140.) Summer resident. Breeds.

It arrives early in March. Their pleasant song is soon heard on all sides, being one of the first signs of spring. During the migrations, especially in the fall, it is found in flocks with other of the sparrow tribe.

It is quite hardy and occasionally one is noted during mild winter weather. It is one of the most common birds in summer anywhere, except in heavy woods. It is an abundant breeder in late May, June, and early July. It nests on the ground in low bushes. Eggs are 4 or 5. It is a common victim of the Cowbird.

Measurements:

Male, 5 1/2–8–2 1/8–2 1/2

Female, 5 3/4–8 1/4–2 1/2–2 3/4

Male, 6 1/2–8 1/2–2 1/2–2 7/8

Lincoln's Sparrow
Melospiza lincolni

(141.) Rare visitor during migrations.

I looked for this sparrow for some time before I finally found it. The Lincoln is very easily overlooked, owing to its habits and resemblance to the Song Sparrow, especially when concealed in the brush and thickets that it haunts.

May 16, 1908, I saw and positively identified, but did not secure a Lincoln. May 14, 1909, at the same place, I saw and secured a specimen. May 12, 1916, at this same place again, I saw a specimen.

I have seen a couple more that I am positive were Lincoln's Sparrows, but I am not absolutely sure, as I could not get a perfectly clear view. The bird undoubtedly occurs more often than is suspected—as it is hard to detect.

May 11, 1928, saw 2 birds, probably a pair. May 14, 1935, saw one.

Measurements:

May 14, 1909, adult male, 5 1/4–7 3/4–2 3/8–2 1/4

Swamp Sparrow
Melospiza georgiana

(142.) Regular migrant. Rare in spring, but common in the fall. Uncommon breeder.

In early October it is sometimes fairly common along the river valley in thickets, reeds, and swampy places—generally in company with Song and other sparrows.

I have never seen it in summer except in the cattails and marsh at the head of the Clarendon Pond on the Tionesta Creek—where a few nest late in May. It no doubt breeds sparingly in a few other suitable swamps.

June 7, 1925, 5 eggs, Clarendon pond.

June 7, 1927, 3 nests, 4 eggs each, Clarendon pond.

May 27, 1927, 8 nests, none with complete sets, Clarendon pond and swamp.

May 23, 1928, 3 eggs, no sets complete, Columbus swamp.

Fox Sparrow
Passerella iliaca

(143.) Regular migrant, spring and fall.

In the spring I have noticed it at different times from March 18, 1893, to April 25, 1892—and May 7, 1909, a very late date. In the fall I have noted it as late as November 5, 1890, and November 8, 1893.

Some seasons it is rather scarce, other seasons it is common. It is found in open woodlands and brushy places, especially thickets containing wild grapevines. It is generally found in company with others of the sparrow tribe. It has a good song.

As of late this sparrow has been scarce and very irregular in its appearance here. In 1944, from March 30 to April 18, I noted quite a few at times.

Measurements:

Male, 7–11–3 1/2–2 3/4

Towhee | Eastern Towhee
Pipilo erythrophthalmus

(144.) Summer resident. Breeds.

Arrives: April 9, 1892; April 14, 1893; April 19, 1901; and March 26, 1904. It is quite common everywhere in brush, barrens, and slashings. I have seen it twice in January.

It nests on the ground amongst brush, on banks and low bushes, and sometimes in thick clumps of hemlock brush. It nests in late May: May 22, 4 eggs; May 26, 4 eggs, 2 sets; May 27, 4 eggs; May 29, 5 eggs; and May 30, 4 eggs—all fresh. These nests were in 1915. Other nests are June 5, 1929, 4 eggs, advanced, and in 1930, all from different nests: May 21, 5 eggs, fresh; May 31, incubation begun; June 1, 5 eggs, incubation advanced.

Measurements:

Female, 7 7/8–10 1/2–3 1/4–3 1/2

Cardinal | Northern Cardinal
Cardinalis cardinalis

(145.) Rare visitor. Breeds.

We are a little too far north for this handsome fellow. He is only seen occasionally. When seen here it is liable to be at any season. I have known them to stay around certain localities for quite a long time.

November 13, 1900, I secured a female that was with a few sparrows and juncos in the brush and willows along the Allegheny River at Cameron's Flats—near Meade Island. July 31, 1904, I heard a Cardinal singing along the river near Meade Island. A farmer told me the bird had been about for a week. April 5, 1906, while duck hunting at Grass Flats I secured a beautiful, adult, female Cardinal.

During the winter of 1912-13, a pair lived about town. The female was killed in January by striking a window. March 3, 1914, I saw a fine male at the head of Highhouse's Eddy. January 18, 1920, a female Cardinal was picked up dead in the deep snow. The weather had been very severe, and the bird appeared to have frozen to death. December 24, 1927, I saw a pair in the brush along the back of Yaegle's barn on the South Side. They were quiet—feeding on weed seeds.

March 11, 1932, I saw an adult male just below town. March 5, 1933, I saw a male Cardinal along the river near the sand pits at the head of Highhouse's Eddy. March 10, 1933, I saw a pair which continued to stick around there, so I kept watch. On May 11, I started a hunt for the nest, as I was certain the birds were nesting. In a short time I found the nest containing 1 egg. It was in a heavy tangle of wild grapevines—about 6 feet up. Two days later, on visiting the nest, I found that something had destroyed the egg or eggs, as fragments of shells were scattered about on the ground.

The birds still remained in the vicinity. On June 8, I found the second nest—5 feet up in a grapevine tangle. It contained 3 eggs. I photographed the outfit. I have long suspected the Cardinal of occasionally nesting here, but this is my first nesting record. A pair nested at Starbrick in early May, 1938, but the eggs were destroyed by some critter. A small party was about the following fall, so I think they tried again and succeeded.

Cardinals have increased considerably in numbers of later years *(1944).* It nests here regularly now. This winter, in January and February, a flock of 15 have been feeding regularly near the house. They are feeding along the Pennsylvania Railroad tracks on grain *(wheat)* that leaks out from the trains hauling past.

Measurements:

Adult male, 8 1/2–11 7/8–3 3/4–4

Rose-breasted Grosbeak

Zamelodia ludoviciana / Pheucticus ludovicianus

(146.) Summer resident. Breeds.

Arrives: May 4, 1889; May 9, 1891; May 6, 1892; May 3, 1899; and May 5, 1901. During migrations it is found anywhere in woodlands, groves, and even orchards. It is rather common at times, and good-sized flocks are sometimes seen.

In the summer it is found in the mountains, in open woodland, second growth, and heavy slashings. It nests in late May and early June: June 2, 1891, 4 eggs; June 9, 1894, 3 eggs; and May 24, 1912, 3 eggs—all fresh.

It nests from 5 to 20 feet up in brush and saplings. Nests are rather loose, bulky, and made of twigs. I have been surprised to find the male sitting on the eggs several times, the female no doubt being off on a visit or a feeding. The Grosbeak is a beautiful bird and a fine songster.

Measurements:

Male, 8, 12 3/4–4 1/4–3

Female, 7 1/2–12 1/4–4–3

Indigo Finch | Indigo Bunting
Passerina cyanea

(147.) Summer resident. Breeds.

Arrives: May 7, 1892; May 7, 1894; May 8, 1901; May 4, 1902; and May 9, 1904. It departs in late September. I have seen it as late as October 3, 1900. It is a rather common bird along the roadways, thickets, edges of woods, and brush lands.

It nests in June: June 5, 3 eggs; June 9, 3 eggs; June 8, 4 eggs; June 13, 4 eggs; and June 11, 4 eggs—all fresh. On June 13, 1909, I found 7 nests—2 held 4 eggs, the others 3 each. It is a common victim of the Cowbird. It nests from 1 to 5 feet up in brush. The Indigo Finch is a fine songster.

Measurements:

Female, 5–8 1/4–2 3/8–2 1/4

TANAGERS

Scarlet Tanager
Pyranga erythromeles | Piranga rubra

(148.) Summer resident. Breeds.

Arrives: May 1, 1890; May 3, 1899; May 8, 1901; and May 10, 1904. During the spring migration this beautiful bird is found everywhere in woodlands. It is also found in groves, orchards, and sometimes in town.

Bad storms and freezes in early May sometimes kill many birds, among them the Scarlet Tanager. During the severe storm and freeze of May, 1917, that almost wiped out the warblers caught in this region, a great many tanagers were found dead. Very seldom was one seen in the woods here the rest of the summer. In early May, 1923, a bad storm occurred that killed many small birds, and the tanager was also hard hit. All the summer birds had not arrived, as this storm occurred early. The damage was not nearly as bad as it was in 1917.

It nests in June: June 16, 1904, 4 eggs; June 19, 1907, 3 eggs; June 8, 1913, 4 eggs; June 10, 1913, 4 eggs; and June 19, 1913, 3 eggs—all fresh. Nests are found from 10 to 60 feet from the ground and generally well out from the trunk on a horizontal limb.

In this region beech and hemlock are preferred as nest trees. Nests are rather flat and loose affairs of fine twigs, and can usually be seen through from the ground. They are not very well fastened, and they are often blown down during heavy windstorms. Blue Jays and Red Squirrels destroy many nests each season.

The Scarlet Tanager is a good songster with a song different than any other bird song found here. It is certainly a beautiful object amid the green foliage.

Measurements:

Male, 6 3/4–11 1/8–3 3/4–3

SWALLOWS

Six species of these graceful and beautiful birds are found in this state and all nest. At Warren all six occur, but up to date only 5 have been found nesting.

Swallows have no particular song—their notes being more of a twitter. They are sociable. They live and travel in flocks and nest in colonies. They are awing most of the time. Much of their time is spent in the vicinity of water. During cool weather they all fly about low over the water, but during warm dry weather they fly high over the surrounding country.

They are very graceful and a welcome addition to any landscape. They are well known to most everyone, but generally there is no distinction made among different swallows. To most they are all just swallows.

Purple Martin
Progne subis

(149.) Summer resident. Breeds.

A few pairs, probably not over 4 or 5, arrive in Warren each spring about the first of May: April 30, 1889; April 21, 1901; and May 7, 1904. They remain throughout the summer.

They used to nest under the old arc lamp shades, but since different arc lamps have been installed, they nest in crevices about buildings. At the State Hospital in North Warren they have several large Martin houses. They always have a nice colony every summer—however they are too scarce to cut much of a figure in the bird world.

Cliff Swallow

Petrochelidon lunifrons | *Petrochelidon pyrrhonota*

(150.) Summer resident. Breeds.

Arrives: May 2, 1892; April 23, 1894; May 3, 1899; May 10, 1901; May 5, 1902; and May 9, 1904. During the migrations, this species, as well as other swallows, is most common along the river. Often after May storms large flocks of swallows of all kind gather along the river, flying about low over the water, especially if the weather has turned colder. If we happen to have high water during migration, swallows are then often plentiful on the overflowed meadows—flying about and feeding.

It nests under the eaves of barns and outbuildings. The nests are made of mud, being entirely different from any other nests found here. Eggs number 3 or 4.

June 20, 1913, at the L.M. Hazeltine farm I saw fully 40 nests under the eaves of a large barn. I noticed a great deal of hay and grass sticking out of the entrance to fully one-quarter of these nests. Getting a ladder, I investigated and found that English Sparrows had taken possession of these nests. They had filled them up with dried grasses and feathers. The nests were filled with eggs and young.

Measurements:

Female, 5 3/4–12–4 3/8–2 1/2

Barn Swallow

Hirundo erythrogaster | *Hirundo rustica*

(151.) Summer resident. Breeds.

Arrives: April 23, 1894; April 19, 1901; April 20, 1902; April 20, 1903; April 24, 1904; and April 30, 1907. During migration it is common in flocks with other swallows. In summer it is found everywhere throughout the farming districts. During wet or cold weather it gathers along the river in flocks with other swallows. It departs with the other swallows in September. It usually nests inside barns, sometimes under the outside eaves. Eggs number 3 or 4.

July 20, 1900, while prowling about the mouth of the Conewango Creek, I saw a perfect albino among a flock of about 50 swallows. I was fortunate enough to shoot the bird, which proved to be a young male Barn Swallow—and a perfect albino.

Measurements:

Male, 4 3/4–10 3/4–4 1/8–2

Tree Swallow
Iridoprocne bicolor | Tachycineta bicolor

(152.) Regular migrant in spring, rare in fall.

The earliest the swallows arrive: April 23, 1893; April 23, 1894; April 15, 1901; April 12, 1904; and April 9, 1914. Several times during snow storms in April, I have found a Tree Swallow in such a state of exhaustion that it could be caught by hand—no doubt many perish by hand.

It is very irregular in numbers, some seasons being quite common, other seasons it is rather scarce. Usually a few are found with the large flocks of swallows that gather along the river during cold or wet weather in May. If we happen to have high water in May, there is certain to be quite a few about the overflowed meadows.

October 13, 1906, I saw a lone Tree Swallow flying about—only two days before we had a heavy 8 inch snowfall. I have seen Tree Swallows here on May 30, 1903, and July 20, 1903. It is possible that they nested nearby, but up to date I have no breeding record. On April 24, 1944, I saw a flock of 25.

Bank Swallow
Riparia riparia

(153.) Summer resident. Breeds.

Arrives rather late: May 12, 1901, and May 14, 1904. It used to be rather common during migrations. Flocks of migrating swallows always contained some of the Banks.

Of late years the Bank Swallow, for some reason, seems to be scarce. A few pairs, but no colonies, used to nest in early June in holes excavated by the birds in the banks of the river, sand pits, and railroad cuts. Few pairs nest here anymore. Eggs number 4, 5, or 6.

Measurements:

Female, 4 3/4–10 3/4–4 1/8–2

Rough-winged Swallow | Northern Rough-winged Swallow
Stelgidopteryx serripennis

(154.) Summer resident. Breeds.

Arrives: April 24, 1893; April 22, 1899; May 2, 1901; May 2, 1902; May 2, 1903; May 7, 1904; and April 30, 1907. It is not at all common, but usually seen in pairs, sometimes in small parties of 4 to 8. While the Rough-wing is not common, it is found as a summer resident all along the river. If a person takes a 5-mile hike along the river, a pair will be met with here and there.

The nests can be located by watching the birds. It nests in holes excavated by birds in banks and sand pits—in the same places used by the Bank Swallow. I have found nests with fresh eggs on dates ranging from May 22 to June 28. Eggs number 4, 5, or 6.

WAXWINGS

Cedar Waxwing
Bombycilla cedrorum

(155.) Summer resident. Breeds.

I have seen the Cedar-bird here several times in winter: February 22, 1908, a flock of 10; January 12, 1912, a flock of 15; and January 16, 1940, a flock of 6. It is quite a common bird, almost always found in flocks or small parties. When awing they fly bunched up and alight in a huddle, often on some dead tree or dead limb.

In July and August it is common along the river, where it sits on wires and trees. It continually flies out over the water to catch insects, which it does in fly-catcher style.

It nests in June: June 17, 5 eggs; June 25, 4 eggs; and June 27, 5 eggs. I have seen a nest containing 4 fresh eggs—as late as August 4 in 1894. Nests are from 6 to 40 feet up in second growth, open woods, orchards, shade trees, and often in town. Nests are quite large and well built.

The Cedar-birds seen here in winter have been looked over very carefully, but the flocks so far have not contained any of the large Bohemians.

June 20, 1928, I found 4 nests all ready for eggs. During the 1941 season this bird nested here in unusual numbers. Four pairs nested right here on our place. All 4 of these nests were high in the oaks and maples.

SHRIKES

Northern Shrike
Lanius borealis / Lanius excubitor

(156.) Winter visitor.

It is occasionally met with in winter along the river valley, on the flats and islands—rarely on the mountains. I have taken it as early as December 19, 1893, and as late as March 14, 1901. Several times I have seen a Northern Shrike flying with a small bird in its bill.

Once at Grass Flats I heard a strange series of notes coming from the brush at the head of my famous Wood Duck swamp. Stealthily approaching, I found the author to be a fine male Northern Shrike. They are usually seen perched on the top limb of a tree, sometimes quite high, and very hawk-like in appearance.

Measurements:

9 3/4–14 1/2–4 1/2–4 1/4

Migrant Shrike | Loggerhead Shrike
Lanius ludovicianus

(157.) Regular migrant, spring and fall.

Arrives: March 28, 1893, and March 21, 1894. In the fall I have noted it as late as December 6, 1900. It is rather scarce and not often met with. Like the Northern, this shrike is also usually perched on some tree or outpost where it has a good view from all around.

This shrike nests regularly at Erie, but up to date I have no record of its nesting here—although I have seen it here in summer. This shrike also has what might be called a song.

Measurements:

Male, 8 1/2–12 1/4–4–3 1/2

VIREOS

Six species of vireos are found in Pennsylvania. Five species occur in Warren County. Four of these five species are more or less common during migrations, and are also common as summer residents. Two of these vireos, the Red-eyed and Warbling, breed regularly in town. The Yellow-throated occasionally breeds in town. The Blue-headed is rarely seen in town, and it only nests in the mountains. They are all good songsters.

Red-eyed Vireo
Vireosylva olivacea | Vireo olivaceus

(158.) Summer resident. Common. Breeds.

Arrives: May 5, 1892; May 3, 1899; May 6, 1901; May 6, 1904; and May 16, 1907. It departs in September with the other hosts of small migrants. My latest fall dates are October 3, 1900, and October 8, 1908. It is one of the most common birds of the woodland in both hill and valley. There are also a few in the shade trees and parks in town *(Warren)*.

It nests in June: June 1, 3 eggs; June 5, 2 sets of 3 each; June 8, 4 eggs; June 20, 3 eggs; June 16, 3 eggs; June 6, 3 eggs; and June 11, 2 sets of 3 eggs. I have never seen but one set of 4, and I have looked into many nests. *(RBS notes show that on June 14, 1925, he found 2 nests of 4 eggs each in the Ott Run area.)* It nests from 4 to 20 feet up—in town, of course, it nests higher. It is a common victim of the Cowbird.

It is a good songster, and one of the few birds heard in the woods on a hot summer day. The Red-eyed suffers severely at times from bad storms in May. The bad storm of May, 1917, which just about wiped out the warblers in this region, also cleaned out the vireos. Hardly a Red-eyed was to be seen or heard the rest of the summer. Other storms that killed many warblers also killed many of the vireos, as well as tanagers.

Measurements:

Male, 5 1/2–10 1/8–3 1/4–2 1/4

Philadelphia Vireo
Vireosylva philadelphica / Vireo philadelphicus

(159.) Irregular migrant.

It is only occasionally met with during migrations. I have noted it several times in late May in the company of other warblers and vireos. Again I have found it late in September with flocks of warblers and vireos. It is a hard bird to identify in the trees, and it probably often escapes detection.

May 19, 1912, I found one in a clump of willows. It stayed close to the ground—appearing very tame and unsuspicious. I approached to within 10 feet and watched it for some time. It was very slow and deliberate in its movements.

It is possible that this species may nest here rarely—once in late May, I saw a vireo gathering nesting stuff in deep woods in the mountains. I got quite close and know it was not a Red-eyed, but it was either a Warbling or a Philadelphia. As I have never found the Warbling in deep woods in the nesting season, I will never believe this bird was anything but a Philadelphia. On trying to follow it up, I lost sight of it and never could find it again.

May 26, 1925, I saw one at Grass Flats.

Warbling Vireo
Vireosylva gilva / Vireo gilvus

(160.) Summer resident, not common. Breeds.

Arrives: May 8, 1891; May 1, 1893; May 3, 1899; May 1, 1903; and May 11, 1907. It is a rather common migrant with the hosts of other small migrants that pass in May. It is not very common as a summer resident.

A few pairs breed in town in the parks and in the large shade trees along the streets. Along the river, where the banks are lined with big trees, a few pairs are found scattered along at intervals. I never saw or heard it in summer in the heavy woods in the mountains.

It nests high—possibly because of its habit of living about such open places—and out so far from the trunk that the nests are hard to find. Once found, it is a difficult matter to get on the limb anywhere near the nest. It nests in June, 4 eggs.

Measurements:
Male, 5 1/16–8 5/8–2 3/8–2 1/8
Female, 5 1/4–8 3/4–2 1/2–2 3/16
Male, 5 3/4–8 3/4–2 3/4–2 1/4

Yellow-throated Vireo
Lanivireo flavifrons / Vireo flavifrons

(161.) Summer resident, rather scarce. Breeds.

Arrives: April 30, 1890; May 8, 1901; May 4, 1902; and May 8, 1904. Only a few are seen during the migrations. As a summer resident an occasional pair is found in town. It is also found about open groves and in open or partly cut over timber in the mountains.

June 11, 1906, I found a nest 60 feet up in a poplar, along the edge of heavy woods at Grass Flats. The nest was beautifully decorated on the outside with lichen—eggs 3, fresh. June 12, 1908, in the grove near the tower on the South Side, I found a nest 20 feet up a large oak—3 eggs, fresh.

At our place in Starbrick in 1941, a pair arrived on April 26. On May 20, I found them building 30 feet up in an oak, but on a small limb close to the trunk. It was a very pretty lichen decorated nest. With the aid of an extension ladder, I photographed the outfit—nest and 3 eggs. June 4, 1942, a pair, probably the same birds, nested here. Again in 1943, they nested at our place in Starbrick—high up in an old, tall maple. In 1945, my pair nested here again this spring—this time 15 feet up in a small maple.

Measurements:
Male, 5 1/8–9 3/8–3–2
Male, 5 1/2–9 1/2–3–2 1/4

Blue-headed Vireo
Lanivireo solitarius / Vireo solitarius

(162.) Summer resident. Breeds.

The Solitary or Blue-headed Vireo is by far the earliest arrival of the vireos, being usually two full weeks ahead of the others, and even ahead of the earliest warblers. It arrives: April 24, 1889; April 29, 1891; April 18, 1901; and May 1, 1904. I have noted it in the fall as late as October 2, 1900.

Almost all the other vireos and warblers, when they first appear, are found along the river valley, where the vegetation is more advanced, and the food is more plentiful. The Blue-headed though is just as likely, or even more likely, to be first heard back in the mountains, deep in heavy woods where it is always most common.

After the migrations are on in earnest, the Blue-headed is quite common, though seldom seen in town. When snow flurries or bad weather occurs during the migrations in May, numbers of warblers and vireos sometimes appear in town about the fruit and shade trees—at such times a Blue-headed can sometimes be seen.

As a summer resident it is quite well distributed in the heavier forests in the mountains where there is plenty of beech and hemlock. In such situations the Blue-headed can be heard singing overhead at most anytime. Its note is like the Red-eyed, but louder, richer, and fuller. Their scolding notes are also deeper and harsher.

It nests in May and early June. I have found a female incubating a set of 4 eggs as early as May 24. Other dates that I have handy in my notebooks are May 27, 1890, 3 eggs, fresh; June 7, 1890, 4 eggs, fresh; June 16, 1907, 4 eggs, fresh; June 2, 1908, 4 eggs, fresh; June 1, 1909, 4 eggs, fresh; June 12, 1910, 3 eggs, fresh; June 3, 1913, 4 eggs, fresh; June 4, 1915, 4 eggs, fresh; and June 9, 1923, 4 eggs, incubation begun.

I have, at different times, come upon females gathering nesting material, and at such times they did not seem to be shy or show fear. I always found it an easy matter to keep the bird in sight until she reached the nest. The male frequently accompanies the female to and fro while nest building. At several nests, where I spent some time on different days watching operations, I found that the male bird helped at times.

They do not nest very high, and I never found one over 25 feet up. I have found several that were only 3 or 4 feet up. Most of the nests that I have found were in hemlocks. Quite frequently a beech is used, and occasionally one builds low in witch hazel or other brush.

Although the nests vary considerably in material and decorations, I never could tell one from a Red-eyed's nest just by its appearance. A nest in a hemlock, though, is certain to be that of a Blue-headed, as I have yet to find any other vireo here nesting in a conifer. Some nests of the Blue-headed are handsomely decorated, for in the deep woods where they are usually found, they have an abundance of lichen, cobwebs, and decorative stuff from which to choose.

The eggs are heavier marked than that of the Red-eyed, although if a number of sets of both species were placed together, I do not believe they could be distinguished with certainty by color and markings. The Blue-headed usually lays 4 eggs, sometimes only 3—with the Red-eyed, 3 is a full set here.

One nest of the Blue-headed that I found was only 4 feet up in a witch hazel in hardwood timber. It was not far from the edge of the woods. In this nest I found 3 eggs of the vireo and 1 of the Cowbird; thereby adding the Blue-headed vireo to the list of the Cowbird's victims in this region. The female I have found to be a close sitter, and if the nest happens to be low she will sometimes allow a person to get within 4 or 5 feet before leaving.

Several times I have found nests in beech saplings and little forked twigs—almost against the trunk. Several years ago I found one way on the end of a long, drooping limb of a big hemlock. It was fully 30 feet from the trunk of the tree and directly over a good-sized mountain stream. In order to examine it I tied a forked stick to the end of a pole and, climbing a nearby beech about 10 feet from the nest, I pulled the hemlock limb with the nest over within my reach.

A few years ago a pair of Blue-headed built in a little hemlock directly under one of my Goshawk's nests. They laid a set of 4 eggs and hatched them. They were not disturbed at all by their big neighbors overhead.

Measurements:

Male, 5 3/4–8 1/2–2 7/8–2 1/4

WARBLERS

Of the different families of birds found in this region, the warblers are my special favorites. Possibly this is because they are well represented here, and because some of the more northern breeders, that only nest in a small part of Pennsylvania, are found nesting here.

There are so many different ones, so much variation in color, and such difference in song and nesting habits, that they have always been of great interest to me. I have spent a great deal of time with them. About 40 species are found or have been taken in Pennsylvania. In the close vicinity of Warren I have so far found 30 to occur. *(In post-1923 notes RBS indicates that the Prairie Warbler increased his species count to 31)* Of the 30 *(31),* I have personally found 19 species breeding here.

Some of the 19 are as a rule rather northern breeders, and they only nest in a small portion of the state. As this region is mountainous and covered with a mostly Canadian growth, it offers a congenial home to many of the more northern breeders—warblers, as well as others. Many of our warblers are amongst our most beautiful birds. Nearly all warblers are fine songsters.

In May when the hordes of small migrants are passing on their way north, large proportions are warblers. During rains and storms in May, warblers are sometimes abundant. When the warblers pass north in the spring, vegetation is much more advanced along the river valley than in the mountains. This causes the earlier part of the migration to follow the river and low lands quite closely.

Large numbers of warblers can be found some days at favorite spots of vegetation in certain bottom woodland areas. The river flat at Grass Flats is a favorite place. Before the "Point" *(see image)* at the juncture of the Allegheny and Conewango Rivers was cut off, it was a wonderful place for migrating warblers.

Severe storms in May, especially if there is snow, often cause great loss of life amongst the warblers. Some of these storms are real calamities. The worst one of my time, and the one causing the greatest loss, occurred in May of 1917. This cold stormy spell practically annihilated all the warblers caught in this region—just about wiped out the breeding warblers.

This storm, coming as it did at the height of the season *(May 14 to 17),* found the warblers here in full force. It rained most of the time and gradually became colder. With the rain was an almost continuous high and—toward the last—bitter northwesterly wind, at times almost reaching the proportions of a gale. This wound up on the night of May 17 with a hard freeze.

The last two days of this storm, the warblers—which I never saw more plentiful here—were compelled to come down into the grass to search for their insect food, which no doubt had disappeared from the trees, brush, and exposed places. They were so chilled and so eager to find food that they could easily be caught by hand in many instances. Redstarts especially were hard hit and came into town in great numbers.

On the morning of May 18, after the previous night's freeze, dead birds were found everywhere. As many as 5 or 6 birds were picked up on one small lawn about town. In the country they lay dead all along roads, fences, and about farm houses. It was not only the warblers, but the vireos and tanagers also perished. Next day hardly a warbler could be seen alive.

An enormous number must have perished. During the breeding season and summer, hardly a warbler, vireo, or tanager could be seen or heard. A person could walk sometimes for half a mile and never hear a warbler.

I spent several days in the field during the nesting season and found only 3 warbler nests, one each of the Hooded, Maryland Yellow-throat, and Yellow. It was 3 or 4 years before warblers really began to be at all plentiful. They have not since nested in nearly the numbers that they did before this storm.

This really was a bad storm, but luckily the warblers had not yet arrived in full force—many had not reached here at all. This storm consisted of rain and wind. This turned to snow, which lay 3 to 4 inches deep in the mountains, and wound up with a hard freeze. This storm even killed off the winter wrens.

Of the 19 species of warblers breeding here, 8 nest on the ground; 5 nest in low brush and bushes; and 6 nest in trees at varying heights. There is a chance of finding one more species nesting here, and that is the Nashville. The Nashville nests in this state but rarely. As I have several summer records, I may yet get a breeding record.

During the past 10 years warblers have become much reduced in number here for some reason—very few occurring during the migrations, especially the more northern breeders during the nesting season. In 1941 and 1942, all the warblers were scarce. In 1943 there were more during migrations and, strange to say, there was a good variety. I saw 27 species of the 31 that I have known to occur here. In 1944 warblers were more plentiful—they may be coming back. In 1945 warblers were scarce again. This was a poor year for all migrants. I saw fewer birds and fewer species than in any year for the past 12 years.

The "Point," confluence of the Conewango Creek and the Allegheny River at Warren, Pennsylvania.

1. Third Avenue bridge over the Conewango Creek.
2. Penna. Avenue bridge over the Conewango Creek.
3. Upper railroad bridge over the Allegheny River.
4. Hickory Street bridge over the Allegheny River.

1949

Photograph by E. Stoke.

Black and White Warbler
Mniotilta varia

(163.) Summer resident. Breeds.

Arrives: May 2, 1891; May 3, 1892; May 2, 1893; May 3, 1901; May 4, 1902; May 1, 1903; and May 11, 1907. It is one of the first warblers to arrive in the spring. Several can usually be seen on the first day of their arrival, and in a few days they are common. It is found in all kinds of woodlands—in hill and valley—and often in town.

Any flock of warblers of any size is sure to contain several Black and Whites creeping over the trunks and larger limbs of the trees. It is rather scarce here as a summer resident, but an occasional pair can be found in suitable situations, in the mountain hardwood tracts mostly—sometimes in mixed woods with not too much hemlock.

It nests on the ground under the roots of a tree, under a fallen limb, under the roots of a stump, and on banks. The nest is always very well concealed, and the female is very hard to flush. It nests in June: June 8, 1909, 4 eggs; May 20, 1913, 5 eggs; and May 30, 1913, 4 eggs. The nests are built of leaves, grapevine, bark, and coarse grasses. They are lined with fine rootlets or hairs.

In West Virginia this warbler was common, and I found a number of nests. Neither here at Warren nor in West Virginia did I have any luck in finding nests by flushing the females. By watching the females building, I have had fair success in finding nests, as they are not hard to follow.

The storms and freezes that have killed off warblers and other insect-eating birds in the past have always hit the Black and Whites hard. In May of 1917, when the big freeze struck, many Black and Whites were picked up dead on the lawns about town.

Measurements:
Male, 4 7/8–8 3/8–2 5/8–2 3/8
Female, 5–8 1/2–2 3/4–2 1/2

Golden-winged Warbler
Vermivora chrysoptera

(164.) Summer resident. Breeds.

Arrives: May 28, 1911; May 23, 1913; May 24, 1915; May 25, 1916; and May 19, 1928. During my earlier field trips here I never saw, heard, or met with this warbler. During the later 1890s I spent the best part of 4 years in West Virginia. It was there that I found the Golden-wing to be a quite common bird in summer. I found its nest with eggs and young, and I became familiar with its song and habits.

On July 25, 1905, five years after coming back from West Virginia, I met it here for the first time. Out that morning, over on the island at the mouth of the Conewango Creek, I heard the unmistakable song of a Golden-wing. Returning with a gun I found a fine pair of old birds with a family of full grown young. I secured both old birds for my collection, and I still have them.

Six years later on May 28, 1911, while on my way out of Morrison Run, through the slashing in the Hertzel Hollow, I heard the "zee zee zee" of a Golden-wing. I followed up, found, and watched this bird for some time. On other visits to this same place I failed to see or hear this bird again.

May 23, 1913, I heard and watched a male for some time on the Ott Run side of the mountain back of the cemetery. May 24, 1915, in this same place, I heard, followed up, and watched a male. Afterward, I was there at different times, and I found that this bird stayed. I saw the female on one occasion. The male roamed about a great deal, and I could not find a nest. I am not certain whether or not this pair nested that season.

In 1916, I watched this place closely, and on May 25, I heard a male singing. I kept close watch. In a few days I found that at least 3 males were on the mountainside—they roamed all over. I had much trouble finding a female.

Because of their late arrival, I expected nesting operations would take place rather late. This however was not the case, as on June 11, while walking along an old grass-grown road on the mountainside, a female Golden-wing flushed at my feet. I was soon looking at a well incubated set of 5 eggs. July 1, within 200 feet of this nest, I found another nest containing 4 large young. This second nest I found by watching the old birds feed the young. Both nests were on the ground in weeds and long grass. They were quite well concealed.

June 5, 1916, I heard a male singing up the Tionesta Valley above Clarendon. In May of 1917, we had the storm and freeze that almost cleaned out the breeding warblers here. I did not see a single Golden-wing that season. In 1918 I found 3 or 4 pairs in the same locality again *(Ott Run),* and by combing every likely looking place, I found two nests each with 5 eggs on June 6.

Since then there has been a pair or two of these warblers in suitable places each season. It inhabits open woodland, brushy areas, slashings, and old grassy, brushy fields. It is found in the valleys and on the mountains.

The male roams about a great deal, spends much time sitting on top of a small dead or living tree, and pours forth his "zee zee zee" at regular intervals. The nests are built on the ground in thick clumps of weeds and long grass—in open places in the brush, and along the edges of old and nearly grown over log roads. The nests resemble the Maryland Yellow-throats very much. They are built of leaves lined with grasses. The nests are usually well hidden, and the female sits very close. Some records: June 7, 1925, Ott Run, 4 eggs; June 12, 1925, Ott Run, 5 eggs; May 31, 1930, 5 eggs, fresh; and June 2, 1930, 4 eggs, fresh.

Nashville Warbler
Vermivora rubricapilla

(165.) Regular spring and fall migrant.

Arrives: May 1, 1903, and I have noted it up to May 24, 1907, and May 29, 1913. It seems to be scarce in the fall, and I have seen but few specimens at that season: September 23, 1903, and September 4, 1905. The Nashville is one of the rarer warblers here. I usually see it singly or in pairs, and generally in company with other warblers.

On May 3, 1901, I found that a small flight of warblers had arrived at Grass Flats. As it was early in the season, the flight was small, but I was surprised to find fully a dozen Nashville. This is the nearest to a flight of this species that I have ever seen.

When migrating here it seems to prefer willows and low stuff along the river and streams. This warbler has been found nesting in Pennsylvania. It is about the only warbler left on the list that I ever expect to find nesting yet in Warren County—unless some more southern warbler should work in this way and settle here, as did the Golden-wing. I have several summer records, but in no case could I find a nest or see young just out, so as to get a breeding record.

June 5, 1915, near the mouth of Meade Run, a tributary of the head of the Tionesta Creek, I found a male Nashville in full song. This place was a rocky region with moss, ferns, and much low brush. There were many scattered trees and second growth poplar. The birds ranged about over considerable territory and sang a great deal. I spent a lot of time following the male around, but I could not get sight of the female. I think from the bird's actions that it was located for the summer—but as it is quite a ways over there, I did not get there again.

During June of 1918, a male Nashville was to be always found in a piece of open, large, second growth hardwood where there was a thick low growth of ferns and huckleberry brush. The bird spent apparently all of its time 20 to 30 feet up in the trees—occasionally moving 100 feet or so to another tree. The bird sang a great deal, especially during the morning.

I was up there a number of times, but never could see a female. I even tried to cover every inch of over an acre of the place where the male hung about the most. I spent two different mornings at it, but no nest could I find.

Late in June the bird quit singing. From then on I couldn't find it, so I am not sure whether a pair nested in that vicinity or whether this was an old bachelor spending the summer.

Measurements:

Female, 4 5/8–6 7/8–2 1/8–1 3/4

Orange-crowned Warbler
Vermivora celata celata

(166.) Rare visitor during migrations.

This warbler is rare anywhere in Pennsylvania. There are but few records. September 28, 1900, along the river at Highhouse's Eddy, I found small migrants very abundant. While looking them over I noticed a greenish warbler that looked odd to me, so I secured it with a light charge of #12 shot. I found that I had taken a very fine, adult male Orange-crowned—my first record.

On September 15, on the Peninsula at Erie, I shot an Orange-crowned young of the year. I found it in company with a few other warblers in the low brush and second growth along the shores of Big Pond.

May 14, 1906, near the head of Highhouse's Eddy, I secured an adult female from a small bunch of migrating warblers that I found in the woodland along the river.

Besides these 3 positive records, I have—at least on two other occasions—seen a warbler that I am positive was of this species. Both of these were seen in very late September.

On September 21, 1946, I saw and fully identified one at very close range in willows along the lily pond swamp.

Measurements:

May 14, 1906, Adult female, 4 5/8–6 7/8–2 1/8–1 3/4

Tennessee Warbler
Vermivora peregrine

(167.) Irregular spring and fall migrant.

It is occasionally met with during the latter part of May: May 22, 1895; May 22, 1898; May 19, 1901; and May 30, 1907. During May, 1913, I saw 5 specimens on dates ranging from May 15 to May 25—it is rather rare, though. I seldom see more than 3 or 4 during a season. Some seasons I have not seen it at all.

I have not seen this warbler back in the mountains, but I have always found it along the river valley, and usually in company with other warblers and vireos. This species sings a great deal while migrating in the spring. I have frequently located it this way. If the Tennessee had not been singing, I no doubt would have passed it by unnoticed.

I have also frequently seen the Tennessee in fruit and shade trees in town. In the fall I have met it in late September and up to October 5, in 1907.

On May 15, 1932, I saw 1; May 17, 1936, saw 1; May 20, 1939, saw 1; May 24, 1941, saw 1; and May 17, 1946, saw 1.

Measurements:

Male, 4 1/2–8–2 1/2–1 5/8

Northern Parula Warbler

Compsothlypis americana / Parula americana

(168.) Summer resident. Breeds.

Arrives: May 2, 1891, May 7, 1892; May 3, 1901; May 6, 1902; and May 1, 1903. This small, neat, pretty, little warbler is a common, sometimes abundant, migrant everywhere in woodland groves—in valleys and on the mountains. Sometimes when we have large flights of warblers during storms, the Parula is often seen in fruit and shade trees in town.

As a summer resident the Parula is not at all common, but is quite well distributed in suitable situations in large timber. They spend most of their time in summer high up amongst the trees. The Parula are more often heard than seen.

It nests in June: June 5, 1908, 4 eggs; June 11, 1923, 4 eggs; June 17, 1923, 4 eggs. I have on several occasions found 5 eggs, but 4 is the usual number. It nests high as a rule, 40 to 60 feet up, and usually in a pine or hemlock, although a deciduous tree is sometimes chosen. June 10, 1943, I located a nest with 5 eggs only 10 feet up in a hemlock. It was at the edge of a thicket of second growth hemlock—an unusually low nest.

When a conifer is chosen the nest is way out amongst the tips of the limb. When a deciduous tree is used it is one with considerable lichen sticking to its limbs—in this case, the nest is pendant and fastened to both the limb and the growing lichen. Such nests are built almost entirely of lichen, with an opening into the nest underneath the limb. Nests in conifers are ball shaped affairs, built of all sorts of vegetable fibers and fine grasses. Nests, once finished, are difficult to find—it is best to detect when the female is building it.

In West Virginia this warbler was quite common, and I found several nests built quite low. One nest in particular proved very interesting. This nest was only 8 feet from the ground and 40 feet from a boiler house. A large top of an oak tree had blown off and lay on the ground. Lichen flourished on the branches of this old top

On May 25, according to my notebook, I noticed a pair of Parula persistently hanging about this old oak top. At first I could not figure out why, but then I found the female was working quite steadily on a nest—for 7 days. She did not finish entirely until June 1, but when finished this nest was a beauty. I spent quite a little time each day watching her.

The female did all the work. The male often followed her back and forth on her trips, but not once did I see him make a trip of his own with nesting material. Both birds were very tame when building. The female often came within 5 or 6 feet of me when hunting nesting material. They did not seem to mind the roar of the boiler at all.

On June 3, two days after being completed, the nest held 1 egg. On June 6, the female began incubating a set of 4 eggs. On June 18, I discovered the old birds feeding the young—the eggs having taken 12 days to hatch evidently. On July 2, I found they had all disappeared.

The male did his share in feeding the young. One morning while this female was incubating, I came along and heard the old bird, together with other warblers and small birds, very much excited and making a great fuss about something.

Stepping up carefully, looking about and on the ground under the old top, amongst the ferns and vegetation, I got my eyes onto what I took to be about the biggest blacksnake that ever grew. I could only see a couple feet of his body, but judging by its great thickness, I thought it must be one of those snakes the old timers tell about—being so long, that after being killed, it could be lapped back and forth several times on a rail fence.

There was a mad dog scare on about that time, and I was packing a gun around with me. This I promptly turned loose on his snakeship and pulled him out. I found it to be a Pilot snake, six and one-half feet long, but fully twice or more as thick throughout its length as a blacksnake should be. If this snake had escaped I would always have thought it was at least 10 feet long judging from its thickness.

Measurements:

Male, 4 1/2–7 1/2–2 3/8–2 3/4

Cape May Warbler
Dendroica tigrina

(169.) Regular migrant in spring, I have not noted here in the fall.

Although I usually see several each season in May, it is one of the rarest regular migrants found here. During mid-May, 1917, I saw 8 or 10 specimens, but other seasons, even when I was in the woods about every day, 2 or 3 or at the most 4 was all I could see in a season.

The following dates on which I have met it here are taken from my notebooks: May 6, 1890, 2 males; May 14, 1890, 2 males; May 13, 1892, a pair; May 2, 1893, a male; May 3, 1899, two males; May 1, 1903, a male; May 10, 1904, a male; May 16, 1904, a pair; May 9, 1909, a male; May 10, 1912, a male; May 14, 1912, a pair; and May 15, 1913, a female.

They are found in company with other warblers along the river valley. They seem to keep pretty well down in the lower branches of the trees and in large thorn trees. They are not hard to detect. I have never met with it back in the mountains, but I have seen it in fruit and shade trees in town.

Recent records: May 18, 1934; May 14, 1935; May 14, 1936; May 12, 1939; May 19, 1940; May 8, 1941; May 8, 1942; May 2, 1944, saw first one and a few more later on; May 15, 1946; and May 3, 1947.

Measurements:

Male, 4 7/8–8–2 1/2–1 3/4

Male, 4 7/8–8–2 1/2–1 13/16

Yellow Warbler

Dendroica aestiva / Dendroica petechia

(170.) Summer resident. Breeds.

Arrives: April 29, 1890; April 27, 1891; April 30, 1892; May 2, 1901; May 4, 1904; and April 30, 1907. The Yellow Warbler is one of the best known warblers. It is one of the earliest of the warblers to arrive in spring. The Myrtle and Pine are about the only ones to beat it here and then usually only by a day or two. It seems to vary but a few days as to the time of its arrival—regardless of the weather.

From records covering over twenty years, during which some warblers varied as much as 20 days in time of first arrival, I find that the Yellow has always arrived between April 27 and May 4—a length of only 7 days.

The Yellow is the most sociable of the warblers and seems to prefer the society of man. It is a rather common summer resident all along the river valley and along the larger streams where the country is settled. In the mountains it is often found about farms, but it prefers the lowlands.

It is also quite common about town in fruit and shade trees. Its cheery song is commonly heard along the streets. It is not found at all in the deep woods, slashings, and wild lands in the mountains

It is one of the early nesters among the warblers: May 25, 5 eggs; May 30, 5 eggs: May 26, 5 eggs; and June 25, 1909, 4 eggs. Many nests of the Yellow contain young by the time most of the warblers are building. It nests from 2 to 30 feet from the ground in fruit and shade trees, orchards, and along the streams in alders, low brush, and willows. Nests are saddled in a fork—solid, compact, and very pretty. They are built mostly of white vegetable materials and lined with down. Eggs are 4 or 5, as often 5 as 4. The Yellow is very often the victim of the Cowbird.

I have found one double storied nest. It was 5 feet up in an alder bush. The first story or original nest contained 1 egg each of the Yellow and Cowbird. The nest had then been built-up another story. The new bottom covered up the first 2 eggs entirely. Four eggs were laid in the second nest or story.

It departs early and is seldom seen after the middle of September. The big storm and freeze of May, 1917, practically exterminated the Yellow in this region—they have never been as common as formerly.

June 5, 1929, 4 eggs fresh, 5 feet up an alder. May 30, 1930, 4 eggs, incubation 1 week, 6 feet up.

Measurements:

Male, 4 3/4–7 1/2–2 1/2–2

Black-throated Blue Warbler
Dendroica cerulescens cerulescens

(171.) Summer resident. Breeds.

Arrives: May 5, 1892; May 7, 1894; May 6, 1899; May 8, 1901; May 13, 1904; and May 7, 1907. This pretty warbler is a common migrant, being one of the late arrivals amongst the warblers. After the warbler migration is on in good shape, the Black-throated Blue puts in an appearance.

When it first arrives, it is common anywhere in woodland—along the river valley with the other warbler hosts, where the buds and leaves are already starting and insect food is plentiful. The Black-throated becomes common as the season advances and the woods in the mountains begin to bud and leaf out.

When the migrations are over and the nesting season begins, it is found as a quite common summer resident. It is common during the fall migrations in September. By October they have about all passed. I have seen one as late as October 10 in 1900, an unusually late date.

In summer they are found anywhere in woodlands in the mountains, both in virgin timber and partly lumbered woods. Woods that contain hemlock, laurel beds, and low brush are preferred. They are also found in second growth and heavy slashings. In fact, they are found most anywhere except on barren, ferny, and huckleberry-covered ridges, where the cover is very short or low.

The males spend much of their time in summer well up in the trees. They sing incessantly. They have two different songs in the breeding season. One song resembles very much the "zee zee zee" of the Golden-wing. The female is rather shy and keeps close to the ground in the brush and laurel most of the time.

Although a rather common breeder, the nests are not easy to find. The males roam at random all about the woods, so that nothing can be learned of the whereabouts of the nest after it is built. The nests, being close to the ground and light-colored, are more or less concealed by the foliage. They are not easy to see or find.

I usually find 2 or 3 each season during my rambles. In June, 1907, I found 8 nests, and in June, 1915, I found 5 nests. Altogether I have found and examined quite a number of nests.

It nests in June. The 1907 nests are June 10, 4 eggs; June 15, 2 sets of 4 eggs; June 16, 2 sets of 4 eggs; June 18, 2 sets of 4 eggs; and June 23, 4 eggs. The 1915 nests are May 31, 4 eggs; June 3, 4 eggs; June 4, 4 eggs; June 7, 4 eggs; and June

10, 3 eggs. June 4, 1920, I located a nest with 5 eggs; and June 10, 1920, 4 eggs *(see photo).* Four eggs is the usual number, occasionally 3. In only this one instance have I found 5 eggs. Five must be a very unusual number of eggs—in this region at least.

The nests are always built close to the ground—usually 10 to 24 inches up, rarely more. I have seen several in brush hemlocks that were but 4 to 6 inches off the ground. In this region laurel beds and low, heavy, hemlock brush is preferred for nests. Sometimes I find one in beech or other brush, but 4 out of 5 that I have found have been in laurel or hemlock.

Most nests of this warbler are pretty structures, some of them amongst the most handsome nests I have ever seen. Nests, found in laurel and deep, heavy, hemlock regions, are usually very pretty. They are quite large and sometimes rather bulky for the size of the bird. The nests are quite deeply cupped.

In such woods there is a variety of nesting material to choose from, and the nests are apt to be quite nicely colored. Fine strips of yellow, rotten wood from old, decayed, moss-covered logs are often used. Also used are fine strips of outer white and yellow bark from birches, fine strips of grapevine bark, and grasses. In some cases the outside of the nests are decorated with cobwebs of white or yellow downy material. The rim and lining of the nest is of fine grasses, black rootlets, and sometimes hair.

In second growth and slashings the nests are usually more plainly colored and smaller. They are not so pretty in these drier situations where the supply of nesting material is not of such variety.

Some of the prettiest nests are large and built almost entirely of fine pieces of yellow, rotten wood and fine strips of birch bark. Decorations of the nest's rim and lining are made entirely of fine and very black rootlets.

The eggs vary greatly in markings. Some sets are simply wreathed; others are heavily wreathed and also spotted and blotched all over. Strangely enough some of the prettiest nests held the heaviest marked and most beautiful sets.

Later records: June 3, 1929, 4 eggs, fresh; and June 6, 1929, 4 eggs, fresh, 2 feet up a hemlock.

Measurements:

Male, 4 7/8–7 3/4–2 1/2–2

Female, 4 13/16–7 1/2–2 5/16–1 7/8

Male, 5–7 3/4–2 1/2–2 1/8

Black-throated Blue Warbler's nest, 4 eggs.
June 10, 1920.

Myrtle Warbler | Yellow-rumped Warbler
Dendroica coronata

(172.) Regular migrant, spring and fall.

Arrives: April 23, 1899; April 25, 1891; April 23, 1892; April 26, 1903; May 2, 1904; and April 29, 1907. This species and the Pine Warbler are the two earliest arrivals amongst the warblers, and it is always a question with me which I will see first each season. It is the most abundant of all the warblers, sometimes after or during storms in May it fairly swarms.

While passing through here it is found all along the valleys and lowlands, but seldom climbs the hills, as the buds and foliage are not advanced far enough to make food plentiful. Very rarely do I see it on the mountain tops. I have noted it as late as May 20, 1903; May 24, 1904; and June 7, 1907. I have never seen a Myrtle Warbler here in summer.

It arrives again from the north during the latter half of September, and it is common about the first of October. I have seen it as late as October 25 in 1903. In the fall they are found a great deal in company with sparrows and other warblers—about old brushy, weedy fields and tangles, as well as with the troop of warblers in the trees.

Measurements:

Male, 5 1/2–8 3/4–2 3/4–2 1/4

Magnolia Warbler
Dendroica magnolia

(173.) Summer resident. Breeds.

Arrives: May 4, 1889; May 9, 1891; May 7, 1892; May 8, 1901, May 13, 1904; and May 16, 1907. It is a very common migrant in the hills and valleys of all woodlands. The Magnolia is a very pretty bird and a good songster. It is by far the most common of all the more northern warblers that nest here. The Magnolia is found in any woods—virgin, cut-over, or second growth—where there is plenty of young hemlock.

It nests in June: June 1, 1890, 2 sets of 3, 1 of 4; June 8, 1890, 4 eggs; June 4, 1891, 4 eggs; May 29, 1894, 4 eggs; in 1895, 5 nests from June 4 to June 9, 4 sets of 4 and 1 of 5; May 27, 1900, 4 eggs; June 3, 1900, 3 eggs; and May 28, 1914, 5 eggs. In 1913, when Magnolia nests were unusually plentiful, I found and examined 25 nests—the first on May 26 and the last on June 5. All nests contained fresh eggs. After incubation had begun, I found that of the 25 nests: 1 full set consisted of only 2 eggs; 5 sets of 3 eggs; 17 sets of 4 eggs; and 2 sets of 5 eggs. From this it can be seen that 4 is the usual number, sometimes only 3, and occasionally 5.

Of course, the season of 1913 was unusually good. Other seasons I have found as many as a dozen nests. I always find at least 5 or 6 nests each season, even if I am only out a few times. Every nest that I have found of this warbler has been in a hemlock. The nests are built in the tops of hemlock brush and saplings, and out near the ends of horizontal limbs on second growth hemlock.

Nests are found from 1 foot to 35 feet from the ground. A nest that I found a few years ago in thick, low hemlock brush was only 1 foot off the ground. This nest was exceptionally low, and usually they would be at least 4 feet up. Most of the nests I have found would range from 6 to 12 feet up. The nests are neat, but rather flat as a rule, and not securely fastened—in most cases being set amongst the twigs, rather than fastened.

The principal materials found in every nest are fine, dry hemlock twigs, mixed often with a few fine grasses or fine rootlets. It is often decorated on the outside with cobwebs. The nests are lined with fine grasses or fine rootlets usually, sometimes hairs. Some nests are rather thin, as the eggs can be seen through the nest from the ground. Other nests are more solid and more deeply cupped, but in any case the bulk of the nest is fine, dry hemlock twigs. Eggs vary much in markings—some sets being heavily marked and handsome.

In June, 1927, Harry Granquist and I found a nest about 15 feet up in brush and briars. This is the only one I have seen in something other than a hemlock.

Cerulean Warbler
Dendroica cerulea

(174.) Straggler.

Sometime in May, 1890, a fine Cerulean was taken on the "Point" by John Truby, a young man interested in birds. Its capture was an accident. He did not know what it was, but had just gathered it in along with some other warblers and small birds. This Cerulean was afterward destroyed by a dog or cat.

May 5, 1891, while hunting at Grass Flats, I saw a male Cerulean with a small bunch of warblers. A pair of Wood Ducks alighted nearby, as I was about to capture it. I watched the ducks for a few minutes, but I lost sight of the warbler. Although I searched for a long time, I could not again locate it.

I found a few nests in West Virginia where the Cerulean was common. I learned much about its habits. It is found as near to us as Mercer County, and it is also found north of us along the lake shore plain *(Lake Erie)* where the elevation is much lower. This warbler may yet occur here and even nest, as the Goldenwing now does.

Chestnut-sided Warbler
Dendroica pensylvanica

(175.) Summer resident. Breeds.

Arrives: May 8, 1892; May 7, 1894; May 3, 1899; May 3, 1901; May 1, 1903; May 8, 1904; and May 16, 1907. This pretty little fellow is a pleasing songster. The Chestnut-sided is a common migrant amongst the flock of migrating warblers in May. It is common everywhere in mountains and lowlands. During storms, when warblers are unusually abundant, it is often found in fruit and shade trees in town.

As a summer resident, it is found anywhere in brush, briars, thickets, and along roads where there is brush. It is common in the slashings and low brush of the deforested regions in the mountains. Its cheery song can be heard on all sides.

In summer it is not confined to high ground in the mountains, but it is found anywhere in suitable brush. It nests in June: June 4, 1907, 5 eggs; June 8, 4 eggs, and June 15, 1909, 4 eggs; May 29, 4 eggs, and June 5, 1915, 4 eggs; and June 8, 1923, 5 eggs.

Nests are built in any kind of low, thick, green brush and briars from 2 to 4 feet from the ground. Nests are small and neat—being built of grasses, thin strips of inner bark, and vegetable fibers. They are lined with grasses, sometimes hair or fine rootlets. Some nests are plain looking. Other nests are quite pretty with decorations of down on the outside.

Four is the usual number of eggs, occasionally only 3, and in only 2 instances have I found 5 eggs. During the nesting season, the male spends a considerable amount of his time pouring forth his pleasing ditty while sitting on some small tree. It is very often a victim of the Cowbird. It is quite tame and fearless in its summer home, much more so than some of the other warblers.

Five eggs is an unusual number for the Chestnut-sided, but in 1928, on May 23, June 5, and June 7, we found 3 sets of 5 eggs.

Measurements:

Male, 5–7 3/4–2 1/8–2

Female, 4 1/2–7 1/2–2 1/8–1 3/4

Male, 5–7 7/8–2 1/2–2 1/16

Bay-breasted Warbler
Dendroica castanea

(176.) Regular spring and fall migrant.

Arrives: May 15, 1894; May 3, 1899; May 18, 1901; May 11, 1904; and May 16, 1907. Among the warblers it is one of the later migrants to appear. Usually about the middle of May there is a considerable flight for a few days. Other seasons it is rather scarce. At times, after warm May rains, I have seen the Bay-breasted here in large numbers. They are very irregular in movement.

The Bay-breasted seems to arrive here in a bunch, being common from the day of its first arrival. It is only found here for a few days, and it is seldom noted up to June 1. An unusually late date on which I found this warbler still here was June 7, 1907, but this was the latest season for birds that we had for many years. All species were much delayed in arriving—of course, all were unusually late in passing.

It migrates through woodlands, valleys and mountains alike, and usually keeps well up in the trees. In late September it is common during the fall movement south.

The season of 1924 was very unusual, being cold until well into June. In early June, as late as June 10, a great many Bay-breasted were here. It looked as if they might possibly remain and breed. Such was not the case, as they all finally left for the north.

Measurements:

Male, 5 5/16–8 3/8–2 3/4

Female, 5 3/16–8 3/8–2 3/4

Black-poll Warbler
Dendroica striata

(177.) Regular migrant spring and fall.

Arrives: May 10, 1899; May 18, 1901; May 15, 1904; and May 20, 1907. It is about the very last of the warblers to arrive. The Black-poll regularly stays the latest of any of the warblers that always breed north of us. Like the Bay-breasted it arrives in numbers. It is common from the day of its first arrival.

During spring in the mountains it is missing from the scenery, but it is common in the woods in the lowlands and the shade trees in town. It keeps high up in the trees as a rule, and it is rather hard sometimes to locate the owner of the lisping song that comes floating down.

It stays regularly into June—June 8, 1904, and June 12, 1907. In the fall it arrives early, coming first in small flights—August 18, 1894; September 1, 1895; and September 3, 1903. They are plentiful, some days even abundant, during the latter part of September and the first few days of October.

In the fall they are very common in the woods in the mountains. They do not confine themselves to the lowlands, as they do in the spring. I noted it as late as October 12 in 1902.

Blackburnian Warbler
Dendroica fusca

(178.) Summer resident. Breeds.

Arrives: May 1, 1888; May 2, 1891; May 5, 1892; May 3, 1901; May 10, 1904; and May 16, 1907. After the warbler migration in spring is well underway, this beautiful species occurs here as a quite common migrant.

It travels along with the other warbler hosts, and it is common in woods in both hill and valley. It has differed greatly during the course of my observations, as to the date of first arrivals each season. Its arrival seems to depend more on the weather than does the arrival of some of the others.

If we have a warm, early spring, the Blackburnian is here soon after the earliest arrivals appear; but if we have a cold, backward season, they are quite slow in reaching us. Often during the height of the warbler migrations in May, we get a bad storm with cold rains and sometimes a little snow. At such times warblers come into town, being plentiful about shade and fruit trees, where the foliage is more advanced. The houses and buildings in town offer more protection against the weather. The Blackburnian is one of the warblers frequently seen at such times. They stay low in the trees—attracting the attention, and arousing the curiosity, of persons who at other times would never see them.

During the severe storm in May of 1917, this beautiful warbler was one of the species hardest hit. Those that were here were practically exterminated. I saw it but rarely after that year. On the last day of the storm, toward evening, a fine male fluttered down onto my back porch. It was in an exhausted condition. I picked it up and put it in a basket in the house overnight, but the next morning it was dead.

After the migrations are over, the Blackburnian is found in the mountains as a summer resident. They are found in the big woods, where the timber is tall and large, and there is plenty of hemlock. The Blackburnians are not at all uncommon, but they keep high up in the trees—therefore, they are hard to see. It is no easy matter to see the male, as his song comes floating down with that of the Parula and Black-throated Green. In the fall I have seen the Blackburnian as late as October 8 in 1908.

Of all the birds that nest here regularly each season, the Blackburnian has proven the hardest to locate. This is because, as a rule, the bird nests high and way out on the outer limb of a hemlock, where it is almost impossible to see the nest from the ground. There are exceptions, of course, and rarely a low nest will be found. About the surest way is to watch the females building.

I was a long time finding my first nest, and they have been few and far between ever since. My first nest was found by watching the old birds feeding their four young. This was early in July of 1901. This nest was 30 feet up and 5 feet out on the limb of a hemlock. The nest was saddled on the limb, which was one and one-half inches thick at that point.

My second nest was found June 23, 1907, in a large tract of mostly virgin forest. This nest I easily saw from the ground, as it was only 20 feet from the ground in a rather small hemlock. It was out 5 feet from the trunk on a horizontal limb. Eggs were 4.

Nest number three was found June 2, 1912. This nest was in a big old hemlock with long, drooping branches. The nest was built way out on one of these long branches, fully 30 feet from the trunk of the tree and 40 feet from the ground. Eggs were 3.

Nest number 4 was found a few days later on June 4, 1912, in the hemlock swamp at Grass Flats. This was a low nest and was seen from the ground. It was 20 feet up in a hemlock and 8 feet out from the trunk, on a nearly horizontal limb. It held 2 eggs when found, but before the set was completed, it was robbed by a jay or a squirrel.

Nest number 5 was found on May 26, 1913. It was 25 feet up and 8 feet out on a limb of a good-sized hemlock. The limb was 2 inches in diameter at the place on which the nest was saddled. Eggs were 4.

Nest number 6 was discovered by watching the female building. She gathered most of her material close to the ground, sometimes going off quite a distance. The male accompanied her on many trips, but did not help at all. The nest was fully 60 feet from the ground in a large chestnut—although there were plenty of hemlocks all around. The nest was only a few feet from the trunk and saddled on a limb 4 inches thick. It was impossible to see this nest from the ground. May 28, 1914, I climbed up. I found the female at home on a beautiful set of 5 eggs.

Nest number 7 was found a few days later, June 6, 1914, by accident. It was 20 feet up and 8 feet out on the limb of a second growth hemlock. Eggs were 4.

Nest number 8 was found June 4, 1916. This nest was in heavy woods. The nest was in a big hemlock. It was 40 feet from the ground and 10 feet from the trunk. Finding this nest was a lucky thing, as it was well hidden by smaller hemlocks growing up underneath. This nest was hardly noticeable from the ground. It held a fine set of 5 eggs.

Nest number 9 was found by myself and a couple of friends. We located this nest by watching the female building; otherwise we never could have seen it from the ground. It was 50 feet up in a large hemlock and saddled on a limb 6 or 7 feet from the trunk. The female, on June 10, was incubating a nice set of 4 eggs.

Out of the 9 nests of this warbler that I have examined, 8 nests were in hemlocks—1 nest was in a chestnut. All were saddled somewhere on horizontal or nearly horizontal limbs—where there were little sprigs among which the nest could be built and fastened. The nests resemble the nests of the Magnolia Warbler a great deal, as they were mostly built of fine, dead, hemlock sprigs.

They have a coarser look than the Magnolias', as the sprigs used are larger as a rule. Usually there are cobweb decorations on the outside, giving the nest a sort of whitish appearance. They are lined with very fine rootlets and fine shreds of inner bark.

The eggs when fresh have a greenish, ground color. They are well wreathed, and sometimes they are well dotted and spotted all over with brown and black.

The female is a very close sitter. In spite of clubs and sticks thrown up past the nests to flush and identify the birds, I have seen them sit tight, until almost knocked from the nest. When I climb up to look at a nest, they will stick until the last second. I have had them stay within a few feet of me all the time I was up in the tree. The males must roam about a great deal while the female is incubating, as they seldom put in an appearance when the nest is being examined.

June 3, 1928, right along Morrison Run, just below the site of the old reservoir, Harry Granquist and I photographed a nest in a hemlock. It was about 40 feet up, near the top, in a cluster of little forks on a limb. Eggs were 4. The photograph is very good.

June 12, 1928, I found a pair of very excited Blackburnians while going through Grunder's Swamp. On investigating, I found a nest in a small hemlock. It was 15 feet up and 8 feet out on a horizontal limb. I saw a 5-foot blacksnake about the nest and on the limb. I went up and found 2 young and 2 eggs just hatching. I also found that a blacksnake can stick very tight to a limb by wrapping his tail end around it a couple of times. While shaking his snakeship loose, one foot accidentally slipped off a limb. This threw me to one side, where I swatted my face against a good-sized limb. I loosened a tooth, which I had to have pulled later—and it was a back tooth, too.

Measurements:

Male, 5–7 1/4–2 1/2–2 1/4

Black-throated Green Warbler
Dendroica virens

(179.) Summer resident. Breeds.

Arrives: April 27, 1889; April 30, 1890; April 25, 1891; May 5, 1892; May 2, 1901; and May 6, 1904. It is one of the earliest arrivals amongst the warblers. During the May migration it is common most anywhere in woods, in groves, in mountain and valley alike. I have seen them in town during the bad storms that sometimes occur in May.

As a summer resident it is not at all uncommon in the big timber in the mountains, but it is especially fond of hemlock and pine regions. This warbler, like the Blackburnian and Parula, usually keeps high up in the trees in summer. It is hard to see, although its peculiar song can be heard commonly enough in all suitable woods.

This warbler, again similar to the Blackburnian and Parula, is a high nester in this region, as a rule. The exception to this rule, the nests that are low, within 25 feet of the ground, are the only ones that a person is apt is see from the ground, while on a nest hunt or just roaming about.

By watching the females during the building season I have found some of the high nests, also some low ones. The females seem to gather most of their nesting material near the ground. As is the case with many others, the male bird often accompanies the female back and forth on her trips, but he does not seem to help much, if any.

The nests range in height from 15 to 60 feet from the ground. The high ones are practically hidden from view from the ground, but the low ones are not hard to see. They nest in hemlocks, in horizontal limbs or limbs nearly horizontal—saddling the nest on the limb and fastening to little twigs.

It also frequently nests in deciduous trees, especially birches, in which case the nest is usually built in the fork of a limb. No two nests look alike. All are well made and quite deeply cupped. Some nests are much bulkier than others. The nests in hemlocks are usually the bulkiest, being built of fine, dead twigs of the hemlock, fine strips of birch bark, fine shreds of inner bark, and lichen. The nests in the forks of birches are usually smaller, neater, and more compact, being built of fine strips of outer birch bark.

Many nests have decorations of cobwebs and downy substances. Nests are lined with fine rootlets, fine dried grasses, and fine shreds of inner bark, hairs, and shreds of lichen. Some nests are very beautiful affairs.

Number of eggs is 4. I have never found 5. I have found quite a number of nests of this warbler here. I found that quite a large percentage of nests are rifled by jays or squirrels before the set is complete.

It nests in late May and June: May 29, 1912, 4 eggs; June 3, 1912, 3 eggs; June 6, 1912, 4 eggs; May 23, 1913, 4 eggs; May 28, 1913, 4 eggs; June 3, 1915, 4 eggs; June 20, 1915, 4 eggs; June 8, 1923, 4 eggs; May 25, 1927, 4 eggs; and May 30, 1927, 4 eggs in a big birch. On June 10, 1928, we found a low nest in a hemlock at Morrison Run that held 4 young ready to leave. This must have been a very early set.

Measurements:

Male, 5–7 3/4–2 1/2–2

Female, 4 3/4–7 1/2–2 1/4–2

Pine Warbler
Dendroica vigorsi / Dendroica pinus

(180.) Summer resident. Rare. Breeds.

Arrives: April 25, 1890; April 25, 1891; May 3, 1901; May 5, 1904; and April 23, 1907. It is one of the very first, often the first, warbler to arrive in the spring. This is one of the rare warblers here. During the migrations it is only occasionally seen, and then usually seen about pines, although sometimes seen with other warblers in the bottom woodlands or edges of old weedy fields.

As a summer resident this warbler does not seem to be found in the real woods here at all. Even in extensive pine woods, I have failed to hear its song. Small groves of large pine trees, such as found in a cemetery, seem to be the only place where it breeds here.

In the close vicinity of Warren, I know of 4 such places where the Pine Warbler annually rears its young. The birds stay high up in these places in summer. Their song, which is a trill—like a Chipping Sparrows, but shriller and higher pitched—comes floating down from the tops of the tall pines, where it is difficult to even get a glimpse of the bird.

At first I did not suspect that this warbler nested here. On May 4, 1902, I was surprised to see a female gathering nesting material on the ground in a small pine grove nearby. By watching her, I located the nest way up in a White Pine. On May 14, I climbed up and found the nest to be 70 feet from the ground. It was out on a limb amongst a clump of sprigs, 6 feet from the trunk. The female was at home on 4 eggs.

Several other nests were found by watching the females building. I found that the birds nest early, and a week or 10 days after their arrival the females begin building. The nesting material seemed to be mostly gathered on or near the ground. The female as usual was doing all the work, as far as I could tell, with the male keeping her company on her trips part of the time.

The nests are very high up and the sets completed early—by the middle of May during an ordinary season. The nests are built neat and compact. They are made of fine bark strips, fine grasses and vegetable materials, and heavily lined with milkweed thistle or willow down.

On April 29, 1915, I discovered a female building a nest fully 70 feet up in a big pine in the Yaegle's grove. A high wind blew this nest down on May 7—the next morning I found the nest on the ground, also the remains of at least 2 broken eggs.

Recent records: May 15, 1940; May 2, 1941; May 6, 1942; May 11, 1943; and April 22, 1944.

Measurements:

Male, 5 1/2–9–2 3/4–2 1/4

Palm Warbler
Dendroica palmarum

(181.) Irregular migrant, spring and fall.

It is one of the rarer migrants among the warblers, and it is not often noted. When seen it is usually early in the season: May 3, 1890; May 6, 1893; May 5, 1899; and May 6, 1901. It is occasionally noted in the fall: October 11, 1900; October 5, 1902; September 27, 1903; and October 11, 1903.

It is found with other migrants in rather open situations, in low brush, and on the lower limbs of trees. Recent records: May 4, 1932; May 9, 1933; April 30, 1935; October 5, 1935; May 9, 1943; May 15, 1945; May 5, 1946; and May 13, 1947.

Measurements:

Male, 5 1/8–7 3/4–2 1/2–2 1/4

Ovenbird
Seiurus aurocapillus

(182.) Summer resident. Common. Breeds.

Arrives: May 5, 1892; May 6, 1901; May 3, 1902; and May 6, 1904. During the migrations in May the Ovenbird is common anywhere in woodland and brush, but as nesting season approaches, it retires mostly to the mountains. It is found commonly in all woodland, second growth, and even brushy regions.

It seldom gets far up off the ground, except to sit on some low limb and pour forth its song. It walks daintily about amongst the fallen leaves. It is very deliberate in its manners, and it wags its tail constantly.

They are rather inquisitive, and if a person sits quietly when one is near, it will usually come quite close to investigate. It nests in early June: June 4, 1910, 4 eggs; June 6, 1910, 5 eggs; June 10, 1910, 4 eggs; May 30, 1913, 5 eggs; May 30, 1915, 5 eggs; June 1, 1915, 4 eggs; and June 5, 1916, 5 eggs.

It nests on a foundation of leaves—roofed over and on two sides with leaves. The nest is lined with dried grasses. It is usually not easily seen. The Ovenbird is quite a close sitter. Recent records: June 3, 1929, 5 eggs, fresh; and June 3, 1930, 5 eggs, fresh.

Measurements:

Male, 5 1/2–9 3/4–3–2 1/4

Water Thrush | Northern Waterthrush
Seiurus noveboracensis

(183.) Summer resident. Rather scarce. Breeds.

Arrives: April 25, 1892; April 30, 1893; May 8, 1901; May 4, 1902; and May 2, 1903. It is a regular migrant during the May migrations, but is not at all common. It travels singly and in pairs. I never saw a flock, but I have seen a small group, a family no doubt, in August and early September.

It migrates along the river and mountain streams, and is never seen far from water. I often see it wading and walking about the edges of pools and ponds in the woods. As a summer resident this species is rather scarce. Along some of the larger mountain streams that are well timbered, a pair can be found here and there. In the big woods on the Four Mile, there are a few pairs scattered in the valley along the creek. They can easily be located by their loud explosive song.

They spend most of their time about the bayous and along the edges of streams. The Water Thrush is rather shy, and it usually does not allow a very close approach. It nests under jam roots and banks, both along the bayous and main streams. Nests are usually well concealed. They are not nearly as easily seen as the nests of the Louisiana Water Thrush.

Nests are composed of about the same material as the Louisiana's—being at first a foundation of leaves on which the nest is built, mostly of grasses. Eggs are about the same as those of the Louisiana, but if anything, they are slightly smaller. It nests in May: May 14, 1915, 5 eggs; and June 10, 1923, 5 young, just hatched. The song of this thrush is a better song than that of the Louisiana.

Recent records: June 7, 1925, on Farnsworth Creek, 4 eggs under the roots of a tree in a bank of a bayou in a wooded swamp, nest of a few leaves, grasses and moss; May 31, 1925, same swamp, nest under bank of bayou amongst roots, well concealed, 1 egg—later nest was deserted. This was a late nesting season for all the warblers.

June 3, 1929, I found a nest and 5 eggs, incubation advanced, on the Four Mile. The nest was entirely hidden under an overhanging bank of a bayou. It was built largely of moss.

Louisiana Water Thrush | Louisiana Waterthrush
Seiurus motacilla

(184.) Summer resident. Rather scarce. Breeds.

When I first began collecting, I only found the Common or Northern Water Thrush. This species did not seem to be found here. After becoming familiar with the Northern, I was almost persuaded that the Louisiana did not occur here at all.

Although I kept a close watch for this more southern form, I did not see one until August 24, 1894, when I secured one at the head of the "gutter," behind the island at the mouth of the Conewango Creek. After several more seasons passed and I could find no more, I carried the Louisiana on my list as a straggler.

Of late years, however, this species—like the Golden-winged Warbler—has gradually appeared in this region, and for some time has been a regular, but rather scarce, resident. This species does not go way back in the mountains, along the laurel and hemlock valleys of the larger streams, but seems to like the valleys of the smaller streams better. It is often found in the smaller ravines of the little runs and streams.

This species, to my mind, does not look as sleek and neat as the Northern, nor is its song quite so good. Its nests are not as well concealed as the Northern. They are found more in a situation such as a Junco would select—in a steep bank along the streams or amongst the roots of an upturned tree. It nests, if anything, a little later than the Northern: May 26, 5 eggs, and May 28, 5 eggs.

On June 1, 1928, along Ott Run, we found and photographed a fine nest and 6 eggs. On May 17, 1930, I found 2 nests of 6 and 5 eggs, fresh. On May 25, 1930, I located a nest of 5 eggs, incubation advanced, on Ott Run.

Connecticut Warbler
Oporornis agilis

(185.) Straggler.

September 21, 1902, while strolling along the river at the head of Highhouse's Eddy, I found small migrants quite common. In some brush, weeds, and tangled vines, I slipped up on a yellowish bird that looked odd to me. I was armed with a 32 caliber revolver and some shot cartridges. With this outfit I secured the specimen, which proved to be a Connecticut Warbler.

Up to date this is the only one that I have ever positively identified here. I have on at least two other occasions, at about this same time in the fall, seen a bird that I am quite sure was the Connecticut; but I could not secure the specimen and identify it, as I did not have a gun on either occasion.

Recent records: September 18, 1927, I saw and fully recognized one near the reservoir on Morrison Run. It was with the other migrants in the brush and tangle along the road; September 25, 1932, saw one near the sand pits; and September 30, 1940, saw one in the jungle down along the creek.

Mourning Warbler
Oporornis philadelphia

(186.) Summer resident. Breeds.

Arrives: May 7, 1892; May 13, 1893; May 3, 1899; May 13, 1901; May 4, 1902; May 10, 1904; and May 18, 1907. It is one of the later arrivals amongst the warblers. It is always quite late in putting in an appearance if the season happens to be backward.

This beautiful warbler is found in much the same localities as the Maryland Yellow-throat. Where you find one, you usually find the other—except that the Mourning is not found along fence rows in open places, such as the Maryland often chooses. The Mourning wants good cover and plenty of it.

Along the river in the bottom woodlands where the alders, skunk cabbage, and nettles cover the ground thickly, the Mourning is not at all uncommon. In the mountains it is well distributed in slashings and brushy regions. At Grass Flats quite a number of pairs nest some seasons on the first flat in the luxuriant growth, but the hordes of mosquitoes make nest hunting there anything but a pleasant task.

The male spends much of his time, sitting in some low tree or high brush, singing his peculiar song. They are easily alarmed and quickly disappear into the brush.

Mr. Thomas H. Jackson and R.P. Sharples, both of West Chester, Pennsylvania, made a week-long trip up here a few years ago. One object of the trip was to observe the Mourning Warbler. On hearing the Mourning singing, both men remarked that it sounded to them like the songs of the Summer Wren and Kentucky Warbler mixed up. About one-half was the song of the wren, and the other half was the song of the warbler. *(Thomas S. Jackson described his successful search with Simpson in the published article:* The Mourning Warbler in Warren County, Cassinea, *1909. Robert P. Sharples published his article in the* Oölogist, *August, 1908, titled:* The Mourning Warbler.*)*

The female is about the most secretive bird that I know. So well do they keep under cover that I have never yet caught one nest building, and I never saw one flush directly from the nest when incubating. It nests in June: June 8, 1909, 5 eggs; June 6, 1910, 5 eggs; June 9, 1911, 5 eggs; June 10, 1911, 4 eggs; June 5, 1916, 5 eggs; June 7, 1916, 4 eggs; and June 5, 1927, 5 eggs.

It nests in clumps of thick grasses and weeds. The nests are built on the ground in these thick clumps, and nests often become raised up a little as the thick vegetation grows. The Mourning very seldom builds off the ground in brush in this region. I have only seen one nest that was built off the ground, and that one was about 18 inches up in a tangle of brush and vines.

The nests are built much like the Maryland Yellow-throat's, but are larger in every way. The nest is built on a foundation of leaves. The nest itself is built of grasses, and it is lined with fine rootlets, grasses, or both.

Although they look much alike when the nests of the Mourning and Yellow-throat are placed together, there is usually a great difference in size. The eggs of the Mourning are larger than the Maryland and are generally well marked, sometimes quite heavily marked.

The female when incubating is very secretive. The nests are always built in little open places in the brush or along old roadways, where the grasses and weeds get the sun and grow thickly. Through this thick cover the female will slip off the nest and away—it never flushes and flies out. For this reason it is a rather hard matter to find the Mourning Warbler's nest.

I well remember the first nest of this warbler that I ever saw. I heard different small birds making a great fuss, and on going over that way I found the cause to be a Red Squirrel. When I first saw the squirrel, it had a young bird in its mouth. I settled the row with my gun, and found the young to be a Mourning. On looking around I soon found the nest, in which there were still two young.

Recent records: In 1928 we found 6 nests, 4 in one day at Grass Flats; and June 1, 1930, 5 eggs, fresh, in a clump of low, thick huckleberry brush.

Measurements:

Male, 5 1/8–7 5/8–2 1/2–2 3/8

Female, 4 3/4–7 3/8–2 5/16–1 7/8

Maryland Yellow-throat | Common Yellowthroat
Geothlypis trichas

(187.) Summer resident. Common. Breeds.

Arrives: May 9, 1892; May 1, 1893; May 12, 1901; May 6, 1902; May 8, 1904; and May 6, 1907. The Yellow-throat is common everywhere in brush, thickets, swamps, and jungles. In the slashings in the mountains, it is one of the common birds. It is one of the few birds to be seen on the windswept barrens and huckleberry ridges.

It nests in June: June 8, 5 eggs; June 9, 3 eggs, 1 Cowbird egg; June 10, 5 eggs; June 15, 4 eggs; and June 17, 4 eggs—all 1908. It nests on the ground in clumps of weeds and high grass. It also nests in brush, sometimes as high as 3 feet off the ground. I have seen one nest in laurel, but none in hemlock.

Nests on the ground are usually well hidden and not easy to find. Nests are built of grasses on a foundation of leaves. They are lined with fine grasses. Eggs are 4 or 5. It is a victim of the Cowbird.

Recent records: June 5, 1929, 4 eggs and 1 Cowbird egg, fresh; June 2, 1930, 3 nests, 4 eggs each, fresh.

Measurements:

Male, 5–7–2–2

Female, 4 1/8–6 5/16–1 7/8–1 11/16

Yellow-breasted Chat
Icteria virens

(188.) Straggler. Summer resident. Breeds.

Professor Homer and several high school students, while on a trip up the Conewango Creek valley, found a pair of Chats that had located here for the summer. Professor Homer is not here now, however, and I have lost this date.

May 28, 1911, while coming out of Morrison Run valley by way of Hertzel Hollow, I heard the call of a Chat—following up I found him perched on a stub. On June 8, I returned and found him located in the same place. I soon got busy and found the nest with the female sitting on a fine large set of 5 eggs. This is the only Chat I ever saw in this county, and strangely enough it also furnished me with a breeding record. *(In his post-1923 recent records RBS notes an additional sighting.)*

Recent records: July 15, 1943, in a slashing up the creek *(Morse Run)* from our house at Starbrick, I found a family of Chats—no doubt they had been reared here; May 16, 1945, I saw one back of the house in Starbrick; and August 1, 1946, I saw another one nearby.

Measurements:

Male, 6 3/4–9 3/4–3–2 7/8

(above) Road up Sugar Run, July 5, 1924.
(below) Morrison Run, before lumbering, June 5, 1908.

Hooded Warbler
Wilsonia citrina

(189.) Summer resident. Breeds.

Arrives: May 14, 1891; May 9, 1892; May 15, 1901; and May 15, 1904. It is one of the later arrivals among the warblers, and usually all are gone by the middle of September. October 8, 1910, I saw one—a very late date indeed.

During the migrations in May, I occasionally see a Hooded along the river in the groves with other migrating warblers; but this is unusual, as it is a bird of the hardwood timber in the mountains. This most beautiful warbler is found in the hardwood tracts and ridges where there is plenty of low underbrush.

The male sits around and sings a great deal during the spring and breeding season. I have seen them up fully 50 feet in the tree, sitting there and singing. The female usually keeps down near the ground in the brush.

It nests in June: June 10, 1910, 4 eggs; June 17, 1910, 4 eggs; May 31, 1912, 4 eggs; June 3, 1912, 5 eggs; June 5, 1913, 5 eggs; June 1, 1916, 4 eggs; and June 7, 1916, 5 eggs and 4 eggs. It nests in brush, vines, and often on fallen limbs—rarely in low hemlock brush. Nests are usually 1 to 2 feet off the ground. I have seen nests within 6 inches of the ground, and I have seen one 5 feet up in a mass of tangled wild grapevines and brush.

The nests are quite solidly built and quite deeply cupped. The nests vary much in appearance. Some are set on a foundation of leaves, especially if built in a tangle of vines. Others are beautiful structures built almost entirely of small strips of inner bark, fine pieces of dead wood from decaying logs, and vegetable fiber. They are decorated on the outside with cobwebs and downy materials, somewhat on the order of a pretty nest of the Black-throated Blues, but more cup shaped.

Eggs are usually 4. I have found but 3 nests containing 5 eggs. I have found one nest of the Hooded Warbler containing an egg of the Cowbird, thus adding this warbler to the list of victims of the Cowbird.

Recent records: May 31, 1930, 2 nests, one 18 inches up, 4 eggs, fresh, and the other 14 inches up, 4 eggs, fresh; and June 4, 1930, 1 nest, 3 feet up, 4 eggs.

Measurements:

Male, 5 3/8–8 1/4–2 5/8–2 1/4

Female, 4 7/8–7 3/4–2 1/2–2 1/8

Wilson's Warbler
Wilsonia pusilla

(190.) Regular migrant spring and fall.

Usually the Wilson's Black-cap is rather rare. I see but a very few, sometimes only 3 or 4, during the migrations late in May. Some seasons they are more plentiful than others.

During May, 1907, a very late season, they were not at all uncommon. I saw the first on May 16, and from then on, up to June 7, I saw several every day I was out. On May 30, 1907, during a trip to Grass Flats I saw 7 or 8.

In the fall I occasionally see one in late September—September 18 in 1901. I never met with this warbler back in the mountains. I have always noted it along the valleys in thickets of willows and thorn trees near the streams. When found here, it seems rather shy and secretive.

Recent records: May 23, 1937, I saw 8 or 10 all together; May 20, 1939, saw 1; and May 14, 1944, saw 1.

Measurements:

Male, 4 5/8–6 1/2–2–1 13/16

Canadian Warbler
Wilsonia canadensis

(191.) Summer resident. Breeds.

Arrives: May 9, 1891; May 8, 1892; May 12, 1893; May 7, 1894; May 6, 1899; May 10, 1901; and May 10, 1904. In May, almost every season, there is a time when, for a few days, the Canadian is very common all along the river valley, in woodlands and groves, in company with vireos and various other warblers and small migrants.

During bad storms in May this species is often seen in town. During the storm of May, 1917, which just about exterminated the warblers here, the Canadian was caught at the height of its migration. It was practically wiped out. Many of them came into town and were found dead on lawns the last day of the storm.

As a summer resident, it is found only in the mountains. Where there is plenty of hemlock, where laurel abounds, where the ground is damp, where ferns grow plentifully about large, moss-covered boulders, along the streams and little ravines; there you will find the Canadian at home. It is not at all common, but still it is far from being scarce. The Canadian is quite well distributed throughout this region in all such suitable localities.

The male is a very good singer with a loud clear song somewhat on the order of the Water Thrush. Nests of this warbler are usually rather difficult to find. The female is very secretive when building, and it is a hard matter to locate the nest by watching her.

Both old birds roam about considerably. They become very excited on seeing a person, whether the nest is nearby or not, so that a person cannot tell by the fuss raised by the birds whether the nest is close by or not. The female is also a close sitter and usually rather hard to flush. Sometimes she almost allows herself to be touched before leaving the nest. I once caught one in my hand, as she sat on her nest amongst the roots of an upturned tree. It was on a bank along an old logging road.

It nests in June: June 11, 1909, 5 eggs; June 7, 1910, 5 eggs; June 19, 1910, 5 eggs; and June 2, 1912, 5 eggs. It nests on the sides of large fern-covered rocks, under overhanging or steep banks, along old roads, along mountain streams, and amongst roots of upturned trees—in very much the same situations that a Junco would choose.

Nests are built on a foundation of leaves. The nest is built of grasses, strips of bark, usually moss, and lined with hair, fine rootlets, or both. It is sometimes lined with fine grasses. Some of the nests are built of mostly moss and are quite pretty. Eggs are as often 5 as they are 4.

In early June, 1926, Harry Granquist and I found a nest near Ott Run containing 6 eggs. This is the only set of 6 I ever saw. Two days later, I returned to get a photo and found that something had taken 3 of the eggs.

1932 was a poor season for warblers with the exception of this species. On May 25, in the Four Mile region, I found 4 nests from half-finished to finished. Later in Ott Run hollow I found two more nests—June 1, 5 eggs, and June 4, 4 eggs.

American Redstart
Setophaga ruticilla

(192.) Summer resident. Breeds.

Arrives: May 12, 1893; May 3, 1894; May 3, 1899; May 6, 1901; May 3, 1902, May 1, 1903; May 5, 1904; and May 11, 1907. It is common everywhere in woodlands except in large and heavy timber. In open or broken timber, in hardwood tracts, where there is plenty of tall brush and little saplings, the Redstart is right at home. They are good singers and active little fellows.

They are always hard hit by bad storms in May. Thousands perished during the storm of May, 1917.

The American Redstart nests in June. In 1895, I found 10 nests from June 1 to June 11—1 set of 3 with 1 Cowbird, 3 sets of 3, and 6 sets of 4. Other nests: June 2, 1912, 1 set of 3 and 1 set of 4; June 3, 1912, 3 eggs; June 6, 1913, 4 eggs; and June 7, 1913, 4 eggs. It nests in the upright forks of brush and saplings, often in dead stuff. Nests are usually 5 to 20 feet from the ground. I have seen a nest within 2 feet of the ground, and on May 26, 1913, I watched a female building fully 60 feet up in the forks of a limb. She gathered her material on and near the ground, so I easily identified her, but this nest was twice as high up as any other nest I have ever seen.

Nests are small, solid, neat, and well cupped—much on the order of the Yellow Warbler. It is built of fine strips of inner bark, fine grasses, and various vegetable and downy materials. It is lined with grasses, sometimes with hairs or a few fine rootlets.

Some nests are quite pretty—being built of different colored vegetable materials, and decorated on the outside with cobwebs and downy substances. Eggs are 4, often only 3. I have on one occasion seen a nest containing 5 eggs.

Recent records: May 31, 1930, 4 eggs, fresh, 8 feet up; and June 3, 1930, 3 eggs, fresh, 25 feet up.

Measurements:

Male, 5 1/4–7 3/4–2 1/2–2 1/4

Female, 5–7 1/2–2 3/8–2 1/2

Male, 5 1/2–8–2 5/8–2 1/4

TITLARKS

American Titlark | American Pipit
Anthus rubescens

(193.) Irregular spring and fall migrant.

I have noted the Titlark here as early as March 28 in 1893, a flock of 50, and as late as May 5 in the spring. April 25, 1901, I had a count of 30 for a flock. In the fall I have seen it from late in October up to November 17 in 1900.

Some seasons it is very scarce, and other seasons quite a few are about. It is usually seen in small flocks of 6 to 20, but I have seen a flock of fully fifty. It is found about plowed ground and overflowed meadows. It is very restless and constantly on the move.

On March 31, 1928, I saw 6 or 8 along the river bank on the South Side. *(Allegheny River.)*

THRASHERS

Catbird | Gray Catbird
Dumetella carolinensis

(194.) Summer resident. Breeds.

Arrives: May 3, 1892; May 8, 1901, May 3, 1902; and May 4, 1904.

The Catbird is a common and well known bird of brush and thickets, both in the valleys and on the mountains. It is quite well known to most people.

It nests in late May and early June. Nests are found from 4 to 10 feet up in bushes, vines, and briars. Eggs are usually 4, occasionally 5.

Measurements:

Male, 8 3/4–11 3/8–3 3/4–3 3/4

Female, 8 1/4–11 1/4–3 5/8–3 3/4

Brown Thrasher
Toxostoma rufum

(195.) Summer resident. Breeds.

Arrives: May 3, 1892; May 2, 1894; May 5, 1901; May 4, 1904; April 27, 1903; and April 26, 1914. It is found about brush, old fields, second growth, and slashings. It is not common, but a pair can be found here and there in suitable situations.

It is a fine songster. The Brown is rather shy and usually does not allow a very close approach. It nests, on the ground and in low bushes, in late May: May 18, 1925, 2 eggs; May 20, 1925, 4 eggs; May 17, 1930, 3 eggs, fresh; June 1, 1930, 4 eggs; and June 2, 1930, 4 eggs.

Measurements:

Male, 11–13 3/8–4 1/8–5 1/4

WRENS

Carolina Wren
Thryothorus ludovicianus

(196.) Rare visitor. Breeds. *(Breeding record is post-1923 journal entry.)*

September 24, 1894, while hunting squirrels at Grass Flats, I heard a strange song. Upon investigating I found the song came from a huge drift pile in the bayou, and the author, a Carolina Wren, was the first I ever saw here.

July 31, 1900, at the residence of Phillip Ittel at King's Eddy, I found a Carolina singing merrily in some vines on the side of the house. One was taken by a student of Professor Homer in May of 1903. August 15, 1903, I found 2 about the head of Highhouse's Eddy. They stayed around there for a week. September 29, 1908, in the same jungle at the head of Highhouse's Eddy, I found one singing.

It is possible that this wren may sometimes breed in this vicinity. In July of 1932, I found what appeared to be a family of these wrens—all well grown, of course. They were in the bottom woodland at the old gun cotton plant up the Conewango Creek. February 26, 1933, I saw one in the grove along the river, about the sand pits at the head of Highhouse's Eddy. During March I found there was a pair about, so I began watching them—expecting them to nest. On April 18, same year, a friend of mine, living at the edge of the grove along the highway, reported a strange nest to me. He had a small, deep basket hanging on his back porch. He had stuffed a few papers in one end, and on the other side was a quite pretty and deep bird's nest. He had not noticed them building, and was at a loss to think what it could be. I suspected the Carolinas, and I went right down to see. One look was enough—it was Carolinas. April 21, it held 1 egg, and on April 26, it held 6 eggs—the female began to incubate.

I got a very nice photo by taking the basket down for a couple of minutes. The wrens raised the brood. Later on they laid a second set of four. This is my first nesting record; although of very recent years it was quite certain that this wren was nesting nearby, as I began to occasionally see a bird or two, usually in July or August.

I saw one December 14, 1943—the first I have seen for several years. April 22, 1944, I saw one.

Measurements:

Male, 5 5/8–7 3/4–2 1/4–2

"Bayou" at Grass Flats, along the Allegheny River, 1928.

Ralph B. Simpson, Feb. 22, 1921.
Among the big rocks at Long Run.

House Wren
Troglodytes aedon

(197.) Summer resident. Breeds.

Arrives: May 7, 1901; May 4, 1902; May 2, 1903; and May 4, 1904. I have seen it as late as September 29 in 1900. It is quite common everywhere except in heavy woods. It is found about farm houses, small groves, slashings, old brush, stumpy fields, heavy thickets, and roadsides. It is common also in town.

It nests in late May and June. It nests in nooks about buildings, bird houses, crevices in stubs and trees, and old woodpecker holes. Eggs are 5 or 6: May 26, 1902, 6 eggs, and June 4, 1906, 6 eggs.

I once discovered a chipmunk robbing a nest in a stump. On another occasion I found a milk snake rifling a nest of young, two of which had already been swallowed.

Winter Wren
Nannus hiemalis / Troglodytes troglodytes

(198.) Summer resident. Breeds.

This hardy little fellow arrives early in April and is met with up until November. When we have an early spring, I sometimes note the first arrivals late in March. If we have a late fall, I sometimes meet with it well along into November. I have never seen it but once in winter. The winter of 1890-91 was a very mild one, and on January 4, 1891, I saw a lone Winter Wren.

During migrations the Winter Wren is apt to be met with in any woodlands; but when settled for the summer, it is found only in the mountains. The Winter Wren is not uncommon as a summer resident in virgin forest and large second growth forest, where there is plenty of hemlock, laurel, and old, mossy logs.

In such places its odd and rippling song, entirely different from any other bird song heard in this region, can be heard in the gullies, ravines, and along the mountain streams. This little fellow is shy and secretive, keeping well hidden among the logs, thickets, and fallen tree tops.

He usually allows a close approach before taking a short flight to dodge into the next hiding place. If one sits down quietly, this wren will soon appear and flutter about, scolding all the time. Remain quiet, though, and he will soon forget you are there.

Nest building begins early in May. The females begin incubating the latter part of the month: May 22, 1910, 5 eggs; June 4, 1912, 4 eggs; May 14, 1913, 6 eggs; and June 1, 1915, 6 eggs.

The favorite nesting site here seems to be under and amongst the smaller roots of upturned trees. It also nests in cavities dug out by the bird itself in the underside of old, badly decayed, moss-covered logs, lying partly off the ground. I have also found nests in crevices underneath large, overhanging rocks and amongst roots on mossy, steep banks along trout streams.

This wren has a habit of building decoy nests. A close search of the vicinity inhabited by a pair of Winter Wrens usually results in the finding of several of these decoys and, if Lady Luck is along, the real nest may be found. The nests are quite bulky. They are built up against the log or dirt of the upturned root, the entrance being a small hole about 1 1/4 inches in diameter.

The nest is a ball of a green moss with a few dry sprigs of hemlock mixed in. The entrance is always rimmed about with these fine dry sprigs. The nests are always thickly lined with feathers. Decoy nests are usually not so large or well made, and they are not lined.

The female is a close sitter and does not flush easily. After the young leave the nest, the entire family roams about together for some time. I have read that this wren will abandon a nest that is disturbed in the least or in which a finger has even been inserted. This, however, has not been my experience. At different times I have felt inside a nest with my finger to determine if they were lined or if they were only decoys, and in doing so have disturbed the entrance more or less. Several times I have found nests all lined and ready for eggs; and on visiting the place later, I have found the female at home on her eggs.

A few years ago Mr. R.C. Harlow of State College, Pennsylvania, was paying me a short visit. One day late in May we were exploring about some large rocks that lay along the brow of a steep mountainside. In a crevice well under a large overhanging rock we discovered a Winter Wren's nest.

Feeling inside with my finger I found the nest to be empty; as it was getting late in the season, I supposed it to be a decoy, so I pulled it out for examination. It came out in fine shape. We were surprised to find it all heavily lined with feathers. It was apparently all ready for eggs. We placed the nest back carefully, and a few days later, happening to be in the vicinity, I paid the nest a visit. I was surprised to see a wren peering out at me. Upon investigating, I found her to be at home on 4 eggs. This instance certainly does not suggest they are quick to desert a nest if slightly disturbed.

This past season the snowstorm and heavy freeze of early May, that killed many warblers, seemed to wipe out the Winter Wren. The wrens were here in usual numbers before the storm, and afterwards they were gone. I have heard only 2 this entire summer. I would hardly look to see this bird frozen out, but such seems to be the case.

Recent records: Farnsworth Creek swamp, May 31, 1925, 6 eggs in a nest in the bank of the creek, amongst the roots of a large tree, hatched out June 7, 1925; and June 3, 1928, we *(Harry Granquist and Simpson)* photographed a nest near Ott Run. It was nicely concealed in the side of a large, rotten log. It held 6 eggs, fresh.

Measurements:

Female, 4–6 1/8–1 3/4–1 1/4

Long-billed Marsh Wren | Marsh Wren
Tematodytes palustris | Cistothorus palustris

(199.) Rare visitor during the spring migrations. I have no fall record.

Although a common bird on the Peninsula at Erie, I have only met with here on a few occasions. I have taken several specimens here and have seen several others about the mouth of the Conewango Creek, Grass Flats, and Honhart's Pond.

Dates of occurrence here that I have handy are: May 14, 1889; April 23, 1894; May 27, 1904; and April 14, 1941.

CREEPERS

Brown Creeper
Certhia familiaris americana | Certhia americana

(200.) Resident. Breeds.

In winter, when the snow lies deep and the bitter winds howl through the leafless trees, bird life is scarce. Here and there a small troop of birds may be found, especially if there is plenty of low hemlock cover or brushy thickets. These little flocks consist of a few Chickadees and Kinglets, a Nuthatch or two, possibly a Downy or Hairy Woodpecker, and usually a creeper or two, or maybe a pair. These little creepers are hardy fellows, as some refuse to leave in spite of the cold and snow.

These small creepers so harmonize with the trunks of the trees, over which they creep, that they easily escape detection. Starting near the ground, they zigzag their way up the trunk seeming to spend considerable time on each tree, but still keeping up with the flock.

Early in April the little creepers are sometimes quite common for a few days, and at such times they are often seen on trees in town. As a summer resident the Brown Creeper is rather rare. In virgin or big timber—in swampy regions about some of the larger mountain streams where large dead stubs and dead trees stand about—the creeper's weak and squeaky, but still rather pleasing, song may sometimes be heard. The Brown Creeper, at all times, seems to be tame and unsuspicious, and pays but little attention to the presence of humans.

It nests in early May: May 10, 1891, 5 eggs, and May 11, 1913, 6 eggs. The only way I could ever find this bird's nest was by watching the old birds building. About April 20 to April 25, of an ordinary season, I have found is the time to locate the nest. About this time of year, by keeping a sharp watch on any creepers seen or heard in a suitable place, I have been able to locate a nest occasionally.

I have found that the male sings, more or less, regularly. A pair may be located by hearing the song, where otherwise they might easily be passed by or overlooked. The female works quite steadily once she has started to build. The male accompanies her on many trips. They work very industriously, are very tame, and once found are easily followed up.

With one exception, the nests that I have found of this bird have been in old hemlock stubs. An old, big stub is selected—one on which the bark hangs loose or is partly fallen off. For a nesting site, the birds select a place where they can get under the bark, through a break or crevice; or under where a piece of bark has fallen off; or where the bark stands away from the trunk a couple of inches. Here, 3 or 4 inches back from the nest entrance, the birds fill up the space—building a perfectly loose nest of fine pieces of dead, rotten wood from old logs, with an occasional fine twig. It is lined with cobwebs, vegetable or downy substances, or feathers. In height the nests range from 6 to 30 feet from the ground.

The exception to this rule, I found in a huge old Yellow Birch. The loose bark of this old birch had curled round in rolls in places, and inside one of these rolls a pair of Brown Creepers built a nest.

The female sits tight. As the nests are so loose, pounding or jarring the loose bark is very liable to wreck the nest. Much care must be used in reaching the nest—to take the eggs or to examine the outfit.

Eggs are 5 or 6. A fine nest and 6 eggs in my collection I took in a swamp near Warren where the birds nest, or did nest, annually. This nest was 30 feet up in a loose-barked, old, dead, hemlock stub. Owing to the conditions of the bark, it was impossible to climb this stub. So I stretched a rope between two trees, so that the rope passed within a foot of the stub. Going out on this rope, with another piece of rope for a seat, I secured this set and the nest.

On May 31, 1930, Harry and I found a nest along the Four Mile in a very large, curly, loose-barked Black Birch. The nest was only 4 1/2 feet up. A few ends of fine twigs stuck outside the opening—eggs laid about 3 inches back in, 5 in number, and fresh.

June 1, 1929, I found a nest behind some loose bark, 35 feet up in a dead pine. The birds were feeding the young. The nest was in the little grove back of where the Yaegle barn used to stand, close to the old Brewery. I never expected a nest in such a situation.

Measurements:

Male, 5 1/4–7 1/4–2 1/2–2 1/2

NUTHATCHERS

White-breasted Nuthatch
Sitta carolinensis

(201.) Resident. Breeds.

It is found the year round, but is more common during the migrations. When not nesting, the White-breasted roams about the woods with troops of other birds, spending much of their time creeping about the trunks and larger branches of trees in search of food.

They are often seen on the ground. They are fond of the kernels of nuts, and will pick out the kernels left in nuts opened and dropped by squirrels. I have caught several in traps baited with nuts that I had set for Flying Squirrels.

It nests early in May: May 4, 1914, 7 eggs, and May 7, 1915, 9 eggs. It nests in natural holes and cavities in trees and stubs. The nests are at various heights from 8 to 50 and 60 feet up. The opening to the nest is usually quite small. Eggs are 5 to 9. A pair nests annually—rearing from 5 to 9 young—in the grove at the head of Highhouse's Eddy. This was in a natural cavity only 8 feet up in a hickory tree.

A pair is always about, more or less every day of the year, at our place in Starbrick. They are the most regular winter patrons at my feeding station. Spring, 1940, this pair began nest building on April 10, in a natural hollow only 4 1/2 feet from the ground, in a large maple close to the garage. On June 4, the young left the nest. The old birds coaxed the young, now fully grown, out one at a time. The young ones had no trouble in climbing up the tree. Soon they were coaxed by the old birds to fly to the nearest tree, which they seemed to have no trouble in doing. They did not have to spend several days learning to fly like most birds do. The old birds and young soon left the vicinity. It was some time before the old ones returned. When they did come back, it was without the young, as they had evidently learned to shift for themselves.

Measurements:

Female, 5 3/4–10 3/8–3 1/2–1 3/4

Red-breasted Nuthatch
Sitta canadensis

(202.) Irregular migrant.

Every 3 or 4 years a flight appears in October and November. They are then common in the woods in the mountains, especially where there is hemlock. At other times they are irregular in their appearance.

They are frequently met with in spring; quite a few are about sometimes in May. In summer, when trout fishing in virgin timber on the Tionesta and Four Mile Creeks, I have seen and heard this nuthatch—not just once or twice—and in different seasons, too. There is no doubt in my mind about it nesting here, but up to date I have no positive record.

June 29, 1901, I saw several of these birds along the Big Tionesta Creek in Forest County.

It is occasionally seen in mid-winter. In February, 1907, during the grosbeak and crossbill flight I saw a few.

Measurements:

Male, 4 5/16–7 5/8–2 1/2–1 3/8

Female, 4 5/16–7 5/8–2 9/16–1 3/8

TITMICE

Tufted Titmouse
Baeolophus bicolor

(203.) Rare visitor. Breeds. *(Breeding record is a post-1923 journal entry.)*

July 26, 1901, in virgin timber near the Warren-Forest County line, I saw 2 of these birds. It is, of course, possible that they nested somewhere nearby. In the spring of 1903, one was taken by Professor Homer and his students. April 13, 1906, I found a pair of titmice at Grass Flats. They were very restless, flying about a great deal, and alighting high up in the tall trees. They called a great deal, and it was these calls that first attracted my attention.

March 16, 1907, I secured a specimen along the river at Highhouse's Eddy. March 29, 1920, I saw and listened to one for some time near the forks of Ott Run. May 9, I heard one, or the same one, near the same locality, but I did not see or hear it again.

April 1, 1928, I saw and listened to one at Grass Flats. Later I saw it again. I began watching and found there was a pair. Afterward I watched for them, and finally I was rewarded by detecting them building. This nest, on June 3, contained 7 eggs. I got a fine photo. It was 30 feet up in a Butternut tree—in an old Downy Woodpecker hole in a dead limb. The nest was a mass of shreds of bark, fur, and fine woody material. This is my first nesting record.

May 21, 1928, I watched one for some time in the swamp just out of Saybrook up the Four Mile. During 1932 and 1933, I have seen this species on several occasions in November, February, March, and April. I think that this bird, with the Cardinal and Carolina Wren, is becoming more common here in recent years.

Since moving down the river *(to the Starbrick home, see photo)*, 3 miles below Warren, in late fall of 1937, I have had a feeding station for birds each winter—amongst other visitors, I have had Tufted Titmice right along.

Of late years, there are a few in this region as residents. In 1946, I only saw one the whole year. They seem to be very scarce again these last few years. In 1947, I saw this species but once—one bird on April 22.

Measurements:

Male, 6–9 3/8–3–2 7/8

The Ralph B. Simpson home, Starbrick, Pennsylvania, c. 1940. In the lower image, the building to the left was Simpson's workshop for his study skins and taxidermy work. Simpson's study skins and mounted specimens remain well-preserved to this day.

Chickadee | Black-capped Chickadee
Penthestes atricapillus | Poecile atricapilla

(204.) Resident. Common. Breeds.

It is quite well known to most everyone. It is often seen about town during the winter months. The Chickadee is common anywhere in woods and brush. It is usually found in small flocks, generally with other birds, roving about the woods.

It nests in May: May 4, 1894, 7 eggs; May 19, 1894, 5 eggs; May 26, 1894, 5 eggs; and June 3, 1928, 7 eggs. It nests in holes excavated in stumps and small stubs at various heights from 2 to 15 feet from the ground. Nests are built of feathers, hairs, and sometimes grasses. Eggs are 5 to 7.

Measurements:

5 1/2–8 1/4–2 1/2–2 1/2

KINGLETS

Golden-crowned Kinglet
Regulus satrapa

(205.) Regular migrant and winter visitor.

Arrives as early as October 9 in 1894. It is found mostly in coniferous woods in company with chickadees and nuthatches. It varies much in abundance, some years being scarce, and again other years being quite common. I have seen it quite late in spring on several occasions: May 3, 1889, and May 2, 1892.

Ruby-crowned Kinglet
Regulus calendula

(206.) Regular migrant.

Arrives: April 14, 1893; April 23, 1894; May 3, 1901; May 4, 1902; April 28, 1904; and May 7, 1907. They are more or less common from the day of their first appearance—some seasons quite common, but they do not seem to linger long. Latest dates I can find are May 12, 1901, and May 16, 1907. It occurs in the fall, from late in September up to October: October 9, 1894, and October 11, 1903. It seems to prefer the lowlands or valleys, where it is found in company with warblers and other small migrants. The Ruby-crowned has a really fine song.

THRUSHES

Eight of this subfamily are found in Pennsylvania, and of this number, I have known 6 to occur at Warren. Of the 6 that occur here, all are breeders. The Gray-cheeked Thrush I have taken in the fall at Erie. It no doubt occurs here, and it could be taken if a search were made for it at the proper time.

Only one of this subfamily, the Bluebird, is brightly colored. The rest, with the exception of the Robin, look much alike in the woods.

The thrushes surely have fine voices. The song of the Veery, Hermit, or Olive-backed—coming near evening from the ravines and mountain sides—is one of the best bird notes to be heard in the woods.

Wood Thrush
Hylocichla mustelina

(207.) Summer resident. Breeds.

Arrives: May 4, 1889; May 5, 1891; May 5, 1902; and May 8, 1904. It is common anywhere in the hills and valleys of the woodlands. It nests in early June in trees and bushes—usually 4 to 25 feet up. I have seen nests 40 feet up. Eggs 3 or 4: June 6, 1909, 4 eggs; May 27, 1927, 3 nests, 4 eggs each; June 5, 1927, 4 eggs, Ott Run.

It is a fine songster.

Measurements:

Male, 8–13 1/2–4 1/2–3

Wood Thrush
Four eggs
Ott Run, June 5, 1927.

Wilson's Thrush | Veery
Hylocichla fuscescens | Catharus fuscenscens

(208.) Summer resident. Breeds.

It arrives about the first of May. In summer a few are found in woodlands in the mountains, but it is not common. It is rather shy and not easily approached.

It nests late in May: May 16, 1893, 4 eggs; June 1, 1894, 4 eggs, and 1 of the Cowbird; June 1, 1910, 4 eggs; and May 21, 1911, 4 eggs. It nests on the ground, often on steep banks along streams or steep banks along old roads in the woods.

Eggs 4. The nest found June 1, 1894, was in the woods near the Oakland Cemetery. It had also been found by a Cowbird, thus adding this thrush to the list of the Cowbird's victims.

It is a fine songster, possibly the best of the thrushes.

Olive-backed Thrush | Swainson's Thrush
Hylocichla ustulata | Catharus ustulatus

(209.) Summer resident. Breeds.

It is quite a common migrant in May, and again in late September—September 22 in 1900. This is one of the more northern breeders that nests in only a small part of Pennsylvania. During the summer months a few pairs remain to breed. In the mountains, in woods containing plenty of hemlock and laurel, the Olive-backed is at home.

It nests in June: May 31, 1901, 3 eggs; June 2, 1901, 4 eggs; June 15, 1909, 4 eggs; and June 8, 1910, 4 eggs. Also July 11, 1892, 3 eggs, probably this was a second laying, as was July 9, 1900, 4 eggs. It nests from 3 to 15 feet from the ground, usually in a small hemlock or laurel, but frequently in green brush.

This thrush builds the prettiest nest of all, as there is usually much green moss used in construction. Some nests that I have found have been built mostly of green moss.

Measurements:

Male, 6 7/8–11 7/8–3 7/8–2 9/16

Hermit Thrush
Hylocichla guttata | Catharus guttatus

(210.) Summer resident. Breeds.

Arrives: April 24, 1891; April 11, 1892; and April 19, 1901. The Hermit is the first of the thrushes to arrive, and it is usually a quite common migrant anywhere in woodlands. It is common again late in September and early October. I have seen it as late as October 25 in 1903.

It occurs as a summer resident throughout the mountains, some seasons more common than others. It seems to prefer woods in which there is hemlock.

It nests in June: June 9, 1910, 2 nests, 4 eggs each; June 19, 1910, 4 eggs; August 9, 1910, 3 eggs, second laying no doubt; June 10, 1912, 4 eggs; and June 16, 1913, 4 eggs. I have seen nests on the sides of large moss and fern covered rocks or boulders more than in any other situation. I have found nests also on the ground, especially on steep banks. I have found several nests 3 feet up in thick hemlock brush.

This thrush is rather tame and unsuspicious. It usually allows quite a close approach.

Measurements:

7–11 1/4–3 1/2–3 1/8

American Robin

Planesticus migratorius | Turdus migratorius

(211.) Summer resident. Breeds.

Arrives: March 1, 1890; March 8, 1893; March 6, 1901; March 1, 1902; and February 27, 1904. It is occasionally seen in mid-winter. On February 6, 1895, with deep snow, a fierce blizzard raging, and the thermometer 25 degrees below zero at 6 o'clock that morning, I was much surprised to see 2 robins in town.

The robin is undoubtedly our commonest and best known bird. I have known two albino robins here, and in my collection I have a partial albino. During migrations the robin is abundant in large flocks. In the fall a great many are found deep in the woods.

It is a very common breeding bird everywhere except in deep woods. It nests anywhere in trees and about buildings. Many robins nest in town. On May 24, 1919, in the grove at the head of Highhouse's Eddy, I found a robin's nest on the ground. The nest was built flat on the ground, amongst the leaves, and partly concealed by mandrakes. The old lady was at home on 4 eggs. Why she ever built on the ground, when she could just as well have built overhead on the limbs, is a mystery to me. This is the only robin's nest I ever saw built on the ground. Although I have looked into many a robin's nest, I have never yet found a nest containing 5 eggs or young.

Eastern Bluebird
Sialia sialis

(212.) Summer resident. Breeds.

Arrives: March 1, 1890; March 27, 1892; March 11, 1893; March 5, 1901; and March 12, 1902. It is quite common and like the robin is well known to most people. It likes open country, but is found most anywhere, except in heavy woods.

It nests in bird houses about farms and in town. It also nests in old woodpecker holes and natural cavities in stubs and stumps.

It nests in May: May 3, 1913, 5 eggs; April 26, 1914, 3 eggs; and April 28, 1914, 3 eggs. I found a nest, June 23, 1912, with 6 eggs.

In 1932, quite a few were here by March 5, but the 3 weeks of blizzard that followed must have killed them, as they were very rare the rest of the year.

Measurements:

Female, 6 3/4–12 /14–4–2 3/4

Species added to Warren County List after October, 1923.

Ring-neck Pheasant
Phasianlus colchicus

(213.) Introduced into this county several years ago by the Pennsylvania Game Commission. It seems to get along quite well in certain brushy and swampy regions, but it does not seem to care for hilly or heavily wooded regions. Regular breeders, but it is not often found here.

Canvas-back Duck | Canvasback
Aythya valisineria

(214.) After years of observing, hunting, and collecting, it remained for a little stroll to get my first positive record of this duck. During all the seasons, when I was out daily hunting ducks or taking migration notes, I never got a Canvas-back, nor did I ever see one that had been taken here. Neither did I ever see, even at a distance, a duck that I suspected of being a Canvas-back.

April 20, 1929, after a rain shower, I took a little walk down to the river at the head of Highhouse's Eddy. Off the point at the foot of the bayou I saw a large duck. Circling out through the woods, I crawled out to the edge of the high bank, and I got to within less than a 100 feet of it. It only took one good look to recognize a very nice drake Canvas-back.

I watched it for over 20 minutes, during which time it simply rested, occasionally turning slowly about when caught in a slight current. It finally drifted away and on down the river. This is a rather late date for this bird to be found in this part of the state in spring.

In the spring of 1934, I saw 2 here—both were fine, full plumaged males. As it happened, I saw both of these birds in very nearly the same place along shore, but on different dates—one on March 18, and the other on April 4.

March 15, 1940, along the river in Grunderville Eddy below Meade Island, I got up to within 50 feet of two, fine, male Canvas-backs. There was much ice in the river yet. This is my fourth record here for this duck.

American Egret | Great Egret
Ardea alba

(215.) August 15, 1929, two large white herons were about the bars at Grass Flats. They were seen by several different parties, who were familiar with the Great Blue Herons. Their accounts were the same. The size and color of the birds, it seemed to me, would leave no doubt as to their identity. One fellow quit fishing and, procuring a gun, tried to shoot one, but missed. Harry and I both looked for these birds afterward, but failed to find them. The shooting no doubt caused them to leave.

During the summers of 1930 and 1931, I had several reports of large white herons being seen, but I could not positively confirm them. August 16, 1932, I saw one at Erie, Pennsylvania, on the Peninsula. I also heard of a couple being about the river near Tidioute.

In 1933, a small invasion occurred here. On July 4, these great, fine, white fellows began to be reported from various points all along the river. On July 9, Harry and I went down the Allegheny River as far as Tionesta. On this trip we saw 3 at one place. About the first week of August they were seen the most often. At Grass Flats and vicinity, 7 were seen at one time on the big bars about the head of Leek Island. A pair, that I watched at times, stayed about until September. The latest date on which one was seen here was September 21.

During 1934, strange to say, I did not hear of or see a single one here, but at Erie I saw 3 in early September. These 3 had been there for some time, I was told.

Prairie Warbler
Dendroica discolor

(216.) Straggler.

After a hard, steady downpour of rain all night, the morning of May 8, 1932, was cloudy and muggy with occasional showers occurring. I found quite a large flight of birds, including many warblers, had arrived. I spent most of the morning looking them over, at the sand pits and along the flats at the head of Highhouse's Eddy.

Among the numerous warblers, I had the great luck to discover a Prairie Warbler. I spent about an hour watching this one bird. It kept feeding in the low brush along the bank, just above the lower sand pit. It did not appear at all scared. Several times it came up to within 8 feet of me—identification was easy.

I was very much surprised to meet this warbler here. I have rather expected, sooner or later, to find a stray Worm-eater or Blue-wing, but hardly the Prairie.

Black-backed Gull | Greater Black-backed Gull
Larus marinus

(217.) *(RBS notes indicate that he omitted this species from the proper place in his journals. It is placed here, species #217, as it is in his journals.)* On the morning of February 9, 1895, I took my gun and went down below town, along the river, to see what the blizzard had driven in—if anything. For a week we had been having high winds, snow storms, and bitter cold, with the thermometer from around zero to minus 25 degrees below zero.

When I left the house it was just zero, with a high northwest wind and fine, driving snow. The snow on the ground was deep, and the river was frozen over, except for the usual open places on the riffles or swift water. While I was going down the road at Highhouse's Eddy, I saw a large gull flying down along the opposite shore. It was a very large one, and it was having a hard time making any headway.

Its wings and back were black, and the rest of the bird was white. There is only one bird it could have been, and that is a Black-backed Gull. Mr. Todd, of the Carnegie Museum, agrees with me in this identification—the adult could not be mistaken for any other bird.

I followed the river 6 miles down to the mouth of the Brokenstraw Creek, but I did not see it again. I found American Mergansers, Goldeneyes, Long-tailed Ducks, and Herring Gulls; but I could not find the big Black-backed Gull again.

Brant
Branta bernicla

(218.) Late sometime in November, 1945, what was taken to be a wild duck of some kind appeared in Crescent Park, in the town of Warren on the South Side. It stayed on, feeding on the grassy lawn, and eating grain and chicken feed that interested residents put out for it. After it was here for some time, there was an article about it in the *Warren Times*, in which this duck was said to be a Merganser.

This Merganser business didn't sound just right to me, so on December 4, happening to be at town, I went over and looked it up. I found it all right. It was busy feeding on grass. I could approach to within 35 feet of it before it would begin walking away. As soon as I got near it, I saw that I was looking at a Brant—the only one I have ever seen or heard of here, and certainly a great rarity at an inland place like this.

On December 6, I went there and took several photos of it, but I couldn't get quite as close to it as I did on my first visit. This was due, I was told, to the boys and dogs that had been after it the day before. They had chased it away repeatedly, until stopped. I flushed it several times trying to get a good close up. I found it to be lively and a good flyer.

Heavy snow came right after this, and one day the bird was missing. It was not seen or heard of until January 2, when acting on a tip, the Game Warden found that a boy in town had it. The wardens took possession of this bird, which now had its wings clipped close. It also had one wing broken, and it was in a bad way from the tough treatment received. It died shortly after the wardens got it. They had tried to feed it and nurse it back to health. Through the kindness of Mr. Norris and Mr. Wilcox *(the wardens),* I was given the bird and a permit to mount and keep it.

I succeeded in making a very nice specimen of it, despite the missing wing tips and abuse it had received. On skinning this bird, I found that it was badly bruised about the body on the side on which the wing was broken. It had evidently been clubbed by the boy or had flown against something before he got it. I also found the bird had been reduced to skin and bones, with hardly any meat on its breast. It showed all signs of starvation. Its stomach was packed with food, as the wardens had given it plenty to eat. It probably fed so heavily when given the chance, that in its weakened and battered condition, it couldn't handle it and passed out. I couldn't determine the sex, but I think it was a young bird.

Ralph Bernard Simpson (left), W.E. Clyde Todd (right).
Todd was curator of the bird section of the Carnegie Museum, Pittsburgh.

EPILOGUE

Ralph B. Simpson had a lifelong respect for the natural world and its inhabitants, particularly those of the avian realm. It's certain that he hoped his journals would instill a spark of this passion in the reader. Not all can become consummate naturalists, but all can endeavor to appreciate nature at a deeper level.

Simpson's success as a naturalist was due mainly to hard work, initiative, and skill. This success undoubtedly demanded physical fitness, endurance, patience, skill with guns, and a very high level of simply making do in the field. The growing science of ornithology, to which Simpson contributed, required these practicalities—resolve, grit, and determination—along with his uncanny talent for field detection and identification.

The professional collector or field scientist needed to be highly skilled at various methods of securing birds. Skinning and preparing the birds has very specific requirements. Simpson was a professional taxidermist, with formulas he refined for his needs in specimen preparation. Today, the Audubon Center, Jamestown, New York, has 200 of Simpson's mounted bird specimens—covering 166 species. These mounts remain in remarkable condition. Recently, a volunteer at the Jamestown Audubon Society discovered a box tucked away for the better part of a century. This box held numerous glass plate negatives, which turned out to be original photographs by Ralph B. Simpson. Plans are in the works for these images, plus information from his species accounts, to be part of the forthcoming Tom Ridge Nature Center at Presque Isle, Erie, Pennsylvania. Also, the Carnegie Museum of Natural History, Pittsburgh, Pennsylvania, has 59 study skins and 94 eggs collected and contributed by Simpson.

Indeed, we are fortunate to have these records. Simpson had not only to care for his growing collection, but his labeling and note taking required minute attention to details. It was all essential. One of the dictums from Elliott Couse's 1890, *Field Guide and General Ornithology*, demanded that one: "Never put away a bird unlabelled, not even for an hour, you may forget it or die." Such were the practicalities of the growing science of ornithology.

Some of Simpson's work may appear as exasperating and tedious, but what he accomplished was an essential part of building any natural history collection. Simpson was prepared to endure large periods of monotony and frustration as long as there was a chance of finding something special and new—an ornithological triumph.

Simpson's 80 plus published papers were most likely written to impress as well as to inform his cohorts. Circulation of these professional papers were in publications such as the *Nidiologist* and *Oölogist*, but one can imagine a group of these professionals gathered together regaling each other with accounts of their expeditions—highlighting hardships endured in the field. Nevertheless, *The Bird Collectors,* by Mearns, asserts that, essentially, the early professional collectors were motivated by the need to discover and classify, thus forming the foundation for a growing science—ornithology. Today's scientists, conservationists, and birders owe a considerable debt to the early collectors.

Ralph B. Simpson's final journal entry was "May 19, 1957—Nighthawk, No. 29." He died two years later at 85 years of age. Simpson's career as a naturalist spanned 67 years.

SCALP ACT

Often birds have been viewed as competing with mankind for food. Historically, some species have been viewed as vermin, something to be eradicated and to be removed from the environment. For some, no more understanding was required, as reported in *The Bird Collectors*:

> There was a time when anything with a talon and hooked beak was regarded as vermin by landowners and gamekeepers. Bounty payments were often paid for birds of prey, for example, in Alaska from 1917–1952 rewards were paid for the corpses of 128,273 Bald Eagles. Bounties have been paid for eagles, falcons, goshawks, sparrow hawks, the list goes on, essentially any bird which competes with humankind for food is liable to be regarded as the enemy, whether its diet is meat, fish, grain, fruit, or grass.

During its session of 1885, the Pennsylvania legislature passed, on June 23, legislation entitled "An Act for the Destruction of Wolves, Wild Cats, Foxes, Minks, Hawks, Weasels, and Owls in this Commonwealth." This legislative act soon became universally known as the "Bounty" or "Scalp Act" of 1885. It read in part:

> Be it enacted...that for the benefit of agriculture and for the protection of game, within the commonwealth, there is hereby established the following premium for the destruction of certain noxious animals

> and birds, to be paid by the respective counties in which the same are slain, namely, for every wild cat two dollars, for every red or gray fox one dollar, for every mink fifty cents, for every weasel fifty cents, for every hawk fifty cents, and for every owl, except the Acadian, Screech, or Barn Owl, which is hereby exempted from the provisions of this act, fifty cents.

B.H. Warren, of Chester County, was ornithologist for the Pennsylvania Board of Agriculture at this time. He is the author of the 1888 book, *Birds of Pennsylvania*, and the 1890 revised edition of the same title. As state ornithologist and a member of the *West Chester Microscopical Society*, Dr. Warren opposed the "Scalp Act." He states in his book:

> In an agricultural district, the preservation of the hawks and owls is a matter of great importance. These birds, with few exceptions, subsist mainly on mice, other small quadrupeds, and various insects, which are so destructive in the fields, orchards, gardens, and about buildings.
>
> Pennsylvania is burdened with an "act" awarding premiums for the destruction of these well-known feathered friends of the farmer. The *West Chester Microscopical Society* recognizes the great wrong and injury which was being accomplished by the enforcement of this odious "Scalp Act," as it is called, and takes an active part in endeavoring to secure its repeal.
>
> Killing of birds is detrimental to the interest of agriculturalists; instead of being destroyed they should be protected. So common are erroneous ideas respecting birds of prey and their relation to the farmer that it is not at all surprising that such laws are enacted.

Quite early in 1886 there existed among farmers, taxpayers, and county officers a widespread dissatisfaction at the workings and effect of the law. Even though the "Scalp Act" was enacted in the summer of 1885, many people were unaware of it for several months; nevertheless the number of bounties collected was astonishing. For example, from November 1, 1885, up to November 1, 1886, the following amounts were paid by these counties for bounties: Warren $1,893.25; Erie $2,746.00; and Venango $952.60. Crawford County had the highest amount paid under the "Scalp Act," $8,022.90. On looking carefully at the legislative act it is odd that wolves are listed in the title, but are not provided for in the body of the bill with a specific bounty.

In many cases, early record keeping in regard to the Scalp Act reveals that the fees of the county magistrates were not included in the total costs. Merely the bounties were counted. As only 34 out of 67 counties made reports by November, 1886, it was thought that the total annual obligations of the counties under this law of 1885 would not be less than $60,000.00. The largest part would be paid for the destruction of hawks and owls.

Accurate figures were later obtained for the first 18-month period of the Scalp Act—county treasuries were depleted to the extent of over $100,000.00! Not less than $75,000.00 was for the destruction of hawks and owls. B.H. Warren, as ornithologist for the State Board of Agriculture, received large amounts of correspondence on the subject. Warren reports the number one reason given by county commissioners in favor of repealing the "Scalp Act" was—"it caused a drain upon the treasuries of the counties, which was not warranted by the results produced." The primary concern was fiscal, not the destruction of wildlife. Another reason for repeal from Warren's summary: "It encourages a certain class to follow hunting as a means of livelihood, and to the exclusion of other labor." Obviously minor social engineering was afoot that did not want to encourage hunting as an occupation.

Replies from the county commissioners to Dr. Warren varied in regard to repealing the Scalp Act. Some typical responses from his summary of replies follow. From Adams County: "The act should be repealed for only hawks and owls." This would have saved the county $2,500.00 of the initial $3,800.00 paid out for bounties. Elk County: "Repeal the whole act; there would be just as many killed." Fayette County: "No complaint from the people at large. It is much trouble to the county officers with the required paper work." Franklin County: "The act ought to be repealed. In the first year we had to pay bounties for 25 wild cats, 425 foxes, 155 mink, 83 weasels, 678 hawks, and 68 owls." Lehigh County: "Repeal the whole act if it can be done; if not, then repeal the portion referring to hawks and owls, by all means." Northhampton County: "We are not in favor of repealing the act and prefer it as it now stands." Warren County: "Repeal the whole act by all means." *(No reason given by Warren County.)*

It was clear that many viewed the Scalp Act as an unwarranted expense upon the county treasuries, particularly in regard to hawks and owls, as these were the most numerous bounties paid out. Reasons *not* to repeal the Scalp Act include the following comments from B.H. Warren's correspondence with the counties of the commonwealth. "Since this is the first year of the act, the vermin are greatest in number. Vermin will be less in the following years and the bounties paid will be less." "By repealing the act the good effects of the bounties already paid would be practically lost." "Destruction of these birds and mammals protects game." Fortunately, not all the populace shared these sentiments.

Farmers' clubs, agriculturists, naturalists, grange organizations, and many knowledgeable individuals knew the preservation of the raptorial birds was of utility to the farmer, as well as gratifying to the scientists who studied them. The Scalp Act was eventually repealed. Much credit went to Senator Harlan, Chester County, who did very much to secure the repeal of this destructive statute. The House of Representatives and Senate of the Commonwealth of Pennsylvania approved, on May 14, 1889, a legislative act for the protection of birds. Various bounties remained, but the wholesale slaughter stopped.

Bibliography

Allegheny Oxbow
Charles E. Congdon
Straight Publishing Company, 1967

Allegheny Pilot
"Containing a complete chart of the Allegheny River, showing the islands and bars and low water channel from Warren to Pittsburgh, also a table of distances for all the principal western navigable rivers."
E.L. Babbit
E.L. Babbitt, Publishers and Printers, 1855
Freeport, PA

Audubon's America
The narratives and experiences of John James Audubon
Edited by Donald Culross Peattie
Houghton Mifflin Company, 1940

The Bird Collectors
Barbara and Richard Mearns
Academic Press, 1998

The Birds of Pennsylvania
Gerald M. McWilliams, Naturalist
Daniel W. Brauning, Ornithologist, Pennsylvania Game Commission
Cornell University, 2000

Birds of Western Pennsylvania
W.E. Clyde Todd, Curator of Ornithology, Carnegie Museum, Pittsburgh
University of Pittsburgh Press, 1940

Ornithology in Laboratory and Field, Fifth Edition.
Olin Sewall Pettingill, Jr.
Harcourt Brace Jovanovich, Publishers, 1985.

Pioneer Outline History of Northwestern Pennsylvania
W.J. McKnight, M.D.
J.B. Lippincott Company, 1905

Stepping Stones
Vol. 20, No. 3, September, 1976
Vol. 21, No. 2, May, 1977
Vol. 23, No. 1, January, 1979
Vol. 46, No. 2, May 2002
Rhonda J. Hoover, Editor
Warren County Historical Society

List: Breeding Birds of Warren County

Acadian Flycatcher
Acadian Owl
American Crow
American Goldfinch
American Goshawk
American Redstart
American Woodcock
Baltimore Oriole
Bank Swallow
Barn Swallow
Barred Owl
Belted Kingfisher
Black and White Warbler
Black Mallard
Black-billed Cuckoo
Blackburnian Warbler
Black-throated Blue Warbler
Black-throated Green Warbler
Blue Jay
Bluebird
Blue-headed Vireo
Bobolink
Broad-winged Hawk
Bronzed Grackle
Brown Creeper
Brown Thrasher
Canadian Warbler
Cardinal Grosbeak
Carolina Wren
Catbird
Cedar-bird
Chat
Chestnut-sided Warbler
Chickadee

Chimney Swift
Chip Sparrow
Cliff Swallow
Cooper's Hawk
Cowbird
Crested Flycatcher
Crimson Finch
English Sparrow
Field Sparrow
Flicker
Golden-winged Warbler
Great Blue Heron
Great Horned Owl
Green Heron
Hairy Woodpecker
Hermit Thrush
Hooded Warbler
House Wren
Indigo Finch
Junco Sparrow
Killdeer Plover
Kingbird
Least Flycatcher
Long-eared Owl
Louisiana Water Thrush
Magnolia Warbler
Marsh Hawk
Maryland Yellow-throat
Meadow Lark
Mourning Dove
Mourning Warbler
Nighthawk
Northern Downy Woodpecker
Northern Parula Warbler
Northern Pileated Woodpecker
Olive-backed Thrush
Olive-sided Flycatcher
Oven-bird
Phoebe
Pine Siskin
Pine Warbler

Prairie Horned Lark
Purple Martin
Quail
Red-breasted Grosbeak
Red-eyed Vireo
Red-headed Woodpecker
Red-shouldered Hawk
Red-tailed Hawk
Red-winged Blackbird
Ring-neck Pheasant
Robin
Rough-winged Swallow
Ruby-throated Hummer
Ruffed Grouse
Savanna Sparrow
Scarlet Tanager
Screech Owl
Sharp-shinned Hawk
Song Sparrow
Sparrow Hawk
Spotted Sandpiper
Starling
Swamp Sparrow
Towhee
Tufted Titmouse
Vesper Sparrow
Warbling Vireo
Water Thrush
Whip-poor-will
White-breasted Nuthatch
Wilson's Snipe
Wilson's Thrush
Winter Wren
Wood Pewee
Wood Thrush
Yellow Warbler
Yellow-bellied Woodpecker
Yellow-billed Cuckoo
Yellow-throated Vireo

INDEX

English Names

Scientific Names

0-595-28749-2

www.ingramcontent.com/pod-product-compliance
Lightning Source LLC
Chambersburg PA
CBHW061341280526
45784CB00001B/84

* 9 7 8 0 5 9 5 2 8 7 4 9 9 *